The Sexuality of Organization

Other books by the editors:

Jeff Hearn

Birth and Afterbirth (1983) London: Achilles Heel.
'Sex' at 'Work'. The Power and Paradox of Organisation Sexuality (with Wendy Parkin) (1987) Brighton: Wheatsheaf; New York: St Martin's.
The Gender of Oppression. Men, Masculinity, and the Critique of Marxism (1987) Brighton: Wheatsheaf; New York: St Martin's.
Studying Men and Masculinity. A Sourcebook of Literature and Materials (with David Ford) (1988, 1989) Bradford: University of Bradford.
member of Violence Against Children Study Group *Taking Child Abuse Seriously* (1989) London/Winchester, MA: Unwin Hyman.

Peta Tancred-Sheriff

Career Patterns in the Higher Civil Service (1976) London: HMSO.
Social Change in France (with Michalina Vaughan and Martin Kolinsky) (1980) Oxford: Martin Robertson.
editor of *Feminist Research. Prospect and Retrospect/Recherche féministe. Bilan et Perspectives d'Avenir* (1988) Montreal: McGill-Queen's University Press.

Gibson Burrell

Sociological Paradigms and Organisational Analysis (with Gareth Morgan) (1979) London: Heinemann.

The Sexuality of Organization

edited by

Jeff Hearn
Deborah L. Sheppard
Peta Tancred-Sheriff
Gibson Burrell

SAGE Publications
London · Newbury Park · New Delhi

Chapter 1 © Gibson Burrell and Jeff Hearn 1989
Chapter 2 © Albert J. Mills 1989
Chapter 3 © Peta Tancred-Sheriff 1989
Chapter 4 © Barbara A. Gutek 1989
Chapter 5 © Nancy DiTomaso 1989
Chapter 6 © David L. Collinson and Margaret Collinson 1989
Chapter 7 © Wendy Parkin 1989
Chapter 8 © Marny Hall 1989
Chapter 9 © Deborah L. Sheppard 1989
Chapter 10 © Rosemary Pringle 1989
Postscript © Jeff Hearn, Deborah L. Sheppard Peta Tancred-Sheriff and Gibson Burrell 1989

First published 1989

All rights reserved. No part of this publication may be reproduced, stored in a retrieval system, transmitted or utilized in any form or by any means, electronic, mechanical, photocopying, recording or otherwise, without permission in writing from the Publishers.

 SAGE Publications Ltd
28 Banner Street
London EC1Y 8QE

HD
58.7
.S49
1989

SAGE Publications Inc
West Hillcrest Drive
Newbury Park, California 91320

SAGE Publications India Pvt Ltd
32, M-Block Market
Greater Kailash – I
New Delhi 110 048

British Library Cataloguing in Publication Data
The sexuality of organization.
1. Organizational behaviour. Sexual differences
I. Hearn, Jeff II. Sheppard, Deborah L.
302.3′5

ISBN 0–8039–8230–5
ISBN 0–8039–8231–3 pbk

Library of Congress catalog card number 89–062871

Phototypeset by Input Typesetting Ltd, London

Printed in Great Britain by
Billing and Sons Ltd, Worcester

Contents

Foreword vii
The Contributors ix

1 The Sexuality of Organization
   Gibson Burrell and Jeff Hearn 1

2 Gender, Sexuality and Organization Theory
   Albert J. Mills 29

3 Gender, Sexuality and the Labour Process
   Peta Tancred-Sheriff 45

4 Sexuality in the Workplace: Key Issues in Social Research and Organizational Practice
   Barbara A. Gutek 56

5 Sexuality in the Workplace: Discrimination and Harassment
   Nancy DiTomaso 71

6 Sexuality in the Workplace: The Domination of Men's Sexuality
   David L. Collinson and Margaret Collinson 91

7 Private Experiences in the Public Domain: Sexuality and Residential Care Organizations
   Wendy Parkin 110

8 Private Experiences in the Public Domain: Lesbians in Organizations
   Marny Hall 125

9 Organizations, Power and Sexuality: The Image and Self-Image of Women Managers
   Deborah L. Sheppard 139

10 Bureaucracy, Rationality and Sexuality: The Case of Secretaries
Rosemary Pringle 158

The Sexuality of Organization: A Postscript
Jeff Hearn, Deborah L. Sheppard, Peta Tancred-Sheriff and Gibson Burrell 178

Bibliography 182
Index 197

Foreword

This book is the product of a rather unusual kind of diffuse network. The idea for the book began in August 1985 in San Diego, California. It was there that we four, along with Robert Quinn, presented the symposium, 'Sexuality, Power and Organizational Theory', convened by Gibson Burrell, to a joint session of Women in Management, and the Organization and Management Theory Divisions of the Academy of Management annual conference. To our great relief and even greater excitement, the symposium went very well. We also got on well with each other. So the questions followed – 'How could we further the study and understanding of sexuality and organizations?'; and 'How could we find a way of keeping in touch with each other?' This book is our answer.

We decided to attempt to put together a collection of what we considered to be some of the most interesting work on sexuality and organizations in the English-speaking world. In particular we aimed to produce a critical and coherent feminist/pro-feminist text on the pervasiveness and power of sexuality in the ongoing production and reproduction of organizations and organizational life. The contributors are from Australia, Canada, the United Kingdom and the United States, and from a variety of academic disciplines – economics, management, organization theory, psychology, psychotherapy, sociology, trade union studies.

Geographical and disciplinary spread has meant that a good deal of learning from each other, and interchange of ideas and information, has taken place – indeed has had to take place. Though we have had the responsibility, as editors, for co-ordinating the production of the book, in practice the process has been more complex and more novel. All the contributions were sent in draft form to all the other contributors, and comments were invited from any or all involved. The commentaries that followed, criss-crossing the world, have been as important as the conventional process of editing. To expedite this process, one person from among us was nominated to act as the main liaising editor for each contribution (including each other's) in moving drafts to a final version. When these were complete we added linking paragraphs at the beginning of chapters and a short postscript. We hope the process of producing this book has mirrored some of the methodological, organizational and political issues raised within it.

As a final word of introduction, we would like to thank Rosemary Nixon, formerly of Sage, for first showing interest in the idea; Stephen Barr and Karen Phillips, for their encouragement and kindness; Sue Jones for her excellent editorial work; Susan Haberis and other staff at Sage; Maureen Froggatt and Sue Moody for typing parts of the script; Kate Russell for the gift of the cover; and Christine Burrell, Jay Hearn, Tom Levy and Guy Paquette for their support, and for putting up with piles of papers in corners of rooms.

May 1989

The Contributors

Gibson Burrell graduated in sociology at the University of Leicester thereafter completing an M.Phil (Leicester 1974) and a PhD (Manchester 1980). After holding a research post at the University of Birmingham, he became Lecturer in Behaviour in Organizations at the University of Lancaster. He is currently Professor of Organizational Behaviour at the University of Warwick. His research interests include the development of organization theory using concepts from social theory and philosophy, as well as 'sexuality in organizations'.

David Collinson is Conoco Lecturer in Organizational Behaviour in the Department of Management at the University of St Andrews, following the completion of his doctorate at the University of Manchester Institute of Science and Technology. He has conducted research and published papers on shop-floor culture, management control, managerial accountancy, sex discrimination in the recruitment process, and the role of personnel management in management. He is co-editor of *Job Redesign* (Gower, 1985), author of *Barriers to Fair Selection* (Equal Opportunities Commission, 1988) and co-author with David Knights and Margaret Collinson of *Managing to Discriminate* (Routledge, 1990). Currently, he is researching workplace culture and safety practices on North Sea oil installations.

Margaret Collinson worked in the finance sector for many years, during which time she became a full-time trade union official. Her responsibilities included all aspects of equal opportunities and she negotiated the first successful equal value claim within the UK financial services sector. She has been involved in management training in England and Scotland for managers from the United Kingdom and Europe. Currently, she is a tutor in Management Studies at the Universities of St Andrews and Dundee and co-author with David Collinson and David Knights of *Managing to Discriminate* (Routledge, 1990).

Nancy DiTomaso is Associate Professor of Organizational Management at the Graduate School of Management of Rutgers, the State University of New Jersey. She received her degree from the University of Wisconsin-Madison and has previously taught at Northwestern and New York Universities. Her current research includes work on organizational culture, managing diversity in organizations, and the occupational structure in organizations. She has published on these and other topics in human resource management and has been active in the Academy of Management and the American Sociological Association, including a recent term as a member of the ASA Council. One of her most recent publications is *Ensuring Minority Success in Corporate Management* (Plenum, 1988).

Barbara A. Gutek is Professor in the Department of Management and Policy, University of Arizona, Tucson; she was formerly Professor of Psychology, Claremont Graduate School, Los Angeles. A 1975 University of Michigan PhD, Gutek has been studying sexual behaviour at work since 1978. Her book, *Sex and the Workplace* (Jossey-Bass, 1985), based on a random-sample survey of 1232 employed men and women in Los Angeles County, was translated into Danish in 1988 (published as *Seksuel Chikane* by Teknisk Forlag). Gutek is co-author or co-editor of nine other books, eight of which are on women and work. She serves frequently as an expert witness in the United States in court cases on sex discrimination and sexual harassment.

Marny Hall has been a psychotherapist and organizational consultant in the San Francisco Bay area for twenty years. She is author of *The Lavender Couch: A Consumer's Guide to Psychotherapy for Lesbians and Gay Men* (Alyson, 1985), and has contributed articles to several anthologies and periodicals, including *The Journal of Homosexuality* (1977, 1986, 1987), *Lesbian Sex* (Joann Loulan, 1985), and *Women and Mental Health* (Bayes and Howell, 1981). She has conducted seminars and workshops in colleges, corporations and in lesbian communities in the US and the Netherlands. She has also written and produced the video *Gays in Corporations* (1981).

Jeff Hearn studied at Oxford University and Oxford Polytechnic, prior to studying organizations at Leeds University and completing his doctorate in social theory at Bradford University. His interest in sexuality and organizations has come from two directions: organizational sociology and men's anti-sexist activities. His recent publications include *The Gender of Oppression* (Wheatsheaf/St Martin's, 1987); with David Ford, *Studying Men and Masculinity* (University of Bradford, 1988); and he is editor of the 'Men, Masculinities, and Leadership' special issue of *Equal Opportunities International* (MCB University Press, 1989). He is Senior Lecturer in Applied Social Studies, University of Bradford, and during 1988–9 was Hallsworth Research Fellow, University of Manchester.

Albert J. Mills's research activities centre on the impact of organization upon people – focusing on organizational change and human liberation. These concerns were formulated on the shop-floor of British industry and through involvement in the movements for social change that dominated the 1960s. Leaving school at fifteen, Mills's early images of organization – images of frustration, of sexually segregated work, of power disparities, of conflict – were experienced through a series of unskilled jobs and given broader meaning through campaigns for peace, women's liberation, environmental survival and social change. In his early twenties Mills went on to full-time study at Ruskin College, Oxford and then to the universities of Durham, Sheffield and Southern California. He is an Associate Professor of Organizational Behaviour and the Associate Dean of the Faculty of Administrative Studies at Athabasca University in Alberta, Canada.

Wendy Parkin is a part-time Senior Lecturer in Sociology and Social Work in the Department of Behavioural Sciences at Huddersfield Polytechnic, and also a part-time social worker in a family centre with Kirklees Metropolitan Council. Research and writing has focused on issues of gender and sexuality within organizations. She has published in Britain, the United States, France and Germany and is co-author, with Jeff Hearn, of *'Sex' at 'Work'* (Wheatsheaf/St Martin's, 1987). She has also written and researched in the field of child abuse, in relation to her current practice, following a number of years as a generic social worker in a social services department.

Rosemary Pringle lives in Sydney and teaches sociology at Macquarie University. When not at Macquarie she divides her time between Bondi and the Blue Mountains where she shares a cottage. She is the author of *Secretaries Talk* (Verso, 1989) and co-author, with Ann Game, of *Gender at Work* (Allen & Unwin, 1983). She is currently interested in statistical discourses and their relation to other levels of reality, in particular the construction of occupations.

Deborah L. Sheppard is a sociologist with degrees from McGill, Carleton and York Universities, Canada. She has taught sociology and organizational behaviour at York and at Concordia University in Montreal. Her research includes decision making in dual-earner families, the relationship between gender and organizational culture, and the implications of teaching and studying from a perspective of personal and social transformation. In addition to sociological work, she has also been involved in arts administration. Sheppard has given many public talks and presentations on issues of particular concern to women. She is a consultant in the Washington, DC area with offices at 5521 Mohican Road, Bethesda, MD 20816–2159.

Peta Tancred-Sheriff has taught sociology at McMaster University, Hamilton, Canada, since 1972. Her early interest in the sociology of organizations has led, via the feminist literature, to a preoccupation with the gender-specificity of organizations. She is currently undertaking research on the impact of computerization on the work of women professionals and she is collaborating, with Albert Mills, on an edited book on gender and organizations. Her previous feminist publications include the editorship of *Feminist Research/Recherche féministe* (McGill – Queen's University Press, 1988) as well as articles in such journals as *Sociologie et Sociétés*, *Atlantis*, and *Australian Universities Review*.

1
The Sexuality of Organization

Gibson Burrell and Jeff Hearn

Sexuality, gender, organizations, organization: these concepts and their interrelationships are the central focus of this book and of this introductory chapter. Gender and gender relations have long been deemed to be absent or relatively unimportant within the study of organizations. The gendered nature of organizations and their management has not been part of the dominant malestream traditions of theorizing on organizational activity. Until very recently, academia, in this case at least, has obscured life rather than reflected it. Even so, we are not just concerned here with gender relations within organizations, but with sexuality and organizations and, more specifically, with the sexuality of organization. For even with the increasing academic, political and personal attention paid to the importance and ubiquity of gender and gendered relations within and of organizations, there has often been and often still is a silence on sexuality. Thus we build upon the fundamental threefold relationship which exists between the realization of the gender-blindness of malestream organization theories; the increasing attention paid to gender and gender relations in organizations; and the persistent neglect of sexuality within the study of gender, the study of organizations, and in the management of most organizational forms.

The approaches we wish to bring to bear on the understanding of gender and sexuality in relation to organizations and organization are unreservedly critical. As men writing on gender and sexuality, we see it as important to learn from feminist theory and practice, not to usurp them; for this reason we describe our own standpoint as profeminist. In these ways we seek to reorientate organizational analysis and move it in a particular direction.

We do not imagine this will prove an easy task; but to begin, we need to clear some ground and make some preliminary remarks on the terms, 'gender' and 'sexuality', and how they are to be used in this chapter and the rest of the book. Since it is through and in these terms that we, as authors, most closely confront the person of the reader, we, and indeed our co-authors, will be dealing throughout the text with deeply held personal values and sensibilities.

Following this next section, we argue for a critical reorientation of organization theory towards concerns with gender, reproduction and sexuality rather than just production and productivity. The third main section links the first two by outlining the sexuality of organization in terms both of the types of literature available, and the contributions to this book. The chapter is concluded with a summary statement of the main common features and key debates in the book as a whole.

Gender and sexuality: sexuality and gender

The first and most important point to be made is that although gender and sexuality are conceptually distinct, they are also clearly closely related. This is particularly so in the sense that it is difficult to imagine (within human society at least) sexuality without gender, or gender without sexuality. The overarching theme of this chapter, and the framework in use, is that sexuality and gender are intimately interrelated with production and reproduction in and of society, and with the production and reproduction of organizations and organization: hence a central element in that process is what we have called the sexuality of organization.

However, the exact meaning of both gender and sexuality, and therefore the nature of their interrelationship, are highly contested. Although there may *appear* to be a high degree of consensus on some sexual questions, on closer inspection the interrelationship of sexuality and gender is just as amenable to the full range of methodological and political interpretations as any other social issue. Moreover, the numerous debates and sub-debates that exist on sexuality and gender are constantly shifting and changing, often reflecting on themselves and each other. These debates include, as noted, what is meant by sexuality in the first place.

Having said that, distinctions between gender and sexuality, while contested, are usually drawn in terms of the generality of the social experience of gender in all social spheres, and the particularity of the social experience of sexuality in relation to desire. Gender is widely used to refer to the social construction of sex and divisions based on differences of sex, however indirectly.

Sexuality is used more variously, though frequently in relation to a notion of desire. Thus sexuality can be defined as the social expression or social relations of physical bodily desires, by or for others, or for oneself. Conceptualization of desire, and of the relationship of desire and sexuality, is a particularly difficult and disputed question. While there are numerous specific interpretations, it is important to note that desire can usefully be thought of as referring to a substance felt to be primordial or aboriginal, but posited by theory to be social and contingent (MacKinnon, 1982:516).[1]

For these reasons, we and our co-editors thought it inappropriate to glide over differences and demand that contributors follow a pre-ordained set of definitions. Instead the authors of subsequent chapters were free to develop their own formulations of these concepts and their interrelations, albeit within feminist and profeminist standpoints.

So how are we to make any sense not just of the concepts of gender and sexuality, but also of their interrelations? Let us outline just four major ways of conceptualizing sexuality and gender, as:

— biological essences;
— outcomes of social roles;
— fundamental political categories;
— communicative practices and discourses of power.[2]

Inevitably, to reduce such a large canvas as sexuality and gender to such a framework involves some considerable simplifications. However, we hope that through these broad approaches we can outline some of the practical questions and conceptual relationships that will be given more detailed consideration throughout this book.

Biological essences
For many, *biological* approaches continue to be the most obvious way of talking about sexuality and gender: sexuality and gender are linked through and explained by the category, biological sex. For example, men's sexuality, the gender of men, and the male sex may be *conflated* so that the ways both the sexuality and the gender of men happen to be are explained away by the male sex (of 'men'). This is clearly so in much that counts as common sense ('men have natural urges, don't they?') or, more grandly, folk wisdom. In addition, biological essentialism has figured strongly in much religious, medical, psychiatric and academic theory and practice on sexuality.

There are of course stronger, that is more deterministic and more essentialist, and weaker versions of biological approaches to sexuality. Such variations are often complicated by moral or normative judgements. According to these, sexuality is not just biological, but may also be naturalized and normalized, so that certain sexual forms and practices become seen as 'natural' and 'normal'. Thus 'normal', 'natural' sexuality may be presumed to be monogamous, procreative, heterosexuality; sexuality may be reduced to sex and sexual acts; and 'normal', 'natural' sex acts may be presumed to entail 'penetrative' genital sex. At worse, 'normal' sex is male sex (see Schneider and Gould, 1987:149).

Since the end of the last century the biological approaches to sexuality have become overlaid with Freudian and other psychoanalytic interpretations. Again, we find intense debates around the interpretation of Freud's and others' ideas on the status of the 'animal', and of sexuality and gender, in relation to biology and culture (see, for example, Mitchell, 1975). Even so, it is reasonable to credit Freud and his followers with extending biological theories of sexuality into psychology, through the concepts of the instincts, sexual drives, the libido – and, moreover, their various projections and sublimations. As in other biologically based approaches, Freudian interpretations of sexuality and gender refer both back to sex, that is, the female or male sex, as the determining element, even though their specific social form is culturally mediated.

Outcomes of social roles
In the biological mode, sexuality and gender are linked together through the physiology of sex, as the sexual difference of males and females. In the *social interactionist* and *sex role* model, [3] sexuality and gender are still linked to sex, but in this case as separable social constructions of sex. Equivalent to the physiological concept of sexual drive is the interactionist concept of sexual script (Gagnon and Simon, 1973; Laws and Schwartz, 1977). Accordingly, sexual behaviour and activity *is social*, yet is also scripted, as in, to continue the dramaturgical analogy, the performance of the sex role (or more accurately gender role). Sexuality, through sexual scripts, is thus one element, relatively autonomous yet also contingent, of gender and gender roles. Gender is then usually seen as the overarching amalgam of sex (or gender) roles, including sexual roles, with their own sexual scripts. Such a social interactionist view does, however, open up considerable room for very detailed and elaborate forms of sexuality, for example in the many different ways that men might flirt with women in the workplace.

Though quite distinct, biological and social interactionist/sex role approaches share a number of features. In particular they tend to:

— conceptualize sexuality as the property of individuals, as relatively unproblematic subjects;
— give insufficient attention to power relations;
— be relatively ahistorical, better able to analyse stability than change.

All these features are open to serious critique. Thus insights around individualism, power relations and historical determination open up a set of more critical approaches to sexuality and gender, with which we wish to ally ourselves.[4]

History and politics
At this point what is meant by sexuality and gender becomes intensely bound up with the history and politics of sexuality and gender (see, for example, Scott, 1986). Our own conceptions of gender and sexuality, in terms both of their social meaning and of the particular forms of their relationship, are determinedly historical. Thus, for example, what counts as 'sexual' in one historical period may vary from what counts as such in the next. In Western society, and especially the Judaeo–Christian tradition, an enormous historical weight of religious, moral and intellectual opinion has accumulated *against sexuality*. Sexuality has historically come to be seen as 'something' frightening, uncontrollable, illegitimate, unpredictable, chaotic. Fear of sexuality has interwoven with men's fear and hatred of women and women's sexuality, and men's association of women with the dangerousness of sexuality. The configuration that *appears* dominant now, in industrialized societies at least, rests on the *apparent* separation of the 'organizational' and the 'sexual', however misleading such appearances are (Hearn and Parkin, 1987). Organizations have historically become a series of sites, where the danger and pleasure of sexuality can be both repressed, and exploited within forms of oppression. Seeing sexuality historically also acknowledges the possibility that sexual interests, sexual communities and sexual identities can be open to change, including conscious political change.

It is difficult to overestimate the importance of the new social movements and debates around sexuality and gender, primarily through feminism but also in the gay movement, in making 'sexuality' and 'gender' problematic. Sexuality and gender have become politics, a process of power relations, in both theory and practice. Thus the study of sexuality, in organizations and elsewhere, has taken place, indeed increasingly so, within the context of the 'new sexual debates' of feminism, gay liberation, post-structuralism and psychoanalysis, to varying degrees contributing to and sometimes oppositional to what Rubin (1984) has called 'a radical theory of the politics of sexuality'. These debates are not unified; indeed their lack of unification, their diversity, is part of their strength; they are, however, unified in problematizing sexuality, particularly in terms of its political construction. These theories and practices centre on the historicity of sexuality, the plasticity of sexuality, and the extent to which sexuality can be seen as the basis of gender divisions and gender oppression. More specific debates have developed around the recognition that men's sexual violence and physical violence to women are empirically and theoretically often difficult to distinguish (Kelly, 1987); the relative autonomy of lesbianism and the 'lesbian continuum' (Rich, 1984); the deconstruction of heterosexuality (Hollway, 1984); the interrelation of heterosexualities and homosexualities; and diverse, sometimes polarized, positions on pornography and their own critique (A. Ferguson, 1984). 'Women', 'men', 'women's practice', 'men's practice' become problematic in the intensity of personal experience.

To make sense of these historical and political developments we shall outline two major critical approaches to sexuality and gender. Both draw on power analysis, but in one, our third general approach, sexuality and gender are themselves fundamental political categories, while in the other, our fourth, sexuality and gender are seen as communicative practices and discourses of power. As before, these are conceptual devices, for in practice particular stances may draw on both of these as well as on other broad approaches.

Fundamental political categories
The conceptualization of sexuality and gender as fundamental political categories, relatively autonomous from biology and individual social roles, rests on the insights of social structural relations, as represented in marxism and materialist feminism. Sexuality and gender are seen as historically constructed, collectivities of interest and community, set within definite relations of power and dominance. Gender and the specific genders are the result of social relations between all people in particular societies, at particular historical times. Thus we can talk of the gender class of women, and indeed of men; and what 'women' or 'men' means, and what it is to be a 'woman' or 'man', is the result of major social forces and changes. A clear example of this is the impact of feminism in both the past and the present on the political category of women. With this third approach it is most usual to see sexuality and sexual change as one component of gender and gender class change.

In addition, the categorical approach has been adapted for the analysis of sexuality itself. This is most obviously seen in the intense interrelation of sexuality and violence, for men at least (Dworkin, 1981). It is also apparent in the historical development of lesbian and gay communities of interest, representing the coming together, at certain historical times, of what were formerly invisible or less visible sexualities. Such developments provide different sets of social conditions within which individuals may subsequently live. Such change may also be seen in terms of sexual(ity) classes of, say, women lesbians or gay men, with contrary interests to others of different sexuality (e.g. Mieli, 1980). Such conflicts of interests, erotic and/or gendered, are, following economic class analysis, usually seen in terms of disputes over control, most obviously control over the body (cf. Diamond and Quinby, 1984, on sexuality; Gilligan, 1982, on gender). Accordingly, while it is more usual to see gender as subsuming sexuality, some feminists, notably Catharine MacKinnon (1982), argue that sexuality and its control is the basis of gender, thus effectively subsuming gender within sexuality. Thus sexuality and sexualities are political, both as categories and in particular instances. This is made explicit in 'political lesbianism'.

This raises a question of special importance in the politics of sexuality, namely the development of sexual identities. These may be seen as the individual equivalent of sexuality communities or classes, and as such may appear to return to the individual possession of sexuality, albeit within a political context. In some cases, sexual identity may involve a conflation of sexuality and identity.[5] Furthermore, 'naming' and 'claiming' have in some situations become invested with a special authority, whereby '(j)ust to *name* yourself as part of a given group is to *claim* a moral backing for your words and actions'[6] (Ardill and O'Sullivan, 1986:33; emphases in original). However, in practice the relationship between sexual community interest and identity is clearly complex, and rarely one of strict equivalences.

Communicative practices and discourses of power
This brings us to our fourth broad approach, in which sexuality and gender are seen as based in *practice* and *process*, and specifically communicative practices and discourses of power. Concern with the categorical politics of the body, as described earlier, has in practice moved the debate to the critique of categories. Not only may the categories not fit politics and experience, but they may impede the analysis of certain practical sexual questions, such as the contradictions of lesbian sado-masochism (Ardill and O'Sullivan, 1986) or 'gay macho' (Kleinberg, 1987).

As an alternative emphasis to practice, the focus on the *process* of communication may cast sexuality not as 'sex' or 'sexual activity' but *as discourse*. The most well known proponent of this approach is the French historian, Michel Foucault. He explained his own *motivation* for working in this field, and in this way, as follows: 'There is a very great difference between interdictions about sexuality and other forms of interdiction. Unlike other interdictions, sexual interdictions are constantly connected with the obligation to tell the truth about oneself' (Foucault, 1988:16). He continued that, following this, 'I conceived of a rather odd project: not the evolution of sexual behavior but the projection of a history of the link between the obligation to tell the truth and the prohibitions against sexuality' (1988:17).

In this view, sexual ideology and gender identities are socially constructed at a very deep level – not just in the interaction of persons or political interests but in the discourses within which those interactions occur. Indeed the very notion that people need a clear-cut identity as a member of one sex or a particular 'sexual orientation' is itself historical and open to deconstruction.

Discourse of and on sexuality is, according to Foucault, like other discourses, maintained through the order of the discourse and the mutually reinforcing interconnections of power, knowledge and pleasure. His concern with how sexuality is constituted in its construction generally ignored women and scholarship on women. His ideas, along with those of other male theorists on sexuality such as Lacan, have been criticized for attempting to produce a 'redefinition of sexual politics', which makes feminism invisible (Stanley, 1984). Even so, discourse analysis has been taken up enthusiastically by some feminist scholars. Seeing sexuality, and indeed gender, as discourse can be difficult and confusing: it can direct the analyst to the structure of the discourse – sexuality as desire for the Other of the discourse – an insight developed much earlier by Simone de Beauvoir (1949; 1953 English edn) in *The Second Sex*; to sexuality as representation (Coward, 1982); and to sexuality as desire in language (Kristeva, 1980). Sexuality can be seen as perpetually in tension with the eroticism of the non-sexual (MacKinnon, 1983), or as a tension between itself and the non-sexual.

It is here that sexuality ceases to be a shorthand: it explodes into numerous discursive elements and practices – sex, sexual relations, sexual relationships, sexual acts, sexual behaviours, sexual activity, sexual feelings, sexual orientations, sexual desires, sexual identities, sexual practices . . . we could go on . . . sexual violences, sexual harassment, sexual fantasies, sexual experience(s), sexual domination, sexual abuse, sexualities. And furthermore, sexuality is not separable but is constructed, as is gender, *in relation to* sensuality, the body, birth, motherhood, fatherhood, violence, and much more. Gender and sexuality do not exist in isolation, but in their *specific* conjunctures with such divisions as age, ethnicity, class and bodily facility. And furthermore, the relationships of sexuality and sex, and gender and sex, are problematic, as are their polarization in certain discourses (Keller, 1987).

These then are some of the approaches to sexuality and gender that bear on our topic. Given that this terrain is both personal and contested, we hope that this book conveys to the reader the importance of the topic of the sexuality of organization, and communicates some of the sense of revelation which comes when one starts to see organizational life in these terms. It is a world which we know well though rarely as followers of disciplines, academic or otherwise. For some readers, this focus will be deemed irrelevant, so for this reason the rest of this chapter is devoted to showing the relevance of the sexuality of organization to the theory and practice of organizations.

The organization of production: the reproduction of organization

Organization theory
The modern academic study of organizations may be dated to the turn of the century, and the work of the classical theorists, such as F. W. Taylor, Fayol and Urwick, and the sociological innovators, principally Weber, but also Durkheim, Simmel and Tonnies. This is not to deny the significant (male) ancestors of modern organization theory, including Machiavelli, Hobbes, Spencer and Marx, amongst many others. These 'founding fathers' and their more modern 'sons' do not do a very good job of gender (relations). For example, while both Marx and Weber have something to say on gender relations, as the first class relation and in terms of patriarchialism respectively, they did little to translate the implications of these structural analyses of gender to the *organizational* level. It was left to others in the postwar period to write of 'organization man' (Whyte, 1956), 'corporate man' (Jay, 1972), and 'bureaucratic man' (Kohn, 1971), even though Weber's theory of bureaucracy is implicitly about male bureaucrats. Furthermore, until relatively recently few women, other than Follett and Woodward, were acknowledged as leading exponents of organization theory, and those involved were usually researchers and collectors of data (Sheriff and Campbell, 1981). This situation was changed little by the impact of systems theory through the latter years of the human relations school, and through Parsonian structural functionalism in the 1940s and 1950s. Indeed, in some ways, Parsons, Bales and their colleagues exacerbated the gender problem in organization theory by moving analysis from implicit assumptions of maleness to more explicit statements about the 'male' and 'female' features of organizations and other social systems.

In surveying the treatment of gender within organization theory (Hearn and Parkin, 1983, 1987, 1988) it is hard to avoid the conclusion that gender has either been ignored, treated implicitly as male, considered an organizational 'variable', reduced to relative stereotypes, or been analysed in a blatantly sexist way. Classics of organization theory such as Crozier's (1964) study of tobacco workers and power, and the Hawthorne experiments by Mayo (1960) and his colleagues are implicit accounts of gender relations and indeed, in the latter case at least, of sexuality. But while sexuality may be the most obvious element of gender relations in terms of common sense, phenomenology and everyday gossip, it has remained the most unexamined within organization theory.

To teach about, indeed sometimes speak of, the sexuality of organization is to invite the sarcasm, embarrassment and hostility of academic colleagues (cf. Smith, 1975; Spender, 1981). For some it is not a legitimate area of study, because of both the anxieties and the deep interest it often engenders in the audience. A form of censorship is sometimes exercised as when, for example, one of us wrote a piece which made some reference to the existence in the Middle Ages of penalties for 'masturbation in church'. The editor of the relevant international journal excised this section because it would, perhaps, alienate 'Mid West accountants'. Funding bodies, too, are unlikely to regard the issue of sexuality in organizational contexts as of paramount importance. The continued moves towards 'big science', with its associated features of a concentration of funding within so-called 'centres of excellence', the positive evaluation given to large research groupings and the process of placing research into hierarchies by 'peer' assessment, point in the direction of a concentrated, centralized system of research. Sexuality is not high on explicit prioritizations advocated by institutional sources of finance. Much more emphasis is placed upon problems with and improvements within the organization of production.

The organization of production
In many ways the growth of organizational analysis has paralleled the rise of interest in issues to do with the organization of production. It asks such questions as 'how is production to be organized efficiently and effectively and what methods are being utilized to increase productivity and enhance smooth organization?' Such a concern is best represented as a constellation of elements, a constellation originally centred around mass production techniques in the United States but more recently around Japanese manufacturing successes, an empiricist methodology, a managerial pragmatism

and the teaching of large numbers of MBAs, and other students of management. Its mouthpiece is the *Administrative Science Quarterly*. Abernathy, Clark and Kantrow (1983) chart the rise of this movement concerned with what we here term the organization of production in their book, *Industrial Renaissance*. They maintain that policy makers and theorists of organization saw economic development as a unilinear process subject to no reversibilities nor cyclicality, in which increased efficiency and productivity would be enhanced by the spread outwards of mass production techniques from the American automobile industry. These processes allowed cost reduction and therefore increased international competitiveness. In short, they led inexorably to success. And therefore they were the Truth imparted to eager MBAs in the business schools of North America.

As the threat of Japanese competition arose, there was an enforced questioning of the *modernism* of organization studies. Modernism, with its assumptions of rationality, progress, the march of history in a unilinear way and the possibility of ever closer approximations to Truth, has provided the context in which most organization theorists have been brought up (Cooper and Burrell, 1988). For some, this led to a crisis of confidence; for others, of course, it did not. Many commentators incorporated the Japanese example without difficulty. Ouchi (1981), Peters and Waterman (1982) and Kanter (1983) all feed upon the so-called lessons of Japan by incorporating the differences between the two nation-states into the modernist project. The story becomes one of utilizing Japanese practice (which is often said to be originally American anyway) in the march of progress. Nipponophobia has *not* put an end to modernism and the organization of production constellation. It has almost certainly rejuvenated it – with 'Just-in-Time', the Kanban system, quality circles, Toyotism and so on.

What we have then within the organization of production is a triangle of supporting forces: modernism, productivity and big science (Lyotard, 1982). Each acts as part of, support to and reinforcement within each of the others. As such, the organization of production finds sexuality a real problem to handle, and the reasons for this we shall look at shortly.

For those concerned to defend the organization of production stance, the argument could at this point develop in two very different directions. The issue of sexuality might be treated in terms of either exclusion or inclusion. In the *exclusion* route, the organization of production perspective relates of a world in which sexuality is simply not a problem. Production concerns are diametrically opposed to issues of sexuality, and indeed to issues of reproduction.

The factory and the office are the obverse of the home. Work time and leisure time are temporally dislocated. Rationality and sexual relations are the twin faces of Janus. Such an exclusionary perspective would maintain that the separation of such discrete features of human life is a natural one, for the world of work is no place for the world of sexuality. One excludes the other. Sexuality is ignored because it is unimportant.

The second explanatory route that might be taken is that of *inclusion*, and this is a much more persuasive argument. Here, the triangle of modernism, productivity and big science are seen as historically including sexuality within their worldview. For, it might be said, isn't the rise of modernism marked by a decline in sexuality, by an enhancement of control over emotion, by the development of a civilizing process? (Foucault, 1979; Burrell, 1988). Doesn't the very success of productivity as a notion depend upon the reality principle and the suppression of libido in organizational contexts? And hasn't the rise of big science meant that resources of time, money and expertise have been directed towards the analysis of sexuality in ways which quite clearly signal that it has become part of the explicit subject matter of the organization of production? (Foucault, 1979). All this would suggest that while sexual relations are not part of the everyday discourse of organizational analysis, this is because they have been 'dealt with', after due consideration, in a previous era. They are not on the agenda because they have been solved as a problem by those who organize production. For them, sexuality is no longer an issue. Their forbears dealt with it by including it in how they built, organized and managed their factories, offices, schools and hospitals.

This argument implies that the organization of production perspective has been quite capable of dealing with sexuality and its analysis – at least it has been in its own terms – otherwise contemporary life would be very different. Sexuality is presumed to be included and resolved within existing frameworks. So successful has its inclusion been that giving it some consideration today may seem to some an irrelevance. Like scurvy, it has been successfully eradicated – the knowledge of how to treat it remains dormant, yet immediately accessible. Thus the absence of sexuality from the vast majority of organizational analyses may be explained as part of a desexualizing of organizations, which developed as discourses about sex grew up in and out of management theory. Sexuality, and indeed reproduction, are effectively seen as functions of production. Such discourses are part and parcel of the triangle of modernism, productivity and big science. Knowledge about how to desexualize the organization in order to achieve enhanced productivity is ever present but seldom articulated. Within such a view of the world, this silent inclusion is one of the great success stories of the civilizing process.

Faced by both explanatory routes, the exclusion and over-inclusion of sexuality in the theory of organizing ignore one crucial point. Within organizations, men and women spend much time thinking and worrying about sex. For them, unlike organizational analysis, it is an important, highly charged, almost ubiquitous issue. For this and other reasons, sexuality appears to be difficult to *reduce* to the framework of the organization of production. This is not to say that sexuality is not *used* within production. It clearly is in, say, advertising; and it may be used in, say, sexual harassment as an oppression that also serves the ends of production, or certain interests of managers or owners. To some, sexuality, in the form of sexual banter, may be seen as a distraction to resistance to exploitation in production. This is all very well, but it is not the whole story. Each of these examples – advertising, sexual harassment, sexual banter – can be *re-seen* by focusing on sexuality and gender, for example, as the display of sexual narratives, as sexual violence of men to women, even as sexual resistance to production. As organization theorists, we wish to argue for a full consideration of sexuality in organizational contexts; in this book we wish to place sexuality in a position of conceptual importance.

Sexuality is an inherently subtle and qualitative issue, and it is not possible to measure 'it', even if one rashly assumes 'it' to be a singular, universal feature of human existence. It is not unusual to consider sexuality solely in terms of sexual liaisons and relationships, taking these as indices of the ongoing 'level' or 'amount' of sexuality, but such a perspective is unnecessarily limiting (Foucault, 1979). Sexuality is a diverse and diffuse process: it is not a 'thing' brought into organizations, there to be organized. Attempts to organize sexuality may be accompanied by disorganization: it is a process that remains *different*. We therefore see it as necessary to broaden definitions of sexuality, in at least two ways: (1) to see sexuality as an ordinary and frequent public process rather than an extraordinary feature of private life; and (2) to see sexuality as one aspect of an all-pervasive 'politics of the body' rather than a separable, discrete set of practices (Foucault, 1977). Thus, sexuality includes a range of practices from feelings to flirtations to sexual acts, accomplished willingly, unwillingly or forcibly by those involved. Whilst we recognise the importance of narcissistic, bisexual and homosexual practices, most of our attention here will focus upon heterosexual relationships. Once one begins to see sexuality as part of a wider 'politics of the body', then we are concerned with its pivotal role in analysis of current imbalances of power between genders. Whilst sexual harassment is obviously of great interest, attention will also be paid here to sexual attraction; in both forms of cross-gender relationship, power is a key concept. Correspondingly, we need to introduce sexuality into discussions of power. But more than this is involved. Sexuality is seen here from within a viable alternative to the organization of production tradition. This alternative we entitle the *(re)production of organization*.

The (re)production of organization

Because sexuality has been both excluded and over-included by those who analyse and direct contemporary organizational forms, it has proved necessary for us to stand back and contextualize our current enterprise. In this section we outline a distinctive mode of organization studies in which this book is located. This we term the reproduction of organization perspective, within which the sexuality of organization is a major element. Rather than focus attention upon how organizations co-ordinate the production of goods, services and outcomes, we ask how the organization of human activity comes to take such patterned forms. How is organization produced on an ongoing day-to-day basis? How do patterns of gender relations become established within the enterprise and, once established, reproduce themselves?

In beginning to formulate this approach, the following assumptions are made. First, rather than focus upon organizations as having an apparent 'factual existence', as legally constituted facticities of unproblematic ontological status, we see organizations as problematic concepts to be discussed and carefully scrutinized before becoming resources for analysis. As Bittner (1965) suggests, we see organizations in the first instance not as resources through which analysis is carried out but as *topics* for analysis in their own right.

Second, the organization of production perspective that has dominated organization theory and the associated disciplines has as its focus the plurality of organizations, but not the concept and form of *organization* itself. Organization is paradoxically taken for granted, as a non-problematic feature of social organization. The focus in the organization of production is on the arrangement, and especially internal structuring, of formal collectivities ('organizations') *in the public domain*. These social constructions in the public domain are conceived to be empirically obvious, self-evidently producers of outcomes and objects, and are almost exclusively seen in a non-problematic way. In contrast, the reproduction of organization perspective is concerned with organization itself rather than the plurality of organizations. 'Organization' is a problematic feature of the dominant relationships of the public and private domains. The emphasis is not on fixed outcomes and products, but on the processes we call 'organization'. The sexuality of organization is a prime aspect of seen, yet often unnoticed, social processes within the organizing of human interaction.

Third, rather than take pragmatic stances on how organization is produced, we would first raise some philosophical issues. Rather than accept the after-dinner dictum that an ounce of fact is worth a pound of theory, we would maintain the viability of the reverse. Given the sensitivity of the subject matter we are about to consider, we have to escape the tyranny of limited data. We would seek to elevate literature, popular fiction, cinema and art to the ranks of proper subjects of study, rather than concentrate exclusively upon social understanding as *science*. The empiricist and pragmatic underpinnings of social science, at least in its organization of production guise, are open to question.

Fourth, rather than be disrespectful of what is old and past in the celebration of what is new in organizational life, we should not be ashamed of searching for the present in the past (Foucault, 1976). Rather than seeing history as an unfolding narrative with a beginning, a middle and an end and a clear story line (Lyotard, 1982), the reproduction of organization viewpoint emphasizes reversals, circularities, incomplete beginnings and unfinished endings. Human society and organizations have historically been and remain sexual, not in a deterministic biological sense but in the persistence of the social presence of sexuality, albeit in different forms and with different degrees of explicitness. Quests for rationality are not performed by asexual actors, but by people in sexually coded positions and locations. Similarly, the notion that organizations are subject to a 'march of rationality' to progressively higher rational forms fails to take account of the reversals, circularities, incomplete beginnings and unfinished endings of organization, such as those which are sexual in nature. For example, the introduction of 'more rational' technological systems may be accompanied by a quite unforeseen set of sexual meanings (see, for example, Cockburn, 1983:139; Game and Pringle, 1983:86). Likewise, historical change to more rationalistic organizations, such as bureaucracies, does not necessarily mean any movement away from sexuality.[7] On the contrary, the creation of bureaucratic organizations may create the spaces, both social and physical, for more sexual activity within the organization. More grandly, the notion of grand historical nar-

16 The Sexuality of Organization

rative, of which organizations might presumably be part, fails to acknowledge the presence of sexuality.

Fifth, much work within the organization of production perspective is narrow in method and focus; in contrast, the reproduction of organization perspective is wide-ranging. This book reflects a cosmopolitan, international perspective with chapters drawn from three continents written by people concerned as individuals to understand the sexuality of organization. Being part of a large multi-dimensional research grouping located in one institution is not essential to this work. Our methodologies are not governed by what is acceptable to funding agencies. We would maintain that communal networks of the kind represented by this text represent an alternative to those in big science.

In these respects at least, we would not turn our backs on *postmodernism*. We would seek to develop new possibilities in organizational analysis, to emphasize mosaic thinking rather than linearity, to concentrate upon lived experience rather than productivity. Analysis rooted in the reproduction of organization perspective begins not from organization theory but from social theory. It would also encourage methodological pluralism – not the emphasis on big science but on the encouragement of individual and small-scale collective research offering a breadth as well as depth.

In summary, the vision we have, in the face of the organization of production viewpoint, is of a philosophically aware stance, non-hierarchical in its structure, pluralistic in its methodology, open in terms of its inspiration, historically conscious, posing problems, eschewing easy answers and 'one best way' solutions, and last, but by no means least, less constrained by regional, sexual, gender, ethnic and age discriminations in its students. Rather than focusing on the plurality of organizations through a unified methodology, we argue for a focus on organization through pluralistic methodology. As we said initially, this creates a framework in which competing definitions and contested concepts are at the centre. Comparing these two visions might be helped by Table 1.1.

The language we have used here is the language of opposition. The two approaches are distinctive and different; they are in tension with each other; but in practice, they are also in some senses in a close relation.[8] Now, in criticizing the organization of production, and arguing in favour of a movement towards the reproduction of organization stance, we should clear away some possible misapprehensions. First, although the organization of production may be represented as or justified as or seen to favour the desexualization of organizations, this is largely illusory. Organizations, or organization theories for that matter, that advocate desexualization, are

Table 1.1 *Contested visions of organization*

	Organization of production	Reproduction of organization
Key concerns	'productivity' rationality	'lived/deconstructed experience' sexuality
Meta-discourse	modernism	postmodernism
Social organization of knowledge	big science	co-operative network
Sources of data	'scientific surveys' experimentation unity of method	art, literature and anecdote action research plurality of methods
Key questions	how are *organizations* to be understood and improved?	how is *organization* produced and reproduced?
Relationship of organization and sexuality	the organization of sexuality	the sexuality of organization

just as sexualized, though perhaps implicitly, as explicitly sexualized organizations. Secondly, and similarly, in arguing for the reproduction of organization perspective and a focus on the study of sexuality, we are not suggesting the increased or more explicit sexualization of organizations. Thirdly, we are not saying that the organization of production is unimportant nor that its students are engaged in a worthless pursuit. Indeed there are occasions when analysis from that viewpoint may well be worthwhile. Nevertheless, for present purposes, we have adopted a defence of an alternative, equally viable stance, supported by the triangle of forces of postmodernism (in part at least), lived experience, and a co-operative network. This book is the product of such a set of forces.

We are clear in our minds that the viewpoint we are developing operates at a deep rather than a surface level. We do *not* claim that the authors are concentrating on the same issues, or the same methods, or are using the same bodies of theory. The reader will find we differ in many places on *issues, methods and theories*. How then can there be a shared view at a deep level? The answer, of course, is to do with a commonality of meta-theory, or worldview, in which the kinds of constellation of elements taken by the authors to be signficant are present. It is at this level that we would seek to reorientate organizational analysis.

But what would this reorientated form look like on the surface? What bodies of substantive literature would it draw upon? Where would we go to detail the sexuality of organization?

An outline of the sexuality of organization

The time and the space of organizations
Clearly then both organization(s) and sexuality are social constructions, existing within specific historical and spatial relations. The historical and spatial relations of organization(s) and sexuality simultaneously act as the social frameworks or contexts within which specific sexual practices in organizations are performed. Furthermore, organizations and organization are themselves reflections of the social organization of sexuality, especially in the public domain. In this way the production and reproduction of organization are part of the social organization of sexuality.

Organizations themselves exist in historical time and physical space; they reflect the social structuring of time and space within their own particular social contexts; they are thus also reflective of the social structuring of the body/bodies within those social contexts. In some of the larger cities there is a clear sexual zoning in terms of lesbian and gay territories, 'red light districts', and so on, in opposition to the spatial domination of heterosexual organization(s) (Rubin, 1984:286–7). There is in effect, 'a geography of access to certain kinds of sexual and erotic experience . . . ' (Rubin et al. 1981); and these geographies are, more often than not, socially constructed around and through organizations.

Though heterosexuality is the dominant form of sexuality in most organizations, there are obviously great variations in the ways in which sexuality is apparent in different organizations. In order to place the status of sexuality in organizations in context, it is sometimes helpful to consider the extent to which sexuality is an explicit element in organizational goals. In some cases, especially sexploitation organizations such as in the pornography industry, the sexual basis of organizations is explicit (Delacoste and Alexander, 1988); more often the sexuality of organizations is obscured by, subordinated to or sublimated to 'non-sexual' organizational purposes.

In many, probably most, organizations, organizational goals may be quite obscure in this respect: they may be presented in apparently asexual language. Similarly, one can ask whose sexual interests are being served or are dominant in a particular organization; who in or outside the organization is the 'prime beneficiary', in sexual terms. At first sight this may be difficult to notice; it may appear that people 'just get on with their work'. However, on closer examination, it may become all too obvious that a particular group – say, in a restaurant, certain types of customer – are those in whose sexual interests the organization is organized. Accordingly, Blau and Scott's (1963) typology of organizations by their prime beneficiary can be modified in terms of how the sexual component of organizational goals is of benefit to managers and owners, clients and customers, organizational members, or none of these (Hearn and Parkin, 1987).

Upon these particular distributions, both organizational and sexual, has happened AIDS, bringing with it the portrayal of sexual practices in government propaganda, a wealth of new organizational policies on sexuality, as well as pain, suffering, death and hope. Meanwhile, the Moral Right restricts the civil rights of lesbians and gay men, urges increased censorship, suspects sex education in schools, and opposes adequate medical advice on sex and contraception to young people, outside parental involvement. Strange alliances occasionally occur between some such factions of the Right, and non-libertarian feminist and Left elements. At such an historical time, and in the changing relations of geographical space not least through electronic and computer technology, we may ask, 'How are we to talk about sex?' Supplementaries to this question are 'How are we to talk in organizations about sex?' and 'How does such talk, or silence, constitute organization itself?'

The movement from the mainstream
In the modernist projects, either sexuality and organizations are opposed, or sexuality is incorporated in organizations; within postmodernism, either sexuality and organization suffuse each other, or organization is incorporated in sexuality. In the remainder of this chapter we will do two things. Firstly, we will review some of the major literature on organization and sexuality, much of it feminist in orientation or inspiration, to demonstrate that a body of work is developing from which one might draw in constructing a viable reproduction of organization perspective; secondly, we will introduce the contributions that follow, in relation to this literature.

It will be obvious when analysing the later chapters that some of them stand between the organization of production and the reproduction of organization viewpoints. Concepts derived from the former are used as starting points for creating an alternative vision through critique. Particular traditions in organization theory are open to criticism, whilst offering useful insights on sexuality in organizations. Thus in Chapter 2 Albert Mills shows the relevance of a wide variety of organizational literature for the consideration of gender and sexuality, especially the production and reproduction of gendered identities. And in the following chapter Peta Tancred-Sheriff both critiques and develops labour process theory, to analyse the relationship between the control function in organizations and the construction of sexuality. Used in this way, concepts from organization theory become transformed into vehicles for opening up the reproduction of organization. Our use of concepts from the organization of production is to transcend their limitations, and so work towards a shared view of the sexuality of organization.

(Hetero)sexual harassment and (hetero)sexual relationships
While the study of organizations with its *agendered* tradition in many ways provides the context for the study of sexuality and organizations, the promotion of sexuality as a topic within that study has come through the indirect route of journalistic sources and political pressures. These have focused mainly on explicit displays of sexuality in the workplace. In most organizations such explicit displays are predominantly heterosexual, or apparently so.

The notion of 'sexual harassment' (probably the only concept of sexual violence to be labelled by women themselves) was recognized in North American journalism, itself operating partly in the context of the modern women's movement of the 1960s and early 1970s (Farley, 1978). From then, sexual harassment has been taken up in workplace and other organizational campaigns, by trade unions, and by women's groups. These campaigns and groups have often though by no means exclusively been led by women office workers; public sector trade union women's sections and committees have often been prominent. To illustrate the development of this political activity, action research and social survey, we may note that the Alliance Against Sexual Coercion based in Cambridge, Massachusetts, published an annotated list of 171, mainly American, publications on sexual harassment to that date, including ten surveys (1980); while the trade union organization Leeds TUCRIC's (1983) study of sexual harassment included a bibliography of seventy-three, mainly British, publications and eleven British trade union publications. In addition, in 1987 the Ministry of Social Affairs and Health in Finland published an excellent review, research and bibliographic text, giving details of 341 publications and ten *bibliographies* on sexual harassment, with particularly useful information on Scandinavian and German sources (Hogbacka et al., 1987). A useful American collection that brings together policy-related material and academic papers on 'romantic and coercive behaviors at work' is Neugarten and Shafritz's (1980) *Sexuality in Organizations*.

Action-based surveys have closely interrelated with and indeed prompted further, more academic analyses. Many of these have been conducted by Barbara Gutek and her co-researchers, and her *Sex and the Workplace* (1985) stands as a landmark text in the development of the academic area. In Chapter 4 she provides a comprehensive review of this and other research on sexual harassment and other social–sexual behaviours, along with policy recommendations for action in organizations. Academic work on sexual harassment has developed from two major directions. First, there are psychological and social psychological studies, sometimes employing the 'imagined situation' as means to the analysis of differential evaluations of and responses to harassment. 'Many of these studies use similar research designs, all classic analyses of variance designs, in which students, employees, or managers are asked to rate one or more scenarios' (Gutek and Dunwoody, 1987). Secondly, there is the increased concern of industrial sociologists and sociologists of work and workplaces with sexuality and sexual harassment, as a necessary development of a general concern with gender relations and power. The major example, of this approach have, not surprisingly, been developed through feminist studies of industrial organizations (for example, Pollert, 1981; Cockburn, 1983). These two approaches are usually somewhat separate, but on occasions their insights converge. In Chapter 5 Nancy DiTomaso brings them together by using the frameworks of both sexual harassment and sexual discrimination to analyse workers' perceptions in three different organizations. (Also compare Gutek and Morasch's, 1982, research and the Leeds TUCRIC, 1983, survey: Hearn and Parkin, 1987:83–5.)

Another set of empirical studies that have helped to establish sexuality as an (almost) respectable organizational issue is the development and inhibition of heterosexual relationships in organizations (Quinn, 1977; Collins, 1983; Gray, 1984; Harrison and Lee, 1986). These often stress the possible mismatch of such sexual practices and organizational norms within an emergent Weberianism (also see Horn and Horn, 1982).

While the range of types of sexuality and sexual practices is immensely varied, the focus in this book is largely, though by no means exclusively, on heterosexuality and heterosexual relations in organizations. The main reason for this is that heterosexuality and heterosexual relations, indeed hierarchic or patriarchal heterosexuality, are the dominant forms in most organizations. Most studies of sexual harassments and sexual relationships in organizations focus on heterosexuality. Furthermore, most studies, certainly of harassment and often too of sexual relationships, point to the impact of the power of men in organizations. These particular avenues are followed more explicitly by David Collinson and Margaret Collinson in Chapter 6, where they explore the domination of men's sexuality in three organizational settings.

Private experiences in the public domain: institutional closure

The acknowledged presence of sexual harassment, sexual relationships, and even sexual rumour is a major element of the sexuality of organizations in many settings. Also important is the way in which sexuality brings private experiences, which do not necessarily involve explicit or visible sexual behaviours in the organization, into the public domain. In one sense this is a common feature in the lives of organizational members in most, perhaps all, organizations. However, the contradictions of private experience and the demands of the public domain are particularly intense in two instances: in closed or total institutions, which are looked at in this section; and in the lives of lesbians and gay men, especially in heterosexually dominated organizations, which are considered in the next section. In both cases, people may be assessed on sexual grounds; they may be conscious of their sexual oppression; and their own sexual behaviour may be severely controlled or proscribed in the organization. Indeed in some organizations such sexual dynamics may not even be explicit or visible in *dominant* organizational discourse. The ambiguities of the private and the public may thus be more intense than for heterosexuals in less closed organizations.

Institutional closure brings into play a particular, and sometimes very powerful, set of organizational controls over time and space, over sexual time and sexual bodies. This is most evident in total institutions, where people eat, sleep, work and play – and have whatever sexual relations they do have – under a formally unified organizational regime. Where the whole of the days or even the life of residents is spent within the institution, private life and sexuality are inevitably important features of public organizational life, with powerful, even if liberal, rulings on sexual conduct. Total institutions are thus primarily institutions where the total control of the bodies of residents is attempted, including their sexuality, sexual relations, sleeping arrangements and night-time practices. In some cases this involves the institutional control of initiation, stripping, degradation ceremonies, strip-searching, and so on. Within the institutional regime of the total institution, the resident is a body. Rules are designed to forbid, control, or even to facilitate social–sexual contacts between residents and non-residents. Attempts to introduce conjugal visits in prisons have been made in Denmark, Sweden, the Netherlands, Mexico and parts of the United States.

The private experience of sexuality in the public domains is of special importance in single-sex institutions, such as prisons, partly because of the importance of policies or lack of policies on homosexuality. In some such military, religious and custodial organizations there is a complex and paradoxical interrelation of official censure on homosexuality, and yet an unofficial facilitation of covert homosexual relations. Homosexuality may be grounds for expulsion from some military and church organizations, yet those organizations may also provide enclaves for lesbians and gay men, and for single-sex sexual activity. Such organizations formalize and institutionalize the social paradoxes of sexuality, and especially the intimate associations of pleasure and danger. These complications of closure are deepened in organizations in the 'intermediate zone', where the dichotomy of the private and public worlds breaks down. This question is looked at in detail in Chapter 7 by Wendy Parkin, when she examines the ambiguities around sexuality, both public and private, facing organizational members in residential care organizations.

Lesbians and gay men in organizations
As already noted, most organizations remain highly complicated and embedded structures, indeed archives, of heterosexuality and heterosexism. Most are dominated by groups of heterosexual men. On the other hand, such men, as managers or workers, may often be socially defined as heterosexual yet be at the least homosocial, and possibly also homo-erotic in their relations with each other: there is a characteristic and routine homosexuality of heterosexual men in organizational situations. In addition, most organizations are arenas for the development of 'heterosexual complementarity' between women and men (Cockburn, 1988). Such heterosexual hegemony tends to construct lesbians and gay men as isolated exceptions, so that they and their sexuality come to be seen, by many heterosexuals at least, as private and individual, even as personal 'problems'.

There now exists a considerable number of empirical surveys and analyses of discrimination against lesbians and gay men and their treatment in organizations, often initially produced as small-scale studies and pamphlets (for example, Campaign for Homosexual Equality, 1981; Beer et al., 1983; GLC, 1985). Some of the reports and surveys of this type have collected information on combined samples of lesbians and gay men, 'making it difficult to determine whether the problem [of employment discrimination] operates differently for the two populations' (Levine and Leonard, 1984:701; also fn.7). A valuable review of the literature on employment discrimination against gay men is Levine's (1979) survey in the *International Review of Modern Sociology*. There have been relatively few studies specifically concerned with lesbians in organizations. *All in a Day's Work*, produced by Lesbian Employment Rights in London (Taylor, 1986), is the only British survey of its type that we know of, and an example of research that deals with both unemployment and employment. Levine and Leonard (1984) identify five empirical studies (Saghir and Robins, 1973; Chafetz et al., 1974; Bell and Weinberg, 1978; Brooks, 1981; Schneider, 1981), plus their own which give some information on lesbian job discrimination. Apart from the finding of relatively high levels of anticipated and experienced discrimination, they offer some tentative conclusions that discrimination is greater in private sector than in public sector organizations, and in medium or large than in small organizations. This may partly be due to strategies of self-employment or specialization in particular areas of work, both of which may involve work in small organizations. Organizations are often hostile places for lesbians to live and work in, and in Chapter 8 Marny Hall analyses in depth the complex interpersonal strategies developed by lesbians for maintaining personal integrity in the face of double oppression. The private experiences of lesbians and gay men in the public domains of heterosexually dominated organizations might suggest that a kind of social 'total institution' is in operation.

In contrast, some organizations do operate with an explicit and conscious ideology, working assumptions and practices, that are not based on heterosexuality. Sometimes this may be an important element in the actual foundation of the organization as, for example, with gay switchboards and gay advice services. In other cases, non-heterosexual ideology and practice may develop over time with changes in the membership of an organization, and the sexual orientation of the membership. Weston and Rofel's (1985) case study of 'Amazon Auto Repair', a small business of lesbian owners and lesbian workers, is a very informative illustration of the complex interrelation of sexuality and work, the possibilities for and limitations on reformulating dominant divisions of people's public and private worlds. Perhaps above all, it shows up the fact that sexual culture and economic class structure cannot easily be separated; each is formed on the basis of the other. While sexuality can be conceptualized as consumption (Lippert, 1977), it is also production; while the politics of sexuality can be practised as struggles over the control of the body, they are also more variable encounters in which control is not necessarily the prime strategic issue (Diamond and Quinby, 1984).

Organization sexuality

Analysis of the ways in which organizations construct sexuality, and sexuality constructs organizations, are necessary conceptually and politically. In addition, the concept of 'organization sexuality' has been developed to convey the paradoxical and powerful form of that interrelation (Hearn and Parkin, 1987). In this view, organization and sexuality occur simultaneously. The very actions of organizing and being organized may carry a sexual cachet – be, in some senses, sexual. Examples of 'organization sexuality' are everywhere in the organizational world – in the movement of people, throughout organizations, in the pattern of emotions, consciousness, language and imagery in organizations. These simultaneous occurrences of organization and sexuality may be seen in the behaviours of managers. Cockburn (1989; 1990) has described the sexual regime in a large retail company, in terms of the power of two managerial forms: one controlled by traditionalist men, 'at best gentlemanly, at worst they saw women as fitted only for kitchen and nursery'; the other controlled by newer modernist men, in which women were expected to 'tolerate, join in, enjoy and retaliate in kind when sexual innuendo and jokes, the stock in trade of modern management, were employed'. In Chapter 9 Deborah Sheppard considers a different set of complexities for women managers, and presents detailed information on their image and self-image, within which the interconnections of sexual presentation, organizational presentation and power are intense.

Other examples of organization sexuality surround the boss–secretary relationship. Consider the 'normal' behaviour of bosses walking *freely* into secretaries' offices, *dictating* to secretaries, their head held bent, both with their own sexual connotations (Hearn and Parkin, 1987:135, referring to Henley, 1977:31,59). Rather similarly, consider the sexualization of the doctor–nurse relationship (Game and Pringle, 1983:108–9). In Chapter 10, Rosemary Pringle attends to the profound and subtle interrelations of organizational and sexual dynamics in the secretary–boss relationship, in the light of feminist and postmodernist theory. The book is concluded with a short postscript from the editors.

Common features and key debates

In this book we seek to allow spaces for discourse on these topics. We aim to encourage speech on gender and sexuality. Since all the chapters stand within a triangle formed by critical, feminist and profeminist theory and practice, certain conceptualizations will recur, being mentioned by some authors, emphasized by others, and then dealt with *sotto voce* in yet other chapters. These conceptualizations are also contested, and the vigour with which definitional and other issues are debated suggests a field which is alive, active and growing. We cannot pretend to be arbitrators in assessing the superiority or inferiority of particular competing views as to the 'correct' meaning of key notions. Instead we can prefigure some of what we have to offer in this book, and some of the common features and key debates within it.

First, at the most basic level is a commitment to critical, *feminist* and *profeminist* stances. From this comes an appreciation of the failure within malestream organizational analysis to consider issues of gender and sexuality. This neglect of these important aspects of organizational life comes partly from a concern for material production and how that is organized in the factory and the office. What one also needs to look at is how organization is produced and reproduced on a daily basis. Each chapter in this book provides this counterview.

However, feminist and profeminist standpoints are likely to be presented somewhat differently. If 'gender' and 'sexuality' are a terrain of conflict, some of it 'personal' and some of it 'political', which is what we believe to be the case, then a source of disputation might well be between feminist women and profeminist men. For while profeminist men may, as a personal and political position, support feminism, this does not resolve conflicts of interest between women and men. Women and men continue to approach their areas of concern, and live their personal experience, from their own gendered stances. Men can learn from feminism, but cannot be feminists.

Second, as already outlined, there will be some talk of the *production* and the *reproduction* of organization(s). Much of the malestream literature focuses upon the former, much of feminist writing concentrates on the latter. Here again, issues will be raised concerning gender and sexuality, for both are intimately linked to the production and reproduction of organizational forms.

Third, there is a concentration on *power* and *control*, as key concepts which illuminate gender and sexuality and their interrelationship. There is an attempt to see discrimination and harassment from within this conceptual arena. Organizations are seen as scenes of power, both gendered and sexual.

Fourth, reference will often be made, explicitly or implicitly, to the distinction between the *public* and the *private*. This antinomy seeks to highlight the world of work, the organization, the street, the individual within society, on the one hand, and the world of the home and of inner-directedness, on the other.

Fifth, some of the contributors speak of organizational *sexualiz-*

ation and *desexualization*. The latter refers to a supposed process whereby sexuality is expressed from and repressed within the public domain to be relocated in the private. Sexualization refers to a supposed counter-trend whereby organizations become the locus and site of increasing sexually based activity and representation. The debate on this particular issue is also featured in the text. Debates on the sexualization and desexualization of organizations have several dimensions: they are fundamentally debates about history and the patterns of change in the relationship of sexuality and organizations at different historical times; they are also about the consistency or unevenness of change between and throughout organizations, and the particular ways in which the presence or absence of sexuality is measured.

Sixth is a *commitment against the hierarchicalizing pressures* of big science, to seek data in non-standard places, to focus on lived experience through sexuality rather than on productivity seen through the lens of rationality. Each chapter seeks to express this commitment.

And finally, given the nature of the last point, another unifying feature in the text is a *concern for practice* and a *fundamental restructuring of power relations*. Critique has to involve lessons for practice – in that to want to criticize is to feel the need to change the nature of the phenomenon under investigation. This orientation, which some might term *praxis*, where critical theory closely informs day-to-day practice, is a common thread throughout the chapters. The weight of sexual oppression can be seen.

Notes

We are very grateful to Sue Jones, Deborah Sheppard and Peta Tancred-Sheriff for their comments on earlier versions of this chapter.

1. In saying that sexuality is related to desire, it is necessary to make it clear that we are referring specifically to feminist work on desire (for example, MacKinnon, 1982; Coward, 1984; Schneider and Gould, 1987). Interpretations of desire as, say, 'mastery' or 'possession' represent particularly male notions, that are possible, but not the only social forms of desire. A considerable amount of recent feminist writing *reclaims* the notion of desire as a useful referent – and not one that can be left to dominant male interpretations (*Feminist Review* Collective, 1982; Ardill and O'Sullivan, 1986).

2. These conceptualizations are a development of the framework used by Connell (1985, 1987). Comparisons may be made with the asexual and agendered typology of organizational analysis and sociological paradigms, presented by Burrell and Morgan (1979), and the typology of literature on gender and organizations, presented by Hearn and Parkin (1983). We present this framework here as an heuristic device, as apart from the problems of over-simplification, any reduction of feminist theory and practice to 'paradigms' is particularly inappropriate, and all the more so

in any analysis by men. Other comparisons can be drawn with Walby's (1988) four approaches to gender politics. Several reviews of approaches to sex and gender are included in Hess and Ferree's *Analyzing Gender* (1987:esp. Part 1).

3. We are using this combination of the social role model and social interactionism with some caution. In particular, social (or sexual) interactionism in the form of the following of sexual scripts has potential for a far more individualist, even phenomenological, analysis than is usual in role models.

4. While much feminist work is broadly critical of both biological and social interactionist sex role models (Eichler, 1980), these approaches, especially the psychoanalytic variants, have been very influential in the development of some feminist critiques (e.g. Coward, 1984). There are also biological essentialist feminisms, sometimes constructed around the concept of bodily sexual difference; as well as a large, especially North American, feminist literature on sex roles.

5. As one example of this, Minson (1981) asserts that 'coming out' to 'homosexuality' is predicated on three assumptions: that sexual practice has to do with personal identity; that the two are one and the same; and that voicing one's identity is the best way to know it. A recent discussion 'on the place of identity in feminist politics' is presented by Adams (1989).

6. Ardill and O'Sullivan (1986:33) go on to suggest that this ideology involves 'an analysis of the world as made up of a fixed hierarchy of oppressions (or a select collection of oppressions) around gender, sexuality, race and ethnicity, age and ability, and notions of the "authenticity" of subjective experience which can be understood only with reference to the hierarchy'. Other critiques of the idea of sex hierarchy are given by Rubin (1984) and Connell (1983).

7. Our uses of 'rational' and 'rationalistic' here refer to dominant malestream views; feminist views of rationality of care or rationality of responsibility (Holter, 1984) offer a quite different perspective, emphasizing the relationship of rationality and reproduction.

8. The connections between modernism and postmodernism are intense; the extent to which postmodernism can be disentangled from modernism is disputed; the former is after all defined in relation and counter-distinction to the latter (Featherstone, 1988). A recent critique of many of the variants of postmodernism on the grounds that they carry their own (modernist) grand narratives is provided by Wickham (forthcoming).

2
Gender, Sexuality and Organization Theory

Albert J. Mills

> These next two chapters introduce some major questions on the relationship of gender, sexuality and organization theory. Here the discussion begins with the long-running debate on organizational culture. This is re-evaluated in terms of the impact of gendered 'rules of control' upon organizational cultures, which can then be seen as contexts in which gendered identities develop. This chapter demonstrates some of the novel ways in which debates around sexuality and gender and debates in organization theory can be of relevance and use to each other.

The rootedness of existing organizational approaches in commitments to the status quo (Burrell and Morgan, 1979) and a consequent inability or unwillingness to address the gendered nature of organizational theorizing (Hearn and Parkin, 1983) has led to the development of a number of radical alternatives. In recent years a number of works have argued the need for a retheorization of the field of organizational analysis (Benson, 1977; Clegg and Dunkerley, 1980; Clegg, 1981) and in particular the development of approaches that adequately theorize issues of sex and gender (Burrell, 1984; K. Ferguson, 1984; Tancred-Sheriff, 1985; Hearn and Parkin, 1987). Analysis of culture and organizations, however, has until recently received only fleeting attention from a radical perspective (Crompton and Jones, 1984; Smircich, 1985; Morgan, 1986). I have attempted elsewhere (Mills, 1988b) to argue that a feminist reworking of Clegg's (1981) rules analysis provides a useful way of conceptualizing the notion of organizational culture:[1]

> Culture is essentially composed of a number of understandings and expectations that assist people in making sense of life. In organizations, no less than other aspects of social life, such understandings have to be learned and they guide people in the appropriate or relevant behaviour, help them to know how things are done, what is expected of them, how to achieve certain things, etc. Indeed, it is the very configuration of such 'rules' of behaviour that distinguishes one social or organizational group from another, it is an essential part of their cultural identity. (Mills, 1988b:360)

But, as Morgan (1986:131) puts it, the structuring of culture involves actors; culture needs to be understood 'as an active, living phenomenon through which people create and recreate the worlds in which they live'. Thus, it can be argued that: 'The culture of an organization can . . . be viewed as consisting simultaneously of a structured set of rules in which behaviour is bounded and of a process, or outcome, resulting from the particular character of the rule-bound behaviour of the actors involved' (Mills, 1988a:4).

Feminist-materialism
Sexual discrimination is a pervasive feature of organizations and there is growing evidence of a need to study not only its *impact* upon women but also its relationship to the process of gender *construction* (Tancred-Sheriff, 1985). Given that gender is a cultural phenomenon (Weeks, 1986) it seems appropriate to question the contribution of organizational cultures to the construction and maintenance of 'male' and 'female' subjects. As Linda Smircich (1985:67) has expressed it, 'an important and necessary aspect of a cultural paradigm for organizational analysis is the addition of a feminist voice', a perspective on culture 'that calls for analysis and critique of the underlying gender basis of the production of knowledge and the prevailing social order'.

A feminist-materialist concern with rules of control seeks to explore not simply the class-structured character of the organization – society interface but also, and in particular, the sex-structured features of that interface. Specifically feminist-materialism is concerned with the sexual division of labour, with explorations of the significance of the public/domestic (Glennon, 1983) divide. Briefly, from this perspective, rules are interrogated for their contribution to the maintenance of gendered identities and the various consequences that arise from that process. Gender is seen as a set of 'master' rules, i.e. 'sense is made of each of a number of rules by reference to a broader, more-or-less coherent class of rules which coalesce in notions of gender' (Mills, 1988a:6). But gender-rule learning needs also to be understood as a process which is developed throughout the life of an individual and in which organizations play a crucial role.

Sexuality
Sexuality is a key factor in the analysis of the relationship between organizational culture and gender construction (Hearn and Parkin, 1987). As Weeks has noted, gender and sexuality have become inextricably linked:

We still cannot think about sexuality without taking into account gender; or, to put it more generally, the elaborate facade of sexuality has in large part been built upon the assumption of fundamental differences between men and women, and of male dominance over women. (Weeks, 1986:45)

A vital aspect of how we develop and maintain a sense of our selves as 'men' and 'women' involves the acting out of sexuality, 'the capacities of the body and psyche are given meaning only in social relations' (Weeks, 1986:15). In a world in which women are viewed as subordinate to men, in which heterosexuality is the norm and in which organizations expect behaviour to conform to a view of 'normal' gender relations, sexuality becomes an embodiment of power relations.

But what is sexuality? Hearn and Parkin use the term to refer to 'The social expression of or social relations to physical, bodily desires, real or imagined, by or for others or for oneself, together with the related bodily states and experiences' (1987:58).

This definition is compelling yet problematic: it serves, however intentioned, to reduce sexuality to those actions and expressions that are directly, or consciously, concerned with physical contact. It is far from clear that this definition adequately reflects the range of historical or contemporary usage of the term. In the work of Weeks (1986:15) sexuality is: 'an historical construction, which brings together a host of different biological and mental possibilities – gender, identity, bodily differences, reproductive capacities, needs, desires and fantasies – which need not be linked together, and in other cultures have not been'.

The way that those possibilities are suggested, acted out and experienced depends upon a range of circumstances, actors and configuration of events:

Sexuality is something which society produces in complex ways. It is a result of diverse social practices that give meaning to social activities, of social definitions and self-definitions, of struggles between those who have power to define and regulate, and those who resist. Sexuality is not given, it is a product of negotiation, struggle and human agency. (Weeks, 1986:25)

It is its very character as a social construct that gives sexuality its relationship of/to power. As Plummer (1975) has suggested, nothing is sexual but naming it makes it so!

It is true that, in large part, contemporary usage of the term sexuality refers to bodily desires but that is only the tip of an iceberg that reaches down to the very essence of human identity. The dominant (heterosexual) view of sexuality in Western societies is rooted in notions of sex and of gender. For example, it is hardly possible for a person to perceive a member of the 'opposite sex' as being 'sexy' without consciously and unconsciously conjuring up the very notion of an 'opposite sex'. One could argue that homosexual attraction also relies on conjuring up the notion of the other's sexual sameness. On the other hand, reference to a person's 'masculinity' or 'femininity' implies a notion of their sexuality.

In understanding the character of sexuality it is vital to understand its association with the concept of sex, which in itself is an historical construct:

> The earliest usage of the term 'sex', in the sixteenth century, referred precisely to the division of humanity into the male section and the female section (that is, to difference of gender). The dominant meaning today, however, and the one current since the early nineteenth century, refers to physical relations between the sexes, 'to have sex'. The extension of the meanings of these words indicates a shift in the way that 'sexuality' (the abstract noun referring to the quality of being 'sexual') is understood in our culture. (Weeks, 1986:13)

'Sex', in its modern usage, is a term that 'refers both to an act and to a category of person, to a practice and to a gender' (Weeks, 1986:13). This definition stands in contrast to Oakley's (1972) influential distinction between 'sex' (as basic physiological differences between men and women) and 'gender' (as culturally specific patterns of behaviour which may be attached to the sexes). The problem with Oakley's definition is, as Tresemer (1975) points out, that the opposition between the two terms presupposes a degree of prior certainty about the separation of innate and environmental differences (quoted in Oakley, 1981:41). Rakow (1986:12) agrees, adding that: 'The relationship between biology and culture can no longer be assumed to be a simple layering of one or top of the other, resulting in cultural differences added on to already biological differences between two pregiven sexes.' Rakow's concern is with a shift from research into the consequences of sex differences to the development of a research focus upon gender construction as a process – 'the doing of gender':

> Sex differences research rests on the assumption that researchers know which traits and behaviours are masculine and which feminine ... Thorne, Kramarae, and Henley ... recommend that research move away from a conceptualization of gender as an individual attribute toward 'complex descriptions of relationship among speakers – sensitive to gender in the context of setting, roles, and other social identities such as age, class, or ethnicity'. (Rakow, 1986:16)

Drawing upon the work of Rakow, Weeks (1986) and Foucault (1979) sexuality needs to be understood as a continual process of power relations, of gender construction, of social and self-definitions; not simply as a reference to our apparent bodily selves but also to the very construction of ourselves as gendered subjects:

> Gender is both something we do and something we think with, both a set of social practices and a system of cultural meanings. The social practices – the 'doing' of gender – and the cultural meanings – 'thinking the world' using the categories and experiences of gender – constitute us as men and women, organized into a particular configuration of social relations. (Rakow, 1986:21)

Gender rules and organizations

In his analysis of organizations and configurations of rules of control Clegg (1981) refers to six major areas of rule behaviour – extra-organizational, technical, social-regulative, state, strategic and reproductive rules. Clegg's focus upon class restricts his subsequent analysis of gender to 'extra-organizational rules', i.e. attitudes about the nature and relative social worth of women which are reflected/reinforced within organizations in such things as low pay, processes of deskilling, the construction of dual labour markets, and low-status work. From a feminist-materialist perspective, gender permeates not only extra-organizational rules but each and every area of rule-bound behaviour. Furthermore, extra-organizational rules are viewed as a central area of rule analysis rather than one of six intersecting areas of rule behaviour.

Extra-organizational rules
What is interesting from a feminist-materialist perspective is how extra-organizational rules are developed and maintained in relation to the construction of organizations. An important area for exploration is the concept of 'public' and 'domestic' spheres of life. Feminist studies indicate that the idea of womanhood is related to the development of the gender division of labour with its ascription of women to family or domestic life and men to public life. It has been argued that an integral part of the image of womanhood is an association of childbearing and child-rearing with domestic life; rooting womanhood in connected ideas of biological reproduction and domestic location:

> The fact that, in most industrial societies, a good part of a woman's adult life is spent giving birth to and rearing children leads to a differentiation of domestic and public spheres of activity that can . . . be shown to shape a number of relevant aspects of human social structure and psychology. (Rosaldo, 1974:23)

In regard to social structure Rosaldo suggests that there is an asymmetrical relationship between domestic and public activities, with the public, in contrast to the domestic, being accorded greater cultural worth. In public life men have become 'the locus of cultural value': 'male, as opposed to female, activities are always recognized as predominantly important, and cultural systems give authority and value to the roles and activities of men' (Rosaldo, 1974:19).

Cultural significance and public activities become intertwined, not simply reinforcing notions of gender but adding yet another layer upon the inequitable distinctions between men and women; women becoming associated with a distinct, yet definitely inferior, set of socio-biological activities. This process of 'gender asymmetry' depends upon male control not only over the material means of production but also over the means of symbolic production (Mackie, 1987:28).

An important dynamic of the gender division of labour is the process of socialization (Chodorow, 1971) which, in the broadest terms, prepares males and females for the fulfilment of different roles; a process which influences the shaping of personality differences (Chodorow, 1978). This has consequences for the development of gendered organizational cultures. As Eldridge and Crombie remind us: 'Roles are ubiquitous in social life. In even the least structured of situations people respond to one another in terms of expectations associated with sex and age roles, and the collective definitions of kinship roles such as son or wife' (1974:114).

But those roles are not simply different; they carry with them notions of inequity (husband over wife, father over children) that are reproduced within organizations and which can be coagulated as less powerful women are confronted by powerful male organization members. Male organizational power tends to exist in the context of occupation of authority roles embedded within male-associated values:

> It often makes a great deal of difference if you're a man or a woman! Many organizations are dominated by gender-related values that bias organizational life in favour of one sex over another. Thus . . . organizations often segment opportunity structures and job markets in ways that enable men to achieve positions of prestige and power more easily than women, and often operate in ways that produce gender-related biases in the way organizational reality is created and sustained on a day-to-day basis. This is most obvious in situations of open discrimination and various forms of sexual harassment, but often pervades the culture of an organization in a way that is much less visible. (Morgan, 1986:178)

The process of gender socialization is a 'culture trap' (Cooper and Davidson, 1982) in which women are relatively ill-prepared for organizational life (Borisoff and Merrill, 1985) and men are relatively ill-prepared to accept them (Dubeck, 1979).

Male domination of the organizational world in the form of ownership and control (Bilton et al. 1983), positions of status and authority (Wright et al., 1982), and in cultural values (Morgan, 1986) and hegemony (Mills, 1988b) has served to restrict the entry of women into the labour force, to filter women into a narrow range of occupations and to channel them into low pay/low status work, and overall to reinforce notions of female inferiority. Domestic location and biological reproductive capacity are reference points that are constantly drawn upon, both implicitly and explicitly, to restrict/throw doubt upon women's ability to be organizationally effective. Women may find themselves concentrated in jobs, such as nursing and child care, that reinforce their sense of self as 'domestic' (Bilton et al., 1983) or in jobs that stress physical 'attractiveness' (Hochschild, 1983) and consequently reinforce male notions of female sexuality:

> Because women are compelled to make themselves attractive in certain ways, and those ways involve submitting to the culture's beliefs about appropriate sexual behaviour, women's appearances are laden down with cultural values, and women have to form their identities within these values, or, with difficulty, against them. (Coward, 1984:78)

Women may also face sexual harassment which, at one level, may insult their sense of self as an autonomous woman while, at another level, reinforcing the notion of woman as inferior and subordinate to man: 'Organizations . . . [are] sites of sexual harassment in which patriarchy and the control it gives over women is reflected in, and enhanced by, sexual harassment' (Burrell, 1984:101).

In the context of organizational power 'the political consequences of male dominance are such that women learn the role of the subordinate, and that role can easily become self-perpetuating' (K. Ferguson, 1984:94). This provides the basis for the worst of situations in which sexual harassment is a regular part of at least some aspect of organizational life (MacKinnon, 1979). It is also a context in which women more often than not find themselves judged incapable of taking on positions of leadership, responsibility and authority:

> The links between the male stereotype and the values that dominate many ideas about the nature of organizations are striking. Organizations are often encouraged to be rational, analytic, strategic, decision-oriented, tough and aggressive, and so are men. This has important implications for women who wish to operate in this kind of world, for insofar as they attempt to foster these values, they are often seen as breaking the traditional female stereotype in a way that opens them to criticism,

36 *The Sexuality of Organization*

e.g., for being 'overly assertive' and 'trying to play a male role'. (Morgan, 1986:178)

Extra-organizational rules, that is, understandings about the respective worth and function of males and females, permeate the cultural arrangements of organizations but they are not fixed; they are mediated in a number of ways as they form part of the cultural processes of each organization. People may enter into organizational arrangements with a sense of gendered self but that self, like the culture itself, is constantly in a 'state of becoming' (Benson, 1977). The specifics of 'doing gender' (Rakow, 1986) may well be linked to the specific rule configurations that compose an organization's culture: notions of femininity and masculinity, developed in a broad cultural context, may be confronted, shaped and reshaped in interaction with a number of other rules. Historical analysis of the notion of womanhood suggests that it stands in dialectical relationship to changes in the character of organizations (Struminger, 1979).

Technical rules
In any formal organization there is 'a job to be done', often in a culturally prescribed way, sometimes expressed as 'the way we do things around here'. The various tasks and mode of accomplishing them – production techniques – incorporate assumptions about the nature of men and women; assumptions that are drawn upon that exclude or undervalue the work of women:

> It can be seen that the market factors and ideological factors leading to women's segregation in the labour force meet in the systematic undervaluation of 'women's work'. Qualities such as close concentration, accuracy and manual dexterity which require obvious skill and training in craft or technician's jobs are relegated to 'natural' and untrained 'aptitudes' in women doing women's occupations. (Pollert, 1981:65)

The nature and extent of female exclusion/undervaluation has varied over time according, among other things, to technical needs and requirements. Physical strength, for example, has often been associated with masculinity, 'men's work', and the subsequent higher evaluation of some male-dominated tasks in contrast to those dominated by females. In the early pioneering days of colonial America the labour-intensive nature of the tasks and the shortage of labour and of women contributed to an image of womanhood that avoided laying stress on physical weakness: 'A casual observer of the colonial household could attest to the strength of women as they routinely lifted heavy caldrons from the fireplace. Accordingly, colonial culture did not delight in calling attention to the delicate frame and petite stature of its women' (Ryan, 1979:28).

According to Ryan, the exacting nature of the tasks at hand during this period relinquished any tendency for the development of any notions of a peculiarly feminine personality: 'colonial culture did not parcel out a whole series of temperamental attributes according to sex. Women were not equipped with such now-familiar traits as maternal instincts, sexual purity, passivity, tranquility, or submissiveness' (1979:28).

Such differences were to come later with the rise of industrial capitalism. In England, meanwhile, notions of physical strength were being embodied in the newly developing textile industry:

> Before the introduction of machinery, the spinning and weaving of raw materials was carried on in the working-man's home [sic]. Wife and daughter spun the yarn that the father wove . . .
>
> The first invention which gave rise to a radical change in the stage of the English workers was the jenny . . . [But] now that the jenny as well as the loom *required a strong hand*, men began to spin, and whole families lived by spinning . . . and, if they had not the means of purchasing a jenny, were forced to live upon the wages of the father alone. (Engels, 1975:307, 310. Emphasis added)

Engels does not appear to question the association of male with strength or 'strong hand'.

Physical strength assumptions underlie many tasks throughout organizations but again can vary according to technical needs. Skill requirements, for example, may supersede strength in certain task cultures:

> In the National Biscuit Company's Pittsburgh plant in 1906 the baking was done by a handful of men, while 1,100 women packaged and frosted cakes. The sexual division of labour was not necessarily based on relative muscle power. In the Pittsburgh metal trades, for example, women heaved sand cores . . . weighing 10 to 50 pounds and hauled them through dusty shops to fuming ovens. Men in the same factory worked only with lighter but more intricate sand cores, having been apprenticed to acquire this high-paying skill. (Ryan, 1979:122)

Nonetheless, as Ryan points out, the industrial character of a particular era can stamp its identity upon the notion of masculinity and femininity. Speaking of 1920s USA she records that:

> It was the age of steel, steam, and then electricity. . . . Powering the industrial machine required massive amounts of human muscle, from mine, metal, and construction workers, most of them male and the majority imported from abroad. It was also the age of the Rockefellers, Carnegies, and the Vanderbilts, who consolidated this industrial power into a few monumental national corporations. In sum, American econ-

omic history seemed its most masculine during this period, characterized by the brute muscular strength of the steelworker and the arrogant aggressiveness of the robber baron. (1979:119)

The concept of skill is a particularly significant area for study in itself as it relates to the evaluation of the work done by females. *Skill* is a concept involving a complex of rules about the nature and value of a person's work. A number of factors combine to ensure that skill is rarely attached to the work of females. Historically, building upon gender divisions, the work of men has been valued higher than that of women (Strumingher, 1979); females are rarely recruited to jobs involving traditional skill training (Abella, 1984); training that does prepare women for skilled positions is grossly inadequate (Mills, 1988a); and the cheapening of female labour has been advantageous to employers (Braverman, 1974). As Tancred-Sheriff shows in Chapter 3 of this volume, within the labour process characterization according to task carries with it gendered statements about worth, space, status and ability.

Social-regulative
Social-regulative rules, according to Clegg (1981), are 'hegemonic' forms of control located within the social arrangements of production and organizational processes. Whereas *skill* refers to the ability of a person to perform a particular task, *social regulation* refers to ways in which that person may be expected to relate to other persons in the achievement of that task and of the organizational purposes as a whole. For the managers of organizations this is usually stated as a problem of commitment, of morale, and of motivation and, as such, it often colours their attitude to recruitment, training, promotion and involvement in the organization. To enter, prosper and survive within an organization can depend upon how a person is viewed by decision makers; whether the person is viewed as a *full* organizational member, as someone who 'fits in', as a 'committed' person. This scenario is highly problematic for women given that they are too often viewed as having a primary commitment to a domestic life outside of the organization (Barrett, 1988).

In Japan, for example, the oft-heralded corporate cultures – that supposedly underlie the 'Japanese economic miracle' – largely exclude women:

> every major firm in Japan has a large category of temporary employees who are mostly women. Even today, it is rare that a major Japanese firm will hire women into professional or managerial jobs. Working class women typically begin work in production and clerical jobs right out of high school. They are expected to work five or six years, get married,

quit work, and raise a family. When the children enter school full time, the women often return to their original employer. Although they may work for the next twenty years, women are considered temporary employees and are immediately laid off in slack periods . . . The central fact remains . . . that women serve as a 'buffer' to protect the job stability of men. (Ouchi, 1981:21)

Within the cultures of organizations a variety of organizational practices can signal to females that they are not regarded as full organizational members; access may be denied to important organizational networks (Simpson et al., 1987) especially where these are rooted in male-centred extra-curricular activities; organizational belonging, in the widest sense, may depend upon involvement in officially sanctioned, but male-oriented social activities (Crompton and Jones, 1984); the availability of mentors may be largely confined to males (Noe, 1988); and the motivating language of the organization may be couched in terms of male-oriented metaphors (Riley, 1983).

Even where the organizational inclusion of women is intended, a number of cultural barriers have become embedded within organizational arrangements. A 'male dominant' style of organizational life, developed out of a number of features (Morgan, 1986), is evidenced particularly in the form of bureaucracy or bureaucratic discourse (K. Ferguson, 1984) which favours males; those who 'think the world' through a female lens (Rakow, 1986) will have more difficulty in an organizational world reflective of male thought and style of communication (Pearson, 1985).

State rules
Organizations and gender operate within, and are in part constructed by, a legislative environment. Definitions of womanhood did not, at one point in the past, exclude the possibility of dangerous and arduous work such as that of mining. Women were accepted as coal miners in the Britain of the early nineteenth century. Changing notions of women, however, led to legal prohibition of women (and children) from the mines in the mid-1800s.

Legal rules have restricted women's participation in organizational life in other ways. In eighteenth century America numerous women engaged in commerce of various kinds but their ability to prosper was restricted by laws relating to property rights:

women entered . . . commercial relationships shackled with the customary restrictions of the second sex. Commerce after all required legal privileges denied women by common law and American legal practice. To mount a successful commercial enterprise required access to credit, the ability to sue to collect debts, the right to possess personal and real property, all of which were severely restricted among women, especially wives. (Ryan, 1979:49)

In the latter part of the twentieth century, thanks to pressure from the women's movement, a number of laws have been passed aimed at the removal of certain barriers to female opportunity (e.g. in the USA, the Equal Pay Act, 1963, and the Civil Rights Act, 1964; in Britain, the Equal Pay Act 1970, and the Sex Discrimination Act 1975). This kind of legislation has had some impact upon the shaping of organizational cultures but through a process that is mediated by organizational decision makers. Referring to the USA, Davis points out that:

> equal opportunity, affirmative action, and a new concern for occupational health and safety have all worked their way into the culture of most corporations. But for all the social change and new laws, the pattern remains the same. The guiding beliefs and root values of corporate cultures come from the top. (1984:9)

In Canada, the Abella Commission has noted that: 'Although they see themselves as being on the corporate 'cutting edge' by virtue of their crown status, and are willing to lead in the introduction of equitable employment pratices . . . [Crown] corporations were mindful of their competition with the private sector' (1984:126).

The report of the Abella Commission is itself significant. Looking into *Equality in Employment* in Canada, the Commission went a considerable way – in their concept of 'systematic discrimination' – towards suggesting that sexual discrimination was embedded within the cultures of organizations: 'Rather than approaching discrimination from the perspective of the single perpetrator and the single victim, the systemic approach acknowledges that by and large the systems and practices we customarily and often unwittingly adopt may have an unjustifiably negative effect on certain groups in society' (Abella, 1984:9).

Nonetheless, as Meehan rightly argues: 'equality at work depends not solely on anti-discrimination policies, but on wider social considerations that go beyond existing or modified equal opportunity laws' (Meehan, 1985:184).

By way of example Meehan (1985) cites a British Court of Appeal judgement which found in favour of the employers in a case brought under the Sex Discrimination Act (1975). In 1977, the company's policy of allowing females to leave work five minutes earlier than males had been challenged by one of the male employees. The company's case was that their policy was concerned with the safety of the women, letting them go early so that they could 'avoid being bowled over in the 4.30 rush (quoted in Meehan, 1985:121). In finding for the employers the judge, Lord Denning, thought:

> it is very wrong if the statute . . . were to obliterate the differences between men and women or to obliterate all the chivalry and courtesy which we expect mankind to give womankind, or that the courts must hold that the elemental differences of sex must be disregarded in the interpretation of an Act of Parliament. (quoted in Meehan, 1985:121)

In this case the intervention of a legal rule had the effect of stressing a particularly virulent form of womanhood (Khan and Mills, 1988).

Strategic rules
Organizations will vary, in extent and character, in the way extra-organizational rules become embedded within organizational practices and thinking. Geographic and market location can be a factor. American womanhood in the seventeenth century for example 'took different shapes with the varying nationalities, climes, and regions': 'Accordingly, there were several modes of early American womanhood bearing the distinctive markings of New England Puritans, southern planters, Pennsylvania Quakers, and the Dutch traders of New Amsterdam' (Ryan, 1979:3).

The ability of an organization to exercise control over its environment may affect its desire either to reflect or to change that environment. This control, as in the case of multinationals or of company-towns, can influence not only the local economy but its particular sexual division of labour: 'These *strategic* rules of control can help to ensure the supply of cheap and submissive female labour, sanctified by local community and religious traditions and in turn reinforced by the power of the employing organization (Mills, 1988a:12–13).

Recording life in the mills of the southern states of the USA in the 1960s Blauner states that: 'most mills are situated in small towns or villages, where the family and the church are the dominant institutions and where traditional patterns and social relationships that reflect the isolation of both the region and the village community still prevail' (Blauner, 1967:74–5).

Far from disturbing those traditions the mills were concerned to maintain 'loyalties of kinship and neighborhood, and a religious sanction on submission to things as they are'; a situation that concentrated women in 'non-involving jobs that permit little control or initiative' (Blauner, 1967:75–6).

In a similar vein the mining, steel and dock communities of Britain tended to be single employment towns but employment which, for traditional and sometimes legal reasons, was largely restricted to men (Young and Willmott, 1962: Dennis et al., 1969). For females caught in the web of strategic rules there was little opportunity to confront different visions of the character and worth of womanhood.

Reproductive rules
Management and organizational theory, far from addressing sexist organizational practices, have tended to reflect and hence legitimate them (Braverman, 1974; Hearn and Parkin, 1983). This has been the case within the organizational culture debate as much as in any other area of organizational analysis. Prominent works in the field have *reproduced* without comment existing notions of womanhood. Ouchi (1981:21), as we saw above, feels able to write off sexist practices in Japanese corporations as mere cultural differences, reflected in 'a unique social and economic structure'. Likewise Hofstede's view about the basis of organizational culture rests on the assumption that 'only behaviors directly connected with procreation (childbearing and child-begetting) are "feminine" or "masculine"' (Hofstede, 1984:177): 'It is not difficult to see how this role pattern fits with the biological sex roles: women first bear children and then breast-feed them, *so they must stay with them*' (Hofstede, 1984:177–8; emphasis added).

Deal and Kennedy (1982) raise concerns about 'ritualistic barriers to the assimilation of [women] into corporate cultures' but do so in a way that reinforces male-oriented and managerial notions of culture. Stating that men have a different cultural outlook from that of women, they go on to suggest that 'a company cannot get the best work from anyone who is an outsider looking in' and, therefore, there is a need for 'traditional, white, male-oriented cultures [to be] more open and accommodating to outsiders', i.e. modified! Underlying Deal and Kennedy's concern is a traditional notion of womanhood that ultimately inhibits their ability to identify barriers to change.

Approaches such as that of Deal and Kennedy (1982), Ouchi (1981) and Hofstede (1984) present a picture of corporate reality which excludes gender from the dynamics of organizational experience and from the construction of organizational culture and human identities. As such they inhibit the potential for change.

Contradictions, resistance and change

To this point, for the sake of simplicity, the related processes of organizational acculturation and gender discrimination have been presented as factors that impact upon females, but women do reflect upon their existence; they do observe contradictions in the way that women are treated differently within organizations; and they do resist those contradictions. Resistance and challenge have taken many forms, from open street riots (Strumingher, 1979) to the development of female subcultures (Pollert, 1981), from the establishment of women's organizations (Ryan, 1979) to the creation of 'counter cultures' (Benson, 1986), from challenges to the law (Meehan, 1985) to critiques of malestream organizational analysis (Smircich, 1985).

Contradictions and forms of resistance are integral parts of organizational culture in its continual 'state of becoming' (Benson, 1977). The organizational analyst has a vital role to play in the process of change, critiquing the gendered nature of organizational reality and legitimating challenges to sexism. Clegg and Higgins (1987) have recently argued that materialist organizational analysis needs to move from simple critique to construction of definite change strategies. The strategy set out in this chapter points to analysis of organizational culture as a key area through which change needs to be addressed. It has been argued that we need to understand the overall process of organizational acculturation and gender discrimination but in a way that recognizes that each organizational culture is configured differently, and thus requires a different strategy for change. Within this process it is essential to understand that actors play a critical role in the maintenance and change of organizational cultures. The importance of the 'role of cognitive processes in creating, sustaining, and changing organizations and society' (Morgan, 1986:230) means that change is possible 'through changing consciousness, by changing the way people think, see, and understand the world' (Mills, 1987:46). As Gareth Morgan has so well expressed:

> The women's movement offers an example of this. The most successful feminist strategy over the last thirty years has been the radical humanist strategy of changing consciousness. Radical structuralist feminists say, okay, so you are conscious of being exploited as a woman, but you still live in a male-dominated society. From a radical structuralist point of view, you move and as you change, the grounds for action change, and the problems which require change become deeper. (quoted in Mills, 1987:46)

Despite Morgan's counterposing of a 'radical humanist' to a 'radical structuralist' perspective of change (Burrell and Morgan, 1979; Morgan, 1980) he is forced to recognize that 'the exploitation and domination of people is often grounded as much in control over the materialist basis of life as in control over ideas, thoughts, and feelings' (Morgan, 1986:230). Change needs to take into account both the structural context of gender construction and the contribution of the actors involved. The two should not be seen as in contradiction. Organizational change should be addressed, among other things, through a raising of people's consciousness about the kind of discriminatory reality construction they are involved in, but it should be done without losing sight of the overall need for social change.

Note

1. My current research leads me to accept the argument of Tolman et al. that, 'as the feminist vision is essentially rooted in the experience of being a woman, it is more appropriate for males who are sympathetic to feminism to describe themselves as "profeminist" ' (1986:61).

3
Gender, Sexuality and the Labour Process

Peta Tancred-Sheriff

> The previous chapter looked at some major ways of relating questions of gender, sexuality and organization theory. In particular it focused upon gendered 'rules of control' as a critique of organizational cultures. This chapter explores some similar issues, but in relation to another tradition in organization theory, labour process theory. Like organizational culture theory, this has also often neglected basic issues of gender and sexuality. In this chapter the location of women in specific organizational settings is analysed, especially through their relationship to 'adjunct control tasks', as a basis for considering the sexual dynamics of organizations. This approach, in which the sexuality or organization is part and parcel of the labour process, moves substantially beyond the work of Braverman and many other labour process theorists.

Within sociology, women's labour force position has attracted a considerable amount of attention over the past decade and a half, and women's work, both domestic and waged, has become one of the main issues of the feminist literature. Yet feminists have largely bypassed certain sociological paradigms which might, potentially, make a significant contribution to an understanding of women's labour force position. The topic has been conceptualized within the framework of the sociology of work, including occupational and labour force perspectives, while the other main conceptual apparatus for the study of the workplace, which is provided by an organizational approach, has been largely ignored.

This chapter constitutes an effort to fill this gap. Is women's unequal workplace participation explicable solely on the basis of the nature of the job or are there explanatory factors in the nature of the organization to which we should direct our attention? In particular, is an organizational framework which emphasizes an analysis in terms of sexuality useful for our understanding of women's workplace position? We know that women are both occupationally and organizationally segregated, and there is at least the suggestion that the latter form of segregation exacerbates the former (Gutek, 1985:27), so that it seems probable that factors pertinent to both forms of segregation have a role to play in explaining women's labour force distribution.

The following treatment is both preliminary and conceptual (though illustrative examples will be cited) and it attempts to provide an explanation for the main tendency in women's organizational location, while recognizing that a minority of women occupy different types of location. Following an extended discussion of women's modal location in the organizational setting, it asks why women (and not men) should occupy such positions. It is suggested that the sexuality of organization, understood in the broadest sense, can be viewed as an important explanatory element; women are viewed both as effecting control and being controlled through sexuality, which becomes a crucial element in the explanation of their modal organizational location.

Towards a gender-conscious approach to organizations

The recent redefinition of organizational reality through labour process theory is a useful way of posing the problem of gender distortion within and between organizations. The conceptualization of organizations as consisting of a certain amount of work (the labour process) that must be accomplished, and one or more control systems which ensure that this work is carried out effectively, is deceptively simple. The labour process includes both individual activity and the instruments and raw materials employed. The control systems encompass (Edwards, 1979) not only the general principles of control, but also the direct control of work tasks, the evaluation of work accomplished and the rewarding and disciplining of workers. Such a definition is quite broad in its organizational coverage and provides a skeletal framework for an understanding of organizational reality.

Within the occupational literature, it has frequently been argued that what characterizes women's wage labour is the nature of the labour process. This has been viewed either as low skilled or as having links with domestic labour. In rebuttal, it has been emphasized that the perceived low skill of women's jobs stems from the wide range of 'invisible skills' which are involved, (e.g. Crompton and Jones, 1984:146) and that two of the main female occupations – clerical and sales – bear only passing resemblance to anything that takes place within the home.

I want to propose an alternative position – that women's organizational location is characterized by their intermediate position between the labour process and the control system. In other words, the defining characteristic of women's work, in both intra-organizational and inter-organizational terms, is that it constitutes an adjunct to the control system. Let me elaborate on this basic hypothesis.

The extension of adjunct control tasks
Glenn and Feldberg (1979) argue that women, over the past seventy years, have moved into those jobs which have expanded most rapidly under advanced capitalism. Recent trends include: (1) the growth and differentiation of organizations of production; and (2) the extension of commodity production to certain services and goods which were previously produced within the domestic sphere. These two trends have extended the distance between the main groups within and relating to the organization and have exacerbated the problems of control. The sheer increase in the size and diversity of capitalist enterprises has meant that the distance between the employer and the worker has become much greater; the simple control, characteristic of the entrepreneurial firm, has given way to the bureaucratic control of these late capitalist organizations, with its need for detailed records and a variety of types of information. In addition, the extension of commodity production means that services (e.g. educational, health, cleaning) and products (e.g. food, clothing) which used to be delivered personally within the family are now delivered organization-to-individual on the market. The distance between producer and consumer has increased enormously, with all the difficulties of control implied by this development.

Glenn and Feldberg take an occupational approach to women's work and continue their analysis with a focus on the content of such work. From an organizational perspective, however, it is clear that women's work, located within the increased space between the various groups that has developed, facilitates control in these new circumstances. The vast army of *clerical workers* (constituting over one third of female wage labour)[1] has been necessary in order to ensure the employer's control over both the employee and the beneficiary or client. Employers would be unable to maintain control over the enterprise without the detailed information collected and categorized by clerical workers, which covers not only the specificities of each employee's contribution but also the overall image of the production rate and the costs involved. Clerical staff, in their personal dealings with clients or beneficiaries, play an important role in channelling the 'group-in-contact' into appropriate behaviour.

The extension of products and services to be purchased on the market has necessitated an army of *sales and service workers* (over one quarter of female wage labour) whose main task is to act on behalf of management in delivering the product or service to the consumer, ensuring that the latter group behaves appropriately – both during the immediate transaction and in becoming 'loyal and reliable customers' in the future (Benson, 1986:75; also Hochschild, 1983; Reiter, 1986). Customers could behave very inappropriately for the enterprise, such that their behaviour could become destructive of all capitalist purposes, were it not for the interface provided by the sales and service workers, their controlling and encouraging presence and soothing demeanour in times of dispute.

The nature of adjunct control tasks
These two groups of workers occupy the newly developed spaces between producer and consumer/client, employer and worker, providing adjunct control over the vast masses with whom the late capitalist firm must deal; taken together, they constitute nearly two thirds of the contemporary female paid labour force. While these female workers are in direct contact with the worker, consumer or client, they have limited personal authority. They *participate* in the authority of management and are often identified with management for that reason. But they have limited say in the determination of policies or in the nature of the product to be delivered. However, participation in the authority of others is seductive and the conviction of committed sales and service workers in imposing management policies on clients and consumers is a familiar everyday occurrence, together with their own recognition that they have little say in the rules to be imposed ('But those are the rules around here'). Clerical workers often have little recognition of the purposes of their data categorization unless they also need to deal with the public at certain points, when the 'explanations' offered are essentially management explanations ('You must fill in this form in five copies in order to be reimbursed'). It follows that these have been some of the hardest groups to unionize; the management identification that comes with the job must be transformed into an opposition to management with respect to working conditions before this can be accomplished – and, in most instances, this transformation to factory-style militancy is never accomplished and muted forms of resistance do not lead to unionization. This is particularly true of the personal fealty positions (private secretary, administrative coordinator; also see Chapter 10) where the personal contact with management and the physical isolation from peers dampens militancy, as David Lockwood so correctly observed in the case of their clerical predecessors (Lockwood, 1958:207).

Gender, Sexuality and the Labour Process 49

The mixture of *types* of control exerted by the two groups of workers is slightly different. While the sales and service workers are required to record information, the main control component of their task is very largely one of socialization. They explicitly encourage and implicitly demonstrate their expectations of appropriate behaviour (as we all instantly recognize when approaching a new service situation in a doctor's office or unfamiliar restaurant). This type of control can be termed *socialization of the group-in-contact*, and very effective control it is.

While clerical workers may have an element of such socialization in their personal dealings with clients (Crompton and Jones, 1984:45), it is mainly through collecting and categorizing information that they facilitate control over workers, and frequently over the consumer/client as well. As Lowe notes with respect to the 'administrative revolution': 'The office as "unseen hand" permitted managers to manipulate more carefully not only market forces, but also the entire production process including human labour . . . increasingly female clerks became the regulatory hand of modern management' (1987:24, 8).

In addition, as Barker and Downing point out, 'capital's acquisition of knowledge about all the human actions within the labour process . . . ' facilitates the designing of machinery 'to pace or replace human motions.' (1980:86; emphasis in original). Generally, one can term the main control component of the clerical task *collection/categorization of information*. As in the case of sales/service workers, clerical workers become the facilitators of management control.

Control by and of adjunct control workers
The organizational spaces occupied by the workers involved in adjunct control can vary in the *extent* of control that is necessary. While we have little information that can assist in delineating this difference, it can be hypothesized that control vis-a-vis the client/consumer group is a vaster task, in organizational terms, than is control of the worker group. Workers, in taking on an intra-organizational status, accept that there will be certain constraints on their activities as part of the labour/financial exchange negotiated with the organization. It is only when such control goes beyond acceptable levels that confrontation takes place between the management and worker groups. The task of adjunct control becomes routinized, except in times of crisis or confrontation.

On the other hand, the consumer/client group is not only more numerous, but the exchange between the organization and this group is more tenuous. It is also enormously threatening to the organization which, essentially, would cease to survive if the exchange of goods/services for finances could not be effected. The organization is dependent on this rather free-floating mass of consumers and clients who, on contacting the organization, may or may not choose to effect an exchange (Benson, 1986:124, 132). Obviously, it is much easier from the organization's point of view if there is a monopoly of a service or product, or if the organization possesses such a desirable product that there is little need for concern. However, one notices that even in the case of monopolies the organization takes great care in its relations with consumers (utility monopolies, for example), for today's monopoly may become tomorrow's competitive market, if consumers become dissatisfied. It is also true that consumer/client tastes change very rapidly and no 'desirable product' can necessarily count on such status into the long-term future. Thus, this amorphous mass of consumers or clients must be controlled in such a way that they behave in the desired manner from the organization's point of view, that is they enter into a satisfactory exchange with the organization and contribute towards its continuing presence in the capitalist economy.

The task of adjunct control is a very difficult one to supervise from the managerial point of view, particularly in its socialization aspect. The expanded space between employer and worker, producer and consumer means that those who exercise adjunct control and who are in contact with the client/consumer or worker are by definition rather distant from those with the authority to originate policies and rules – otherwise the latter could clearly effect the control themselves and would not require adjunct staff. In addition, managerial control over adjunct workers attempts to control intangible skills: '[managers] attempted to harness skill in social interaction, a most unmanageable quality and one even harder to control than manual skill' (Benson, 1986:126). Lacking direct control, management must seek reliable workers who can be counted upon, even when distant from management, to act on its behalf.

Intra- and inter-organizational distribution of adjunct control workers
Adjunct control workers share in common that they participate in the authority of management, but do not themselves hold such authority; they control through varying combinations of socialization of the group-in-contact and collection/categorization of information; the need for workers engaged in adjunct control will probably be greater in relation to a numerous and amorphous client/consumer group than to a numerous worker group; and fin-

ally, they themselves must be trusted or encouraged to act as management would act if present, for the so-called 'invisible' skills are all the harder to manage.

From an intra-organizational perspective, in positing a labour process and one or more control systems, labour process theorists ignore the fact that the process of control constitutes a task in and of itself. This is the secondary, though very important, task of controlling the core labour process. While it is true that many elements of control are built into the labour process, it is simultaneously true that many control activities constitute tasks in and of themselves. It is here that the depressed female pyramid is located in organizational terms – clustered in the strata where the jobs involve maintaining and enforcing the control of management.

As to *inter*-organizational concentration it can be hypothesized that women are concentrated in those organizations where control is most problematic, because the group to be controlled is too distant and/or too numerous for control to be easily executed. As has been indicated, control over the consumer/client group is particularly problematical for many organizations, and it is in such organizations that the greatest proportions of women are concentrated. Women are also likely to be employed in organizations where workers do not easily accept the degree of management control that is imposed; or where the worker group is geographically dispersed, giving rise to additional problems of control; or where the client group is particularly numerous or recalcitrant to control for some reason. While the basic thread running through inter-organizational differentiation by gender is the requirement for organizational control, certain facets of the worker or consumer/client groups could exacerbate or diminish the female adjunct control presence as indicated.

This categorization of women's tasks within and between organizations still does not really explain why they should be located at a depressed level within the organizational structure, except insofar as tasks of 'execution' are identified with management less than tasks of 'conception'. This takes for granted, of course, rather than explaining that the classical head/hand division demotes tasks of the latter variety; I do not intend to take on such a hoary problem at this point except to note its existence. It also does not explain why it is mainly *women*, rather than men, who occupy these jobs and it is to the latter topic that I now turn.

Sexuality and gender distortion

In a fascinating discussion of the development of American department stores from the late nineteenth century to 1940, Benson argues that the hiring of a majority of women for sales positions included a process of co-opting 'their gender-based characteristics' (1986:128). While there is a great deal of force in her argument, her focus on gender emphasizes women's presumed personality characteristics, neglecting the elements of sexuality which also come into play. Complementing this gender approach, I am going to underline that women's *sexuality* is harnessed for general purposes of adjunct control by the employing organization – and that, in fact, the multiple facets of women's sexuality, understood in the broadest sense, are utilized in this location between the labour process and the control system(s).

In including a wide range of human states and actions within the definition of sexuality, I share Burrell and Hearn's general approach to sexuality (Chapter 1 of this volume) and with Mills (Chapter 2:30–3) the understanding that gender and sexuality are inextricably linked. Furthermore, I recognize that there are certain organizational contexts where sexuality is more overt. DiTomaso (Chapter 5:88) suggests that where women transcend traditional subordinate roles in the workplace they will experience more overt sexuality, while Gutek formulates a similar proposition by linking the degree of sex segregation of the workplace to the extent of 'sex role spillover', where roles encouraged within the private sphere spill over into the public (1985:40). At the other end of the spectrum, sexuality is merely implicitly present, and the skills that are associated with the 'sexually desirable' female are those very skills which are harnessed for the adjunct control location.

The most telling examples of the harnessing of sexuality for the purposes of control come from the airline industry, where Hochschild underlines the sexuality of advertising ('Fly me, you'll like it') or the way in which the flight attendant's omnipresent smile is sexualized when accompanied by the advertisement: 'We really move our tails for you to make your every wish come true' (Hochschild, 1983:93). The adjunct control aspect of this sexuality is brought out by one flight attendant who explains that the sexualized cabin atmosphere is expressly designed to diminish male passengers' fear of flying: 'they figure mild sexual arousal will be helpful in getting people's minds off of [sic] flying' (1983:94). The extent to which the sexuality is deliberate is underlined by Hochschild's observation that a ' "sexy" look and manner are partly an achievement of corporate engineering – a result of the company's emphasis on the weight and (former) age requirements, grooming classes [etc:] . . . ' (1983:182). In the extremely sexually segregated context of (mainly) male passengers and (mainly) female flight attendants, organization sexuality becomes overt.

In a slightly less overt manner, adjunct control workers are often encouraged to draw on their 'sexual skills' in order to facilitate the operation of the capitalist enterprise. Hearn and Parkin talk of the 'presumed identity of "work-role" and "sex-role" ' in traditional jobs for women (or what I am calling adjunct control jobs) such that 'the job itself is sexualized' (1987:83). They also refer to the 'institutionalized flirting relations between women boundary staff and men customers' (1987:84) and the 'selling of sexuality' on the part of women in a range of adjunct control positions such as secretaries, receptionists, salespersons (1987:102). What is frequently omitted in such discussions is that such implicit sexuality is both encouraged and welcomed on the part of management in both its short-term and long-term interests. One has only to attempt to visualize a homely or frumpy receptionist to recognize the effort invested in the selection process and the constant encouragement/ reinforcement of sexually attractive appearance that must take place. It is also clear that from management's point of view such sexuality should not become too explicit; a low-level 'simmer' is desirable, but excessively overt sexuality no longer serves to control, but, on the contrary, gets out of control.

At the implicit end of the continuum, those aspects of female appearance and behaviour which are associated with sexual desirability are generally harnessed to the adjunct control task. Benson talks of agreeableness as a desirable quality for sales positions:

> On the selling floor, manner was at least as important as cumulative result; it mattered little if a worker stamped out a widget while in a high temper, but it made a great deal of difference if a saleswoman sold a pair of stockings while in a grouchy mood. (1986:127)

She also refers to 'gender characteristics' as desirable traits for saleswomen:

> Qualities which had for a century been encouraged in women – adeptness at manipulating people, sympathetic ways of responding to the needs of others, and familiarity with things domestic – fit nicely into a new [turn of the century] view of selling . . . Empathy and responsiveness constituted the irreducible core of selling skill. (1986:130)

It is tempting to argue, as does Benson, that the characteristics sought were those linked to gender – that 'feminine' qualities were required for an adjunct control position. But when one sees such characteristics located within the context of increasingly explicit sexuality, they take on a new meaning; they become part of the sexual skills of womanhood, part of the 'intangible social skills' which are, in practice, more highly rewarded than actual technical skills (Barker and Downing, 1980:75, 77), as the relative status of private secretary and copy typist indicates. The result, as Thompson indicates, in some confusion with no further elucidation, is that: 'There is something clearly *special* about the characteristics associated with female wage labour' (1983:182, emphasis in original). One can suggest that at least part of what is 'special' is women's sexuality, which is firmly harnessed for workplace purposes.

Sexuality and gender control

Women's sexuality not only constitutes part of the skills of the adjunct control task, but it assists in the solution of one of the managerial problems which is built into the capitalist enterprise. As suggested earlier, the adjunct control tasks are extremely difficult to control, particularly in their socialization manifestation. The frequent gender contrast between those occupying managerial positions and those in adjunct control positions facilitates the use of sexuality in order to maintain control.

For example, Pringle underlines that bosses 'like their secretaries to be able to work largely unsupervised' and outlines the way that they use 'symbolic family and/or sexual dimensions as the best way of overcoming the "discipline" problem' (Chapter 10 of this volume, p. 169). Other writers make reference to the utilization of female sexuality for control purposes through verbal gifts – flattery, giving a sense of indispensability, implicit sexual innuendo (Barker and Downing, 1980:74) – or concrete gift-giving and material rewards which connect to 'the dominant themes of consumerism, family and sexual attraction in women's lives' (Thompson, 1983:197). Hearn and Parkin make reference to the use of sexuality – through harassment, sexual joking and sexual abuse – as a means of controlling women and of maintaining authority (1987:93). In this connection, the increase in sexual harassment, when juxtaposed with the increase of women in managerial positions, can be linked not only to a more sexually heterogeneous workplace (see Chapter 5 of this volume, p. 88) but also to the use of harassment to control threatening women, to remind them of their ultimate position as sexual objects (Balsamo, 1985:11–12). In short, women's sexuality assists in gaining, maintaining or re-establishing control over adjunct control workers.

In this chapter I have argued that women are located in organizational settings as adjuncts to the control system(s) and that their presence is concentrated in those organizations where control is particularly problematic, for some reason. Mass consumer/client groups pose very important problems of control, though the control of a distant and numerous worker group, particularly in times of confrontation, can give rise to similar problems.

I have suggested that two facets of adjunct control – socialization of the group-in-contact and collection/categorization of information – run through the main female organizational locations in different combinations. These facets are differentially emphasized in the jobs in which two thirds of women are located – specifically clerical and sales/service occupations.[2]

The sexuality of organizations is harnessed to the purposes of adjunct control in two ways. Women's sexuality is utilized in adjunct control tasks in order to carry out the most effective possible control at the interface with workers and/or consumers or clients. In addition, women's sexuality is employed to exert control over the adjunct control task, given that managerial control is tenuous in these circumstances, by allowing women to be controlled through sexual domination. In general, organization sexuality is at the very least a contributory explanation for the selection and maintenance of women in adjunct control positions.

Notes

A previous version of this chapter was developed for the Symposium on Sexuality, Power and Organizational Theory of the American Academy of Management Meetings, San Diego, California, August 1985. Since that time, I have had the opportunity to discuss various facets of the paper at seminars, both in Canada and in Australia. I am grateful for the assistance of those who participated in these various forums and, in particular, to Rosemary Pringle, Albert Mills, Deborah Sheppard and Jeff Hearn for their extensive and helpful comments on later versions.

1. I am using general proportions in citing the main groups of female workers so that the resulting image could apply not only to the Canadian situation in the 1980s, but also to women's work in countries with a similar economic conjuncture. For those who are interested in the specific data for Canada, as of 1980, 34.6 per cent of women worked in clerical occupations and 28.5 per cent in sales and service occupations for a total of 63.1 per cent (Armstrong and Armstrong, 1983:Table 5).

2. I am not suggesting that all women's organizational locations are covered by this discussion, though there are clearly certain semi-professional jobs (e.g. nursing, social work and teaching) which are associated with women and which include a strong adjunct control component. It is also possible that many women in 'non-traditional' jobs, both professional and manual, are specialized into an adjunct control location within organizational settings. In this chapter, as indicated earlier, I am concerned with explanations of women's modal organizational location, covering the great majority of women.

4
Sexuality in the Workplace: Key Issues in Social Research and Organizational Practice

Barbara A. Gutek

> Whereas the last two chapters have approached gender, sexuality and organizations in the broad context of organization theory, the next three are more concerned with the detailed expression and occurrence of sexuality in organized workplaces. The first is a wide-ranging review of recent research on heterosexual social–sexual behaviour at work, with particular emphasis placed necessarily on research on sexual harassment in organizations. The chapter concludes with a statement of some key issues for current practice and policy in organizations.

The discovery, labelling and study of sexual harassment a decade ago and the more frightening recent spread of AIDS has helped to redefine sexual behaviour at work and elsewhere from being invisible, private and individual to being visible, public and organizational. In this chapter I will discuss some key issues that emerge from research about sexual behaviour at work and its implications for organizational practice. In doing so, I will rely on the research, especially my own, on heterosexual social–sexual behaviour at work. I define social–sexual behaviour as non-work-related behaviour with a sexual component. My research programme consists primarily of quantitative surveys of representative samples of workers in California supplemented with experimental research. The major study of male–female relations at work, a representative sample of 1232 working people in Los Angeles county, is described and summarized in *Sex and the Workplace* (Gutek, 1985; translated into Danish as *Seksuel Chikane*, 1988). The research I have conducted with colleagues and students has resulted in both data-based (Gutek, Nakamura et al., 1980; Gutek and Morasch, 1982; Jensen and Gutek, 1982; Gutek et al., 1983; Cohen and Gutek, 1985; Konrad and Gutek, 1986; Gutek and Cohen, 1987; Gutek et al., forthcoming) and theoretical/review publications (Gutek and Nakamura, 1982; Gutek and Dunwoody, 1987).

The early research on sexual behaviour at work focused on description of the frequency of sexual harassment, description of harassing encounters, people's reactions to harassment, the behaviours that are defined as harassment, and the like. While this research is useful to lawyers and policy analysts who are trying to establish and enforce laws and policies, researchers (American researchers in particular) have done much less to try to understand sexuality at work as an organizational phenomenon. For example, there is little systematic description of non-harassing sexual behaviour at work and few attempts to understand sexuality at work aside from determining whether some particular class of behaviour is or is not harassment.

I would like to frame my discussion of key issues of importance for organizational researchers, human resource professionals, and managers around the gradual transition that is taking place from viewing sexual behaviour at work as private, individual and largely invisible to public, organizational and somewhat visible. In doing so, I will provide some partial explanations for the conventional view of sexual behaviour as private, individual and invisible. I will also show why the research (and public concern about sexual harassment, discrimination and AIDS) supports an understanding of sexual behaviour at work as public and organizational.

The issue of sexuality and sexual behaviour as public and organizational versus private and individual is discussed extensively by Hearn and Parkin (1987) and by several authors in this volume (see also Gutek, 1985: Chapter 1). If sexuality is defined as private behaviour, then there is no reason for an organization (or organizational researchers) to be concerned with it. It is outside the scope of organizational behaviour. As non-organizational behaviour, it need not be discussed, handled or even acknowledged: for all practical purposes, it is invisible. As several authors have noted (cf. Chatov, 1981; Burrell, 1984; Gutek, 1985: Chapter 1; Hearn and Parkin, 1987), sexuality within organizations is invisible, if not to managers and employees, certainly to most organizational researchers and theoreticians. As a topic of study, it is notably absent from textbooks and journals (see Burrell, 1984; Zedeck and Cascio, 1984).

Sexuality in organizations: personal, individual and invisible

In my research (Gutek, 1985: Chapter 6), I found that most employees view sexual behaviour at work as benign or even positive. Men were somewhat more likely than women to view sexual behaviour at work favourably (Gutek, Morasch and Cohen, 1983; Gutek, 1985: Chapter 6). In general, employees tend to believe that people will be flattered by sexual overtures from the other sex, and men will be somewhat more flattered than women. The same was true for students evaluating an incident of possible sexual harassment (Cohen and Gutek, 1985). A factor analysis of a series of responses about an incident of possible sexual harassment showed that students tend to focus on the positive interpersonal aspects of the encounter. For example, if a person walking down the hall passes someone of the other sex and pats that person on the rear end, students tend to believe that the two people are friends and perhaps dating partners. They tend to assume that whatever happens is agreeable to both parties. It does not readily occur to them that they may have witnessed sexual harassment.

There are two key aspects to people's evaluation of real or hypothetical social–sexual encounters between men and women who work in the same organization. First, people tend to think positively about sex: sexual encounters affirm one's sexual desirability and probably indicate that the two people are interested in each other and perhaps already intimate. Second, people tend to evaluate social–sexual encounters as interpersonal rather than as organizational. They do not see sexual overtures as a product of the organization's culture or norms (see Chapter 2 of this volume). Consistent with the research on attributions showing that people usually attribute causality to actors rather than to the characteristics of their environment, people in organizations seem to underestimate the impact of organizational environment on their behaviour. Most workers seem to think social–sexual behaviours are unaffected by the structural characteristics or the climate of the workplace. For example, in my research, female victims were likely to blame the individual harasser or even occasionally themselves for the harassment (Jensen and Gutek, 1982; Gutek, 1985: Chapter 4). Only a minority reported that the psychological climate was a noticeable influence. With respect to attitudes about sexuality at work, workers played down the effects of gender role expectations and tended to report that people who were propositioned encouraged it.

Some findings from another study also show that workers think social–sexual behaviour is unaffected by structural characteristics such as organizational hierarchy. In a survey of workers for the State of California, we (Dunwoody-Miller and Gutek, 1985) found that when people were asked what they would do if they were sexually harassed at work, most said they would tell the harasser to stop. In contrast, real victims of sexual harassment rarely tell the harasser to stop. Their organizational position vis-a-vis the harasser usually makes them feel uncomfortable telling the person to stop because they are generally powerless to enforce their demands and may suffer retaliation for their complaints (Schneider, 1984; Dunwoody-Miller and Gutek, 1985; Crull, 1982; see also Gutek, 1985: Chapter 4).

Thus, sexual behaviour is often viewed as personal and individual because people see it as positive, none of the organization's business, and they are not particularly aware of the effects of organizational structure and expectations on their own behaviour or on the behaviour of others in organizations. When people see sexual behaviour in the workplace, they attribute it solely to individual's wishes and actions and ignore the influences of hierarchy, work roles or organizational norms.

Sex-role spillover
A role analysis also can provide information on the reasons why sexual behaviour in organizations has been viewed as personal, individual and invisible. Role concepts have proved useful for examining the behaviour of people in organizations in general (Katz and Kahn, 1978), and women's experiences more specifically (Nieva and Gutek, 1981: Chapter 5). A work role is the set of expectations associated with a particular position such as manager or secretary and can be compared with other roles that people occupy such as parent role and spouse role. Roles can conflict with one another and one role can spill over to another as when a parent stays home from work (work role) to care for a sick child (parent role). Another, broader role is sex role, which is usually defined as the expectations, norms and rules associated with being male or female in our society.

Nieva and Gutek noted that 'most of the rules concerning male–female interaction have been formulated solely for social–sexual behaviour' (1981: 59). In theory, these rules – sex roles – are not particularly useful guides for behaviour in the workplace. In practice, however, sex roles are used to shape men's and women's behaviour in the workplace (for a number of reasons discussed later).

Nieva and Gutek (1981) use the term 'sex role spillover' to denote the carry-over of gender-based expectations into the workplace. Some of these gender-based expectations are rooted in stereotypes about men and women. Among the characteristics assumed by many to be associated with femaleness (such as passivity, loyalty, emotionality, nurturance) is being a sex object (see Williams and Best, 1982). Women are assumed to be sexual and to elicit sexual overtures from men rather naturally (see Schneider, 1982). In a 32-

nation study of sex stereotypes, the characteristics of sexy, affectionate, and attractive were associated with femaleness (Williams and Best, 1982; see also Abbey et al., 1987). What is equally important is the fact that *there is no strongly held comparable belief about men*. For example, of the forty-nine items that were associated with maleness in at least nineteen of the twenty-five countries studied by Williams and Best (1982), none was directly or indirectly related to sexuality. While it is generally assumed that men are more sexually active than women (see Glass and Wright, 1985) and men are the initiators in sexual encounters (Kinsey et al., 1948; Grauerholz and Serpe, 1985; Zilbergeld, 1978), the cluster of characteristics that are usually associated with the male personality does not include a sexual component. Rather the stereotype of men revolves around the dimension of competence and activity (Constantinople, 1973; Deaux, 1985). It includes the belief that men are rational, analytic, assertive, tough, good at maths and science, competitive, and make good leaders (Bem, 1974; Spence and Helmreich, 1978; Williams and Best, 1982). The stereotype of men – the common view of the male personality – is the perfect picture of asexuality. It is a view that does not reflect reality. As mentioned above, men are as – or more – sexual than women. Why should the stereotype of men lack a sexual component? Who benefits from the asexual stereotype of men? This is a point to which I will return. For now, the important point is that the carryover of sexrole stereotypes into the workplace introduces the view of women as sexual beings in the workplace, but it simply enforces the view of men as organizational beings – 'active, work-oriented' (Deaux, 1985). It should also be noted that these stereotypes of female characteristics and male characteristics have remained quite stable throughout the 1970s and thus far in the 1980s in the United States (Ruble, 1983).

A variety of subtle pressures may encourage women to behave in a sexual manner at work, and this then conforms to their supposedly essential sexual nature. Because it is expected, people notice female sexuality, and believe it is normal, natural, an outgrowth of being female (Lipman-Blumen, 1984). Unfortunately, women do not seem to be able to be sex objects and analytical, rational, competitive and assertive at the same time because femaleness is viewed as 'not-maleness' (Foushee et al., 1979; Major et al., 1981; Deaux and Lewis, 1984), and it is the men who are viewed as analytic, logical and assertive (Constantinople, 1973; Spence and Helmreich, 1978). Despite the fact that the model of male and female as polar opposites has been severely criticized on several grounds (Bem, 1974; Constantinople, 1973; Spence and Helmreich, 1978), a dichotomy is used by researchers and laypersons alike (for example, we speak of the 'opposite' sex). Not only are the sexual aspects of the female role carried over to work, but also they swamp or overwhelm a view of her as a capable, committed worker. As Kanter (1977) noted, a woman's perceived sexuality can 'blot out' all other characteristics. Thus, sex role interferes with and takes precedence over work role.

What is doubly troublesome about this inability to be sexual and a worker at the same time is that women are not the ones who usually choose between the two. A female employee might decide to be a sex object at work, especially if her career or job is not very important to her. More often, however, the working woman chooses not to be a sex object but may be so defined by male colleagues or supervisors anyway, regardless of her own actions. A woman's sexual behaviour is noticed and labelled sexual even if it is not intended as such (Abbey, 1982, 1987; Schneider, 1982; Carothers and Crull, 1984; Goodchilds and Zellman, 1984; Gutek, 1985). In this regard, research by Abbey (1982; Abbey and Melby, 1986; Abbey et al., 1987) is particularly relevant. She found that women's actions are often interpreted as sexual by men, even though the women meant them to be friendly but not sexual. This is especially true when the behaviour takes place in a bar or when a woman is wearing sexually seductive or revealing clothing. Men's and women's assessment of the situation is more discrepant – with women rating the woman's behaviour friendly, men rating her behaviour sexy – when the non-verbal cues are ambiguous or women wear revealing clothing (see also Saal, 1986). In order to avoid being cast in the role of sex object, a woman may have to act completely asexual. Then she is subject to the charge of being 'frigid', a 'prude', an 'old maid', or lesbian. In her attempt to avoid being a sex object, she is still stereotyped by her sexuality or, more accurately, by her perceived lack of sexuality – or wrong kind of sexuality if she is labelled a lesbian.

The situation for men is entirely different. Benefiting from the stereotype of men as natural inhabitants of organizations – goal-oriented, rational, analytic, competitive, assertive, strong or, as Deaux (1985) put it, 'active, work-oriented' – men may be able to behave in a blatantly sexual manner, seemingly with impunity. Even when a man goes so far as to say that he encourages sexual overtures from women by unzipping his pants at work (as reported by one man in Gutek's 1985 study), he may escape being viewed as sexual or more interested in sex than work by supervisors and colleagues. While the image of women acting in a seductive manner and distracting men from work is viewed as a detriment to the organization, many employers know of men in their organization who are 'playboys' and harassers, yet they may not see that these men are a detriment to the organization. Although these men may hire the wrong women for the wrong reasons, make poor use of female human resources in the organization, squander the organization's resources in their quests for new sexual partners, and make elaborate attempts to impress potential sexual partners, all this may escape the notice of employers. In short, men's sexual behaviour at work often goes unnoticed – for at least three reasons. First, their behaviour is viewed as a personal proclivity rather than as work behaviour, i.e. it is personal, not organizational. Second, as noted earlier, there is no strongly recognized sexual component of the male sex role.[1] Thus, men's sexual behaviour is neither salient nor noticed. Third, perhaps sexual pursuits and conquests, jokes and innuendos can be subsumed under the stereotype of the organizational man – goal-oriented, rational, competitive and assertive, which are expected and recognized as male traits. Men may make sexual overtures in an assertive, competitive manner. Likewise, sexual jokes, metaphors and innuendos may be seen as part of competitive male horseplay (Hearn, 1985). Thus the traits of competitiveness, assertiveness and power-orientation are noticed, whereas the sexual component is not.[2] Finally, if a man's sexual behaviour is noticed, it may be overlooked or tacitly accepted if he is envied or admired as a 'ladies' man'.

Using sex at work
The above analysis brings up the issue of who uses sexuality at work? Most people do not 'use their sexuality' at work, but to the extent that people do, women, not men, are expected to do so. I argue that men are as likely – perhaps more likely – than women to use their sexuality to foster their workplace goals.

The stereotype that some women use their sexuality to advance at work probably developed because women's sexuality may be viewed as a greater resource than men's sexuality. Thus women are assumed to be sexy, flirtatious, seductive (Abbey et al., 1987) and their sexuality is a resource to be used. Women's presence and behaviour then elicit a sexual response from men. The frequent comments of men in my studies (Gutek, 1985) ('she was asking for it') and women ('I was wearing red pants') express this point of view. When a woman wears a tight skirt, a sheer blouse, no bra, or makes a comment to a man, she is viewed as 'using' her sexuality. Women can use their sexual resource at will, giving them an unfair advantage over men or less attractive women who lack the resource, or so some people appear to believe. Some men and women in my

Los Angeles surveys suggested that, by use of this resource, women do receive organizational rewards they would not otherwise obtain. When the stereotype is carried to an extreme, it leads people to believe that any woman who had advanced did so by using her sexuality. By implication, she does not deserve the position she occupies, and people may ostracize her or treat her with hostility.

My surveys found relatively little evidence that women routinely or even occasionally use their sexuality to try to gain some organizational goal. There is even less support for the position that women have succeeded or advanced at work by using their sexuality. Only one woman out of over 800 said she used sex to help her achieve her current position, and she said she was 'thankful' that she did not have to do that any more. In comparison, many women reported that they were fired or quit after they got involved with a man at work. Of the men who reported that women made overtures towards them, presumably in order to get better or easier tasks, all said that they did not give the woman a better or easier job and several men said that they fired those women. Thus my surveys revealed virtually no evidence that women either want to use or are successful at using their sexuality at work to gain an unfair advantage over other workers, although the surveys also revealed that some employees are concerned because they think some women do receive privileged treatment for 'putting out'. It is also intriguing that virtually everyone who has such a concern blames the woman for making the offer rather than the man for accepting.

By contrast, men appear to use sexuality more than women and in diverse ways. (They may also be more successful in doing so, perhaps because they often come from a position of power rather than subordination.) A sizeable minority of men say they dress in a seductive manner at work, including the man who said he encouraged overtures from women by unzipping his pants. More frequently, according to many women in our survey, some men offer organizational rewards to women in exchange for sex (e.g. 'He told me we could be managers together.') Some men use sex in a hostile manner, i.e. either to try to intimidate women to have sex with them or to force a woman to quit her non-traditional job. These actions are rather unusual, involving a small minority of men.

More common are the sexual jokes, use of explicit sexual terms to describe work situations, sexual comments to co-workers, and display of sexual posters and pictures engaged in by many men at work. (Sex and sports, some observers claim, are the two major metaphors of business.) The use of sex can be more subtle than either hostile sexual remarks or sexual jokes. Although this tactic is often assumed to be used exclusively by women, some men, too, may feign sexual interest to gain some work-related advantage. Instead of trying to get a new typewriter, a lighter work load, better working hours, or a free trip to San Francisco, men may try to extract extra work from women by engendering loyalty in them. A man may use the bonds of affection to ask a woman to work overtime or perform tasks unrelated to work (stop at the cleaners, buy presents, clean his apartment). Since men are not expected to use sex at work, their behaviour is hardly ever interpreted as sexual and the work that is done through their use of sex may instead be attributed to their ability as leaders or to some other factor. Thus, in comparison to women, men may not only use sex more often at work, they may be more successful at it! The ultimate measure of their success is that their use of sex is not interpreted as a use of sex, but as their ability to get the job done.

Macromanipulation versus micromanipulation
How can men use sex more than women and be more successful at it when people who are concerned about employees using sex perceive the problem almost exclusively as women using sex? How could my analysis of the situation lead to conclusions so counter to 'common knowledge'? Lipman-Blumen (1984) made a useful distinction between macromanipulation and micromanipulation that bears directly on this issue. Lipman-Blumen contends that 'When the dominant group controls the major institutions of a society, it relies on macromanipulation through law, social policy, and military might. . . . The less powerful become adept at micromanipulation, using intelligence, canniness, intuition, interpersonal skill, charm, sexuality, deception and avoidance to offset the control of the powerful' (1984:8). Macromanipulation is not viewed as manipulation because it is embodied in social institutions; people are unaware of its influence. The emphasis on sexual aspects of the female sex role in some work environments (for example, cocktail waitresses, women in show business, flight attendants) is an indication of macromanipulation by the dominant (male) group of workers. This macromanipulation is not obvious or transparent to either the dominant male group who control these industries or the subordinate female group. Because it is embodied in social structure, this macromanipulation escapes being attributed to the biological or psychological needs of the dominant group. The sexualized work environment is not viewed as an outgrowth of the male psyche. Instead, it is considered part of the background, taken for granted and unquestioned.

On the other hand, the micromanipulation of women is noticed by both women and men; it is not ignored, and its roots are traced, correctly or incorrectly, to women workers and their biological and psychological make-up. A woman worker's response to an environment that encourages seduction is viewed as an outgrowth of her psyche: she is viewed as enjoying being an exhibitionist, and she may be viewed as a nymphomaniac. Yet this micromanipulation may also be viewed as a response to macromanipulation – one response to an environment that promotes and encourages sexy behaviour and seductive dress.

As Sheppard (Chapter 9 of this volume) notes (see also Kanter, 1977), many women feel that they must manage their femininity at the workplace. If they are too feminine they may be viewed as sexual, which may lead to problems for them. On the other hand, if they are insufficiently feminine, they may pose a threat to some men. If they are insufficiently feminine they may be labelled lesbian and ostracized by fellow employees (Schneider, 1982). Thus, women are left to handle organizational behaviour as if it were personal behaviour, on a personal level. Although their attempts to manage their sexuality is a response to organizational structure, policies or norms, they frequently have to deal with it on a personal level and treat it as an exclusively interpersonal encounter.

Trivializing sex at work
A subtle effect of viewing sexual behaviour in organizations as personal is to trivialize the work environments where sexuality and physical attractiveness are emphasized. Sexuality can also trivialize a person's accomplishments. Some women in our surveys clearly understood this when they said they would personally be insulted by a sexual overture from a man at work (as 63 per cent of them did). They want their accomplishments, not their sexual attractiveness, to be noted and they expect that only one but not both will receive attention. When their sexual attractiveness is noticed, they feel their work will not be. When being physically and sexually attractive is an explicit part of the job (as it may be for flight attendants, cocktail waitresses and many receptionists), people assume the job does not require a lot of other qualifications. The extent to which the importance of physical attractiveness is emphasized over the job holders' specific skills, motivation and educational credentials determines how much the job will be devalued and trivialized. The work is viewed as so simple 'any pretty young woman will do'. When only attractive women are found in a job, others will assume that (1) physical attractiveness is the most important prerequisite of the job; and (2) the job does not require other skills or abilities. In this case, the job is trivialized.

Similarly, when an employee is complimented for physical

attractiveness or a good personality, a subtle side effect may be to draw attention away from work accomplishments. Our finding that the majority of women say they would be insulted by a sexual overture from a man at work (but think that other women are flattered) may reflect their basic understanding that they make a trade-off between being sexual and being skilled workers. The effect of the sexual compliment is a trivialization of their work. Although few jobs held by men require men to be physically attractive, the same dynamics probably apply to those men. Most men in jobs not requiring physical attractiveness claim to enjoy sexual compliments from women and probably view them as unrelated to their work competence.

Pervasiveness of sexuality
One inescapable conclusion of the study of sexual behaviour and sexual harassment at work is that sexual behaviour in various forms is present in the workplace, despite the fact that work organizations do nothing officially to encourage sexual overtures among employees. In our research, 76 per cent of men and 80 per cent of women said they had experienced on their current job some kind of sexual overture, comment or touch that they did not consider sexual harassment (Gutek, Cohen and Konrad, forthcoming). These social–sexual acts occur despite the fact that many organizations – such as the military – try to control sexuality through strict rules against 'fraternization'. In my representative sample of working people in Los Angeles, California, I found that about 62 per cent of the people asserted that their organization tolerated employees dating each other (Gutek and Cohen, 1987). Few people, however, assert that one goal of work organizations is to satisfy people's sexual interests or that the workplace should serve that function. Thus, sex at work occurs in an arena generally viewed as inappropriate to the expression of sexuality, which might cause one to ponder whether any sexless environments exist. If the workplace, a setting that symbolizes rationality, efficiency, productivity and business, engenders so much sex, is it possible to design an environment where gender would be irrelevant and sexual overtures would not be made? Is it possible to create a social setting that actually conveys the message that 'sex is inappropriate here'? Probably not. This may be the reason why organizations like the military traditionally prefer only heterosexual men. Having only same-sex heterosexuals at least in theory precludes any sexual behaviour.

Summary

I have argued that there may be multiple reasons why sexual behaviour in organizations was viewed, until recently, as personal, individual and was relatively invisible. In general, people view sexual behaviour as personal and private because, among other reasons, they are rather oblivious to the effects of the organization's hierarchy, rules, norms and policies on people's behaviour which they see as self-motivated rather than a response to organizational contingencies and constraints.

The view that sexual behaviour is personal and private is facilitated by the fact that people also view it as positive. When people see other employees engaging in sexual or intimate behaviour, they tend to assume that both parties welcome and enjoy the interaction, rather than that one may be harassing the other. Because sexual behaviour in organizations is viewed as personal, in positions where it occurs the labour of the worker is trivialized. Work is viewed as easy or unskilled in jobs in which people are expected to act sexy or dress seductively.

Using a role analysis, I have argued that when sex was visible, it was woman's sexual behaviour but not men's that was visible. Aided by gradually evolving organizational policies, norms and hierarchy that are largely controlled by elite men, the interests of those elite men are served when their sexual behaviour remains invisible. It preserves the view that they are consistently analytical, rational, active and work-oriented. It also facilitates the transfer of any blame for sexual encounters to women, who must be particularly careful to 'manage' their sexuality in the workplace.

The above analyses suggest many possibilities for researchers. Recognition that sexual behaviour at work is a public, organizational phenomenon means that it deserves as much study as other kinds of organizational behaviour such as leadership, performance or negotiation. Too many researchers in the United States have narrowly focused on frequency and definition of sexual harassment, performing a service to the legal profession, but scarcely enriching organizational psychology. The pervasiveness of sexual behaviour at work and its very broad implications, only some of which have been covered in this chapter, suggest that it should receive the kind of broad attention it has in this volume.

Implications for organizational practice

Once sexual behaviour at work is viewed as a public, organizational phenomenon, it needs to be made visible so that it can be managed like other organizational behaviour. It becomes the organization's business. A certain amount of sexual behaviour in organizations may well remain in the private sphere if it is mutually entered into and does not have negative repercussions for workers or for the organization. Some organizations seem very concerned that they will impinge on workers' personal behaviour by setting some standards about sexual conduct in the workplace. Yet by not setting some standards of conduct, they allow, for example, sexual harassers to harass with impunity. Until recently, sex was a 'freebie' for employees who chose to cajole, seduce, pressure or harass others at work into sexual relationships with them. There were no sanctions against people who used work to find willing or unwilling sexual partners. Some harassment appears to be intentionally hostile and is an attempt to intimidate women and force them out of certain jobs (O'Farrell and Harlan, 1982). Some harassment is a display of power, of 'showing who's boss'. In other cases of harassment, the harasser probably does not realize the extent of his effects on the victim and may be completely unaware of the subtle effects of his behaviour. Some harassment may be unintentional, a response to a worker who is viewed through traditional gender roles as an attractive female rather than a capable worker. And some harassment is a response to an environment that encourages sexual overtures; the same man in another, less sexualized workplace might behave quite differently toward women.

As long as it is culturally acceptable to treat women as sex objects, some sexual harassment is bound to occur. Organizations need not wait, however, for a change in cultural norms. Management can alleviate the problem within its own organization by applying sanctions. If sexual harassment is no longer free, I believe that most of it will disappear. Relatively few people are likely to risk their job or promotion opportunities in order to make sexual overtures to co-workers or subordinates. Organizations can establish many practices that will discourage unwanted sexual overtures and can change the consequences of sexual harassment so that it will no longer be a free option. If unwanted sexual overtures are facilitated both by sex-role spillover and by organizational structure, then both should be the target of organizational change efforts.

I recommend five steps:

1. Establish a policy on sexual harassment (or review the current policy) and establish a set of procedures to implement the policy. The set of procedures should include explicit steps whereby complaints by women can be investigated and dealt with

appropriately. In addition, it is important that not only should complaints be taken seriously, but that people who complain should not be punished for making a complaint.
2. Provide employees with knowledge about sexual harassment in special training sessions, if necessary, and in new employee orientation. Also include information about the negative effects of emphasizing sex role over work role.
3. Vigorously pursue allegations of harassment and act on the basis of evidence found in an investigation.
4. Include sexual harassment (and other unprofessional conduct) in performance appraisals and act on those results.
5. Promote professional behaviour and professional ambience throughout the organization. Do not wait until the organization is faced with a lawsuit; get at root causes. A sexualized workplace and unprofessional ambience facilitate sexual harassment.

All of these steps will yield more satisfactory results if they are embraced in earnest, rather than as window-dressing measures to avoid being sued (as has happened in many companies in the United States). They will be understood as serious steps only if top management provides clear support for them and acts in a manner consistent with them, for example not promoting men who sexually harass women. Employees understand the difference between policies that are important to top management and the organization and policies that exist merely to comply with government regulation.

In responding to concerns about sexual harassment, employers may focus on programmes for women, since harassment is a greater problem for them than for men. While women may appreciate advice about how to avoid sexual harassment, deflect comments and overtures, and file a formal complaint of harassment, organizational efforts to reduce sexual harassment and the amount of flirting and sexual joking might most profitably be directed at men, particularly male supervisors who have the power to reduce an oversexualized environment. To a great extent, men control the amount of harassment in the workplace since they are more likely than women to be harassers, and as supervisors they exert control over work environment.

Finally, social–sexual behaviour that is not harassment may also cause problems in organizations. Therefore, organizations might set up specific gender-blind rules regarding sexual conduct in the workplace to protect employees from being sexually exploited. Such rules may vary with the needs of the organization, but could include standards of dress and behaviour. An organization might want to caution employees about excessive touching, for example, and make sure female employees are not required to wear revealing or low-cut outfits (as frequently happens in restaurants and bars). An employer might also establish some rules of conduct and guidelines for people who are mutually involved or married, for example intimate behaviour is inappropriate at work, between spouses as well as between other employees. Likewise, it is usually inappropriate for an employee to provide a performance appraisal or determine the salary of an employee with whom he or she is sexually involved.

In the past, if a man and woman at work became involved or married, the woman was transferred, fired or asked to quit. This was the most likely outcome even if the overtures were unwelcome by the woman. In short, the woman bore the burden of the relationship. As women become more equal partners with men in the workforce and as social-sexual behaviour at work gradually undergoes a transition from private, individual and largely invisible to public, organizational and somewhat visible, new policies and guidelines are necessary. The alternative of ignoring sexual behaviour at work until it becomes a major problem can be more expensive – in time, money and lowered morale among employees.

Notes

I would like to thank Deborah Sheppard and Aaron Cohen for their helpful comments on an earlier version of this chapter.

1. Many gender researchers acknowledge the sexual component of the male role. See for example, Hearn (1985) and Hearn and Parkin (1987).
2. It has been repeated so often that rape and sexual harassment are motivated by power, not sex, that we may forget that rapists and harassers choose to exercise their power through sex rather than some other mechanism. Yes, sexual harassment is a power play; but it is a *sexual* power play.

5
Sexuality in the Workplace: Discrimination and Harassment

Nancy DiTomaso

> This chapter follows the research review of the last by engaging with some of the complexities of sexuality in particular organizations. Workers in three organizations – heavy manufacturing, service and a public agency – were interviewed in terms of their experience of the job. Subsequent analysis by gender and by ethnicity revealed that it was those women who earn most, often working with men, who were most conscious of sex discrimination and sexual harassment. From the comments of women, men's behaviour appears often to go far beyond flirtation, and is as much an exercise in power as in sexuality.

One of the most pointed discussions of how sexuality in the workplace affects women is presented by Catharine MacKinnon in her argument that sexual harassment should be acknowledged as a form of sex discrimination. MacKinnon argues:

> Sexual harassment breaks the marketplace nexus . . . The woman's financial dependence on a man – this time her employer in place of her husband – is again sealed on a sexual basis. Gender and sexuality become inseparable as the dynamics of the home and marketplace converge. Sexual harassment on the job undercuts a woman's autonomy outside the home by sexualizing her role in exactly the same way as within the family: sexual imposition combined with a definition of her work in terms of tasks which serve the man, sanctioned by her practical inability to create the material conditions of life on her own. (MacKinnon, 1979:216–7)

If, as MacKinnon says, sexuality in the workplace imposes on women tasks which serve men and thus reproduces at work the role relationships from the home, then one would expect that its function in the workplace is intertwined with women's financial dependence on men in the workplace, namely, sexual discrimination. Yet, as MacKinnon notes, precisely because sexuality as it is introduced into the workplace often reflects the pattern of sexual expression in the rest of society, the US courts were initially reluctant to include sexual harassment under legal protection against sexual discrimination. Based on arguments that sexual harassment was a 'personal' matter between the individuals involved, that sexual advances are a 'normal' part of the relations between males and females, and that sexual harassment is not exclusively a female problem (in that it could also happen to a male), the courts refused to provide legal protection for victims of sexual harassment under Title VII of the Civil Rights Act, until the Equal Employment Opportunity Commission finally issued guidelines holding employers responsible.

As is implied by MacKinnon's description, the image of sexual harassment is usually of a subordinate woman in a typical helping role being placed in a compromising position by a male boss. Also implied is that women who are economically at risk are more likely to be victimized by sexual harassment than those who have secure and well-paying jobs. As MacKinnon notes, financial dependence on men undermines women's autonomy outside the home as well as in. In this chapter, I want to show that the experience and consciousness of sexual harassment among working-class women is more complex. If the results of this study are typical, then it is only when sexuality becomes part of the agenda of the workplace that women become conscious of both sexual harassment and sex discrimination, and this apparently occurs when women reject the subordinate occupational roles they have most often held and instead seek 'men's' jobs. Under such conditions, I will seek to show, men in the workplace engage in a type of power play by which they use sexuality to put women in their 'proper' subordinate role in relation to men. It is in this struggle that women become conscious of sex discrimination and that they recognize its manifestation in the various forms of sexual harassment. Otherwise, it appears that women do not interpret their experiences of sexual harassment as a reflection of sex discrimination on the job.

In this analysis, I usually refer to men and women or male and female roles to indicate gender differences on the job, but use the terms sex and sexuality to refer to the introduction of actual or implied physical interactions among workers. Sexuality on the job, as is true for sexual harassment in general, indicates a range of possible behaviours, from verbal comments about sexuality to demands for sexual intercourse. One exception to this general differentiation, however, is that I continue to use the term sex discrimination (because this terminology is far more prevalent in the literature than is gender discrimination) to refer to the unequal rewards that men and women receive on the job because of their gender differences.

The theoretical perspective which underlies the analysis in this study assumes that gender relations on the job, including sex discrimination and sexual harassment, and the sexualization of the workplace are rooted in the structural positions that men and women typically hold in the labour force. It is assumed that the power differences existing in most organizations, which give men more authority and access to rewards and sanctions than women, enable the sexualization of the workplace and make it possible for men to exploit women sexually for their own benefit. Most important in this respect, however, is that sexuality can be used as a power tool for those in positions of authority, and because males are more often found in such positions in the workplace, men tend to exploit women sexually as a means to keep them in subordinate positions and to limit the access women have to good jobs.

The study

The data for this study are taken from a survey of 360 workers in three companies: a heavy manufacturing firm, a non-manufacturing service firm, and a public agency. In each company, 120 non-professional and non-managerial workers, equally divided by race/ethnicity (black, white and Hispanic) and gender were interviewed in face-to-face interviews on a variety of topics regarding their experiences on the job. Within each organization a random sample was selected of each of the six race/ethnic and gender groups. Most questions on the survey were closed-ended, but some open-ended questions were included. A number of questions were asked about discrimination and unfair treatment, but nothing was explicitly asked about sexual harassment. Data on the latter emerged from some of the general comments women made about their work experiences and in their descriptions of what they considered discriminatory experiences. All interviews took place in the same urban labour market during 1980, and all were conducted on company time and premises. The surprising result from the study is that it is only in the predominantly male manufacturing firm, where women were more likely to be found in non-traditional jobs and where they received non-traditional wages, that they complained of either sex discrimination or sexual harassment.

The primary purpose of the study was to compare the internal and segmented labour market effects on the work experiences of women and minorities compared to white men. Therefore, by design the companies differed in terms of several major factors (see

Table 5.1 for a summary of these differences). Because there are only three companies and by design they are quite different from each other, it is difficult to identify a single factor as the cause of discrimination in a given company. Even so, by exploring the work experiences of women in different types of setting, it is possible to raise specific questions about the conditions under which women have to confront the sexualization of the workplace. The differences among these three firms tend to reflect the options available to working-class women in the labour force. Women who work in traditional female settings have to accept low wages, while women who work in non-traditional settings frequently have to accept unpleasant working conditions.

Table 5.1 *Selected characteristics of firms in the sample*

	Manufacturing	Non-manufacturing	Public agency
Type of firm	Heavy industry	Service	Public
Unionized	Yes	No	Yes
Job structure	Job ladders with defined promotion sequences	Job grades but no defined promotion sequences	Jobs defined by union contract but no promotion sequences
Average annual income			
Males	$23,968	$10,126	$15,456
Females	$18,560	$9,836	$11,236
% Female	10	70	70
% Black	20	12	60
% Hispanic	20	5	3

The organizations

The manufacturing firm was in heavy industry. The workforce was 90 per cent male, but the company had agreed to increase its hiring of women over the next several years. The firm was unionized by a strong union (or at least one considered strong until recent economic difficulties in the industry), and the wages and benefits for employees in the firm were among the highest in the US for blue-collar workers. An important characteristic of the internal structure of the firm was that jobs were organized by union contract into a series of job ladders. Workers came into the company in a general labour pool and then, after a number of years, were usually assigned to the lowest level of one of the job ladders or sequences. The work was dirty and physically demanding, especially in the lower levels of the job ladders.

Promotions were earned through seniority in a job sequence. The burden of proof was on management to show that a worker was not qualified if they chose to violate the seniority rules. Grievances over rights to specific jobs in this company were frequent. The company followed the letter, but not the spirit, of the law by making a distinction between a permanently assigned job and a temporarily assigned one. A 'temporary' job, however, could go on for years, and as many as 20 per cent of the workforce worked 'out of sequence' at any one time.

A major complaint of women in the company and a major fear by management was that many women could not physically do the lower-level jobs, either in the labour pool or at the beginning of some job sequences. At the higher end of the job sequences, however, jobs were often both more highly skilled and easier physically. Many women in the company wanted access to those jobs without having to go through the usual training steps up the job ladder. For this reason, the women in our sample felt far less sanguine about union seniority rules than did the men in the company. The women wanted access to the jobs which they themselves felt they could do, while at the same time they did not want to be forced to do jobs they felt were too physically difficult. These attitudes clearly made management in the company nervous, because they firmly believed that moving up the job ladders was necessary to give adequate training for higher-level jobs. Whereas management may have been concerned about the overall productivity effects of having less well trained workers in some types of job, it is likely that male workers in the plant were concerned about the effects, for example, of group bonuses which depended on departmental productivity and possibly about the safety implications of allowing exceptions for women.

Because of the kind of environment in the manufacturing firm, the women, at least in our sample, were different from the women in the other two companies in the study. Table 5.2 summarizes these differences. They were more likely to be divorced or never married and more likely to be supporting children by themselves. More than in the other two companies, they were also likely to be the sole wage earner in their households. Most had waited for jobs with this company for up to two years.

Because the women in our sample, on average, had less seniority than the men, they were also more likely still to be in the labour pool and not permanently assigned to a job sequence. Of those who were not yet assigned, many expressed an interest in ending up in a clerical job, and the largest proportion of the women outside the labour pool were already in clerical jobs. In other words, many

Table 5.2 *Selected characteristics of females in three sample firms*

	Manufacturing	Non-manufacturing	Public agency
Average age	37	34	45
Average years seniority	6.0	5.5	9.5
% Married	32	42	25
% with dependants	62	43	43
% with female supervisors	3	75	65
% Clerical or service	57	97	85
% Major wage earner	48	25	38

of these women were working in traditional jobs in a non-traditional setting; those who were not in such jobs often wanted to be. The major difference, then, between their jobs and those of the women in the other two companies was that they were getting paid 'male wages' for the jobs they held, whereas women in the other companies with comparable jobs were getting paid 'female wages'.

The males in the manufacturing firm, in contrast, were older, on average, than those in the non-manufacturing firm and comparable to those in the public agency. They were also more likely to be married and supporting families than the males in the non-manufacturing firm, and again were comparable on this dimension to males in the public agency. Because of the nature of the work, there were many more skilled occupations in the manufacturing firm than in either of the other two organizations. Wages, as noted, were substantially higher in the manufacturing firm than in either the non-manufacturing firm or the public agency. See Table 5.3 for a summary of the differences.

Table 5.3 *Selected characteristics of males in three sample firms*

	Manufacturing	Non-manufacturing	Public agency
Average age	37	25	41
Average years seniority	12.3	2.9	8.4
% Married	63	25	53
% with dependants	77	32	68
% with female supervisors	0	48	17
% Clerical or service	10	77	67
% Major wage earner	73	25	70

Top management in this firm was exclusively male, with a few women professionals in staff positions. In addition, almost all first-line supervisors were male. In other words, although the work was segregated by gender, few women had female supervisors or any experience with female management at this company.

The non-manufacturing firm was on the other end of the scale for most of these characteristics. The work in the firm was predominantly office work, and 70 per cent of the firm was female. Many of the males in the firm were doing semi-clerical work, at female wages. For this reason, the company had difficulty keeping male employees, many of whom were in their first jobs. The company did not have a union.

The women in the firm were more likely to be married, with their spouse as the primary wage earner. This company, like the manufacturing company, had assigned job grade levels to different jobs, but they were not organized into job ladders or sequences with defined promotion patterns, as in the manufacturing company. There was very little difference in pay between one job grade level and another in this company. Assignment to a job was completely at the discretion of the company, and workers perceived arbitrariness in many of the company's decisions.

A large proportion of the professional and managerial staff in the non-manufacturing firm was female, but the very top management was both male and white. About two thirds of the first-line supervisors were female, but a larger proportion of the female than male employees had female supervisors. The firm could be characterized as stereotypically women doing 'women's work' and males doing women's work. Even so, all of the few 'male jobs' in the company were held by males. It was typically the case from our interviews that males entered the company at a low job-grade level and were assigned to a much higher job-grade level within a short time, whereas women entered the company at comparably low levels and stayed there. Thus, there were no disadvantages – aside from the low pay – in being male in a female company, and no special advantages in being female.

The characteristics of the public agency were in between those of the manufacturing and non-manufacturing firms. Like the non-manufacturing company, its work was labour-intensive and fell within the service category. The workforce was about 70 per cent female, but there was much more gender segregation of work within this agency than in the non-manufacturing company, because there was a wider variation of types of job within the public agency than in the private service firm. The workers were organized, with five separate and relatively weak unions. The agency paid about one third more than the non-manufacturing company, but much less than the manufacturing firm. The average tenure of the employees in this agency, however, was similar to that of the employees in the manufacturing firm.

The women in the public agency were, on average, much older

than the women in either of the other two organizations. A larger proportion had been widowed, and the family size of the other women in this agency was substantially smaller than for women in the non-manufacturing company. About the same proportion as in the manufacturing firm were the major wage earners, and there were substantially fewer wage earners in the family, on average, than for the women in the non-manufacturing firm.

The union contracts in the public agency specified rules of job assignment, but there were no defined promotion sequences for the agency as a whole. Males were more likely to be in male jobs and females in female jobs here than in the non-manufacturing firm. About 40 per cent of the first-line supervisors were female, but their assignments were obviously gender segregated. About two thirds of the females in this agency had female supervisors, but less than one fifth of the males did.

The three organizations also differed in terms of race/ethnic composition. The manufacturing firm was 60 per cent white and other, 20 per cent black, and 20 per cent Hispanic. The non-manufacturing firm was 83 per cent white and other, 12 per cent black, and 5 per cent Hispanic. The public agency, in contrast, was 60 per cent black, 3 per cent Hispanic, and only 37 per cent white and other. Both private firms had a predominantly white management, while the management in the public agency was predominantly black.

The findings

We asked an explicit and straightforward question regarding sex discrimination on the job, namely, whether the employee had ever experienced it. The pattern of response was very uneven across the three organizations. Very few women in the non-manufacturing company or the public agency said that they had been discriminated against because of their gender. Relative to women, more men in the non-manufacturing firm, and nearly as many in the public agency, said that they had experienced sex discrimination. In contrast, a third of the women in the manufacturing firm said that they had been discriminated against because of gender, but none of the men in that firm said sex discrimination had been part of their experience on the job (see Table 5.4).

Another sixteen women in the manufacturing company made comments on open-ended questions which indicated that they felt that either sex discrimination or sexual harassment existed within the firm, but they did not claim that they themselves had been discriminated against when asked directly. For example, one woman said that supervisors 'treat women on a more controlled

Table 5.4 *Percentage who said that they had experienced sex discrimination at some time in their jobs*

	Manufacturing	Non-manufacturing	Public agency
Female	30	2	7
	(18)	(1)	(4)
Male	0	5	5
		(3)	(3)

Number of employees in parentheses.

basis than men', such that she felt like 'a prisoner'. She also said that 'the company chooses who they want after too many black women started working there'. Yet she said 'no' when asked whether she had ever been discriminated against because of her gender. The proportion of female employees in the manufacturing firm who noted the introduction of sexuality into the workplace is 57 per cent, if we combine those who claimed that they had experienced sex discrimination with those who otherwise made comments about being a woman in the plant. Similar comments were not made by the women in the other two organizations, in reply to the open-ended questions.

The reason that this is a surprising finding on the face of it is because the women in the manufacturing firm were making so much more money than the women in the other two organizations. We generally think of sex discrimination as restricting women to low-paying jobs, but in this case the women with the lowest-paying jobs across the three firms were least likely to say that they had been discriminated against. There are several possible reasons for this apparent anomaly.

First, in separate regression analyses of yearly personal income (not given here), controlling for education, tenure, experience, weeks and hours worked, and even occupation and hourly wage rate, women were found to have approximately a $1200 to $1800 a year disadvantage (depending on race or ethnicity) compared to men. This disadvantage, however, is primarily accounted for by differences between men and women's incomes in the manufacturing firm. Given the controls included within the analysis, however, this does not mean that only the manufacturing firm discriminates. Rather, the difference in that company is most likely to be due to the departmental incentive pay which is added to the individual earnings for workers in some jobs in that company. It is apparent that men in the company are more likely to hold such jobs than are women. For example, if one did not control for occupation and hourly wage rate, women would have a $4000 a year disadvantage in both the manufacturing firm and the public agency. In other words, in both organizations there is significant gender segregation across occupations and, in the manufacturing firm, some of the jobs held primarily by men have an added advantage of a departmental incentive.

In the predominantly clerical non-manufacturing firm there is no statistically significant disadvantage for women (and, in fact, some women actually do better once one controls for the variables listed above), but in this firm it is also the case that many men are working in 'women's jobs', because there are so few 'male jobs' in the company. (But what few male jobs exist in that company, as noted, are held by men.) There is less gender segregation in this company, then, because there is less differentiation of the occupational structure in the firm.

Second, a major difference exists across the three firms in terms of the proportion of female supervisors of female employees. The physical segregation of women's work from men's work in the non-manufacturing firm and the public agency does make it different from the manufacturing firm, where women are doing mostly women's work, but in close proximity to men. But this alone should not be enough to account for the difference in response regarding sexual harassment. For example, a survey by *Redbook* (a popular American women's magazine) found that 88 per cent of those women answering the questionnaire had experienced some form of sexual harassment on the job. Other surveys have found similarly high proportions of women experiencing sexual harassment. Thus, even though the women in the non-manufacturing firm and the public agency are more likely to work with other women, this does not mean they are exempt from the possibilities of sexual harassment from the 30 per cent or so of men in each firm. (See Konrad and Gutek, 1986, for an analysis of perceptions of sexual harassment related to the gender composition of the job and work setting; and Leeds TUCRIC, 1983).

In addition, the nature of the comments which women in the manufacturing firm made about their job experiences suggests that there is more to their charges than just that they come into contact more frequently with men than the women in the other two organizations. For example, one Hispanic woman said, 'There is definitely sexual harassment problems. I'd like to see an investigation of this. The men are different here than on the street. It's like they have been locked up for years.'

Another woman who said that she did not want to date men from the plant also indicated that there was much more aggressiveness in their approach to women than would occur outside the plant. She said that so many men asked her out, 'It's like a field day.' A third woman said that she thought her supervisor treated her better because she was a woman, and that, 'A majority of the men here go out of their way to make you feel uneasy about being inside the plant and being a female; nice guys are a minority.'

These comments and others suggest that the behaviour of the men in the manufacturing firm was not of the character of everyday flirtation. It was not 'normal' behaviour between men and women. In fact, the women who commented on their experiences in this regard were quite clear that the men in the plant acted differently than they would if they interacted with these women in any other context. Their behaviour, in other words, was very much related to the work context itself. It appeared to provide a licence for offensive behaviour and an occasion for attempting to take advantage of many of the women in the plant.

Given the pervasiveness of the problem for working women, I would assume that sexual harassment took place in the two organizations where women did not report it, but that they did not perceive it in the same way (see Konrad and Gutek, 1986). Most likely they thought of it as a nuisance or perhaps as normal, everyday flirtation, but they evidently did not think of it as sexualizing their jobs. Indeed, in the comments of the few women who reported discrimination in those two organizations, none mentioned anything about sexuality or harassment. Their comments were directed, instead, toward unfair supervisor evaluations, promotion and pay.

In contrast, in the manufacturing plant, the introduction of sexuality into the workplace was the most frequently mentioned topic among those who charged that there had been some sex discrimination in their jobs. As one woman said, 'Men should mind their own business here; they make a big deal of a woman being in the plant.' Sex itself was mentioned by a number of women as a negotiating tool, used by both men and women in the firm. Several talked about women in the factory who slept with men to get easier jobs or to get promotions. The direction of power was always clear, however: it was women who were giving and men who were receiving the sexual favours, for it was always men who had it in their power to grant privileges and rewards.

The use of sexuality as a means to control the demands of women in the plant, however, was not uniform for all of the women there. By and large, younger (but not necessarily very young) women were the ones to make complaints, and it was also the younger women who were more threatening to the men in the sense that they were directly competing for the same kinds of job. Many of the older women in the plant had held jobs there since their entry during the Second World War or during the post war periods of labour shortage. Because the company sought these women to facilitate their production schedules, they also accommodated most of them in 'easy' jobs, or otherwise placed them in positions that were non-competitive with those of the men in the plant. In fact, a number of the older women in the plant said that there was no sex discrimination against them; instead they talked about how grateful they were to the company for making it possible for them to continue working. One woman told us that her husband had been killed, so the company provided a job for her. Also, most of the women who had said that their jobs were easier than others did not say that they had experienced sex discrimination.

But there also seemed to be a double edge to the gratitude. For example, one woman said:

> 'The company is very considerate of their employees, especially when there is sickness, family problems, and the way they help alcoholics. They have programs to help us learn jobs. I wish there were more programs for Latinos. We don't know or have available the programs the company has, but need and would like to participate in them. Especially, I would like to be trained as better than a janitress.'

Another older woman was made conscious of her age and saw it as age discrimination rather than as sex discrimination. She said that her boss had replaced her one day without warning. He had told her that he 'wanted to look at a younger woman' so his 'spirits could be lifted'. She said that her age (54) had never bothered her until he mentioned it to her.

Except for the manifestation of sex discrimination in the form of age discrimination, most of the older women did not say that they had been discriminated against because of their gender. But many of them also indicated that they had easier jobs, or as one woman said, a job 'suitable for a woman'. These women, it seems, were beyond consideration for placement in a job sequence where they would compete with men. They accepted their roles as subordinate in relation to men, and consequently, did not experience harassment. The situation was best explained by the woman who claimed to have a suitable job. She said that 'with women and men working side by side, men act differently toward all women'. Thus, she said she did not like 'the changes in the company'. She also emphasized that she did not want 'a daughter of mine working here; it is no place for a woman'. Another said that the 'company demands more from women because of ERA and in a way it has hurt them'.

Black women also experienced discrimination differently than either white or Hispanic women. Table 5.5 summarizes all of the

Table 5.5 *Whether employee thinks there has been some job discrimination against him or her by race/ethnicity and gender. Manufacturing company*[1]

	Age	Gender	Race/ethnicity	Language	Any reason[2]
Black males	0	0	50% (10)	0	50% (10)
Black females	0	15% (3)	25% (5)	0	30% (6)
White males	10% (2)	0	15% (3)	0	25% (5)
White females	5% (1)	40% (8)	15% (3)	0	50% (10)
Hispanic males	10% (2)	0	50% (10)	5% (1)	55% (11)
Hispanic females	10% (2)	35% (7)	10% (2)	0	35% (7)

1. Percentaged within each cell, representing the proportion who said yes to each question; number of employees in parentheses.
2. Represents non-overlapping proportion.

types of discrimination about which we asked. As can be seen, white and Hispanic females were most likely to say that they had been discriminated against because of their gender, whereas black women were more likely to say that they had experienced race, not sex, discrimination. A possible reason for this difference can be seen in Table 5.6. We asked all of the employees whether they thought that they were treated differently than other employees by

Table 5.6 *Whether employee thinks supervisors treat him or her differently from others with similar jobs. Manufacturing company*[1]

	Treats different	Treats better	Treats worse	Just different	Don't know
Black males	45% (9)	15% (3)	25% (5)	5% (1)	0
Black females	15% (3)	0	15% (3)	0	0
White males	35% (7)	15% (3)	15% (3)	5% (1)	0
White females	35% (7)	25% (5)	5% (1)	5% (1)	0
Hispanic males	25% (5)	15% (3)	10% (2)	0	0
Hispanic females	40% (8)	15% (3)	15% (3)	5% (1)	5% (1)

1. Percentaged within cell, representing the proportion who responded as indicated; number of employees in parentheses.

their supervisors and, if so, whether they were treated better or worse. Most of the white women who said that they were treated differently said that they were treated better, while half the Hispanic women said better and half worse. All of the black women who said that they were treated differently, however, said that they were treated worse. The same pattern exists for black men, with a larger proportion saying that they had been treated worse than either white or Hispanic men. Although a smaller number of black women indicated different treatment, the pattern is still revealing. Many of the black women who made comments about discrimination said that favours in the company were based on 'who you know', or as one woman said, 'if they like you or not'.

This raises the general question about the structure of power within the plant. Even with the guarantees of the union contract, the first-line supervisors had a lot of discretion in the assignment to jobs on a daily or on a permanent basis. The work was hard and difficult, even for the men, and most thought that women could not do the jobs in the plant. Furthermore, most of the women who had been working for the company until recently were secretaries in the office – which was physically separated from most of the factory – or older women who had started during the war years.

The entry of younger women into the plant was a direct result of the growth of the women's movement and the protection against discrimination provided by Title VII (the section of American law guaranteeing civil rights to minorities and women). These new women workers were in direct competition with some of the men for access to desirable job sequences and they indirectly threatened others by questioning the seniority rules that allocated people to jobs. Women had to undergo extensive testing by the men in order to make it in the plant. Much of this testing had to do with their sexuality.

The difficulty a woman experienced depended a lot on her supervisor. Some supervisors purposely tested women by giving them the most difficult jobs to do, while others gave women preferential treatment and allowed them to do the easiest jobs. In either case, it was emphasized to them that they were women in 'men's jobs'. When they were asked to do more than anyone else, it was to show them that they could not handle jobs in the plant because they were women. When they were asked to do less, it was to show them that they could only handle the jobs if men helped them. As one woman said, 'You have to demand that people respect you "sexualwise" or you are continually confronted.' Another said that she would have doubts about recommending her job to a friend because, 'You have to put up with a lot of bull and prove that you can do the work.'

In both cases, women were dependent on men within the plant: to get their help in work which was too difficult or to get their approval for work accomplished. Women were not treated as co-workers, but as women per se. Sexuality became part of the workplace negotiations in this company. Sexual favours became a currency which women could trade for easier jobs, promotions, and job 'security'.

Although none of the women in our survey admitted that they themselves had slept with a foreman or a co-worker to get ahead, many mentioned that other women had done so. Most talked about having to 'know somebody' and 'playing up' to the 'right' people to get a promotion. Others simply talked about having to go to bed with someone. As one woman said, 'Some of the women use their sex to get easy jobs, to get promoted.' Others talked about foremen getting 'involved personally' with some of the female employees. One said flatly, 'Getting promotions are by who you know or go to bed with, like the foreman.' Several of the women indicated that they were not able to get ahead because they did not treat the foreman the same way. One said that she was not able to get a promotion because she did not 'laugh and talk with the supervisors like other women'.

Many of the comments the women made indicated that men were hostile toward women in the plant, while also testing them and making demands – often sexual demands – on them. It is the combination of these comments which makes it clear that the differences between this company and the other two is because women in the manufacturing firm were not properly in their subordinate roles, and so men saw the need to play games of power. The stakes were good jobs. Many said that they were not offered or not given access to some jobs they wanted because the foremen assumed that they could not do the jobs. Even when they protested to the contrary, they were often not allowed to try – because they were women.

The women discussed this struggle in terms of the need to show that they could 'pull their weight'. One woman said that her supervisor made 'sarcastic comments', because 'he doesn't consider that I am the same as men on the job'. She also told us that the males around her 'want her to be a man sometimes and a woman sometimes, but you can't be a woman in this job'. Another said that her supervisor had 'yelled and screamed at me for not doing my work fast enough'. Another was to the point: 'The supervisor does not like me because I am a woman, and they don't want women in these jobs.' She said, 'I am everything he evidently doesn't like.' Some of the women thought that they could do their jobs better, 'if the supervisor offered encouragement sometimes, instead of just negative remarks'.

The use of sexuality as a negotiating tool was complicated by the desperate need that most of these women expressed for keeping their jobs. The women knew that, as women, the jobs in the plant were the best jobs that they could get. Most said that it would be 'very hard' for them to find other jobs with similar wages and fringe benefits. Because so many were supporting themselves and their children, some expressed anger that they were confronted with the choices they had. One said that being in the plant was 'the pits'. Another said that 'It's too bad that women have to work in places like this to get good pay.' As she said, 'It is a hell of a way to earn a living.' Ironically, many of the women looked forward to the day when they could get married and leave the plant. They sought a husband to protect them from the sexual harassment of men in the plant.

Management in this firm was motivated in two directions. They expressed fear of having to face lawsuits, and so wanted to find some way to end the harassment of women before it reached the grievance level. But they also suggested that such behaviour was 'normal' between men and women and could not be policed by them. In discussing the issue, one manager went through the whole scenario which Farley (1978) suggested was the typical reaction to charges of harassment. He said, 'It doesn't happen. If it did happen, the men were probably joking. If they weren't joking, the women probably asked for it. Most women can't do these jobs anyhow and use sex to help them get through their probationary period.' He seemed completely unselfconscious about the stereotypes he was reflecting when he made this comment.

Managers in the plant were concerned about more than lawsuits. They were also convinced that it cost them more to have women in the plant. Two issues were of particular concern. First, management claimed that women were absent more often than men, and, therefore, that they caused inefficiency in the plant. In some ways this was a peculiar charge, because another manager told me that as many as 5 to 10 per cent of the workforce was absent on any one day, and so the company had overhired by this much to keep the plant running. In other words, absenteeism was already a major problem and not one that was being created by women in the plant. Furthermore, an analysis of absenteeism in our sample (not shown here) indicated that it was those in the labour pool who were most likely to be absent, and women were disproportionately in the labour pool because they were new hires. When I mentioned this to the manager, he simply reiterated that women were costing the company money because of their absenteeism.

The second issue was pregnancy. The company was very unhappy when they had to cover pregnancy under their disability plan. The manager I talked with claimed that women typically got medical slips from their doctors which said they were unable to work in their second month. The company was then liable to pay them their full wages until six weeks after the baby was born. Because the wages were so high in this company, the management was sure that women being covered for pregnancy was a significant contributor to the recent productivity declines experienced by the company and the industry (see also Chapter 9).

Management was also concerned about the future. They said that it had been possible up until the time of our survey to find 'niches' of 'women's work' for women to do in the plant. They said this had been the way that they could accommodate women working in the plant during the Second World War. With the tremendous pressure for women to gain access to non-traditional jobs, however, they feared that they had run out of niches. Among other things, they were afraid that they were going to be faced with a large number of women, past their probationary period, who 'plugged up the sequences'. In other words, they thought that women would get access to entry-level jobs in a job sequence and then be unable to handle the next job. In practice, this means they would be likely to decline an offer of promotion, but because of the nature of the seniority system, according to the managers, this would effectively prevent anyone else from having access to the jobs as well. The design of the job sequences was supposed to be that each lower-level job provided training for higher-level jobs in the sequence, so if along the way some workers did not move 'out of the way', it denied the training necessary for workers to do the next higher-level jobs. When management was asked why they did not rearrange the sequences or renegotiate the work rules regarding them, they said it could not be done.

Two additional observations should be added to this story. As noted by Kerr and Siegel (1954), people who work in dangerous occupations tend to develop solidarity with each other. The overwhelming sense of being in this plant was that it was dangerous. The company was very conscious of this and made 'safety' a primary campaign, and the union had considered safety the major issue of concern during bargaining talks that year. Also, a large number of the employees mentioned to us that they were concerned about safety in the plant. In this environment, 'male bonding', expressed in an explicit camaraderie, was prevalent (see Cockburn, 1983). Furthermore, as Kanter (1977) suggests, trust among males is developed with other people 'like themselves'. Women, by the definition of the males in the plant, were women, not co-workers in solidarity. In other words, the men did not trust the women in these jobs to do their share of the work, nor to have the necessary competence in some of these physically demanding jobs to prevent accidents which might threaten the safety of men working in nearby or related jobs.

Another issue is also a general one, namely, that authority and symbols of authority have always been sexualized. The notion that 'men in uniform' are somehow more attractive than others is a good illustration of this. That virtually all of the supervisors in this plant were male may also have contributed to the problem of sexual activity, as well as to sexual harassment between the supervisors and female employees. The important factor, in this situation as in others where sexual harassment is prevalent, is that the males in this plant could both sexualize the workplace and take advantage of their authority, because they had all of the critical discretionary decisions in their hands. (See Carothers and Crull, 1984, for a discussion of the hostility engendered when females challenge male power and work roles; also, Konrad and Gutek, 1986.)

Summary

I have tried to argue in this chapter that women who transcend their traditional subordinate roles to men in the workplace by working in 'male jobs' or otherwise challenging male authority in the workplace are most likely to become conscious of the sexualization of the workplace in the form of both sexual harassment and sex discrimination. Harassment and discrimination also take place in the context, and in relation to, patterns of class and ethnic subordination and oppression. By entering the male job market women place themselves in competition with men, who then attempt, if they have the power, to secure their dominant roles by emphasizing the 'womanness' of their female co-workers and subordinates. In contrast, women who work primarily with other women or who reproduce their subordination in the workplace in relation to men are less likely to be conscious of the sexualization of their workplace roles and more likely to claim that they have not been discriminated against because of their gender, precisely because the reference group they use in regard to their jobs is not men but other women. Sexual harassment is a form of sex discrimination, because its manifestation in the workplace affects those women who by their location or action refuse to enact their subordination to men. As the stories of the women related here indicate, these women are subjected to a particularly aggressive form of sexual harassment, even when the monetary compensation for the jobs they hold is far above that of women doing women's work around other women.

We know much more about sexual harassment through recent research which has explored some of the dimensions of the workplace interactions which are examined here. For example, Konrad and Gutek (1986) have found that women more than men consider sexual behaviour at work to be sexual harassment. They argue that this is so because women more than men are often the recipients rather than the initiators, have more often experienced negative consequences because of sexual activity at work, and are affected more often by subordinate roles off the job which are carried over into the workplace. Although informative about the dynamics of sexual harassment, these theories do not explain why sex becomes the medium through which power games are exercised in the workplace. It is surely tied in some way to sex discrimination in rewards. If women were not so dependent on men for their jobs and so often desperate to keep the jobs they have, then most likely their victimization through sexual harassment would be made more difficult. It also clearly has to do with the fears that men have about losing their privileged place in the labour force. For example, Carothers and Crull (1984) confirm that male workers are overtly hostile to women who challenge or compete with them for jobs, and that this hostility is expressed in terms of sexual harassment.

In addition, it is probably linked to the fact that sexual behaviour is assumed to belong in the private realm. By publicly calling attention to a woman's sexuality or by threatening to make public acts which are supposed to remain private, men have an especially powerful restraint on the ability of women to fight back. At the same time, men have more latitude in most cultures in having their own sexuality made public. For men, public evidence of sexual behaviour is supposed to be a mark of manhood, whereas for women it is often degradation. Added to this, sexual ritual in Western culture often equates sexual excitement with male control over women. Whether men in the workplace intend consciously or unconsciously to use sex at work for these purposes would require further research of a different nature than that reported here. Whatever the causes and however complicated the dynamics or the motivations, the consequences for women in the labour force are significant in adversely affecting their access to good jobs, good training and sufficient rewards.

Note

I would like to thank Marisa Alicea, Nancy Hartline, Audrey Henderson, Charles Kyle, Patricia Passuth, Alicia Ordonez Sequeira and David Torres along with others for their assistance in the data collection. I would also like to thank Barbara Heyns and Judith M. Gerson for helpful comments on an earlier version of this chapter. This research was supported in part by grants from the US Department of Labor, Grant No. 21-17-78-66, from the Rockefeller Foundation, Grant No. GA-EO, C EO 8208, and from Northwestern University's Center for Urban Affairs and Policy Research. An earlier version of this chapter was presented at the Society for the Study of Social Problems annual meeting, San Francisco, California, 1982.

6
Sexuality in the Workplace: The Domination of Men's Sexuality

David L. Collinson and Margaret Collinson

> Like the last, this chapter compares three different organizational settings – in this case an industrial shop floor, a trade union organization and an insurance company. However, in contrast, here qualitative methods, especially participant observation, were used to focus on men's sexuality. Thus in several ways these case studies provide some examples of the type of qualitative research material suggested in the conclusion of the previous chapter. They also indicate something of the nature and complexity of the domination of men's sexuality in many organizations.

Within organization theory there is now an increasing awareness that sexuality is a neglected but crucial issue. Yet empirical research in this area is highly problematic. Sexuality is a particularly sensitive, delicate and indeed often invisible issue within the workplace (Hearn and Parkin, 1987; Gutek, Chapter 4 in this volume). Accordingly, despite the growing literature on the subject, there is a relative absence of detailed *case study* data concerning sexuality in contemporary organizations in the UK. By examining in depth three empirical case studies, this chapter is intended to contribute to an understanding of the complex relationship between power and (hetero)sexuality in organizational practices.

Yet these case studies are not the result of research directly designed to explore sexuality. The significance of this issue emerged during the course of two research projects conducted over a ten-year period. The first project was concerned to examine management/shop-floor relations in a lorry-producing factory in the northwest of England over a four-year period. Here the importance of men's discourses about sexuality for an understanding of shop-floor relations developed as the project progressed (see also Collinson, 1981; 1988a). The second project was funded by the Equal Opportunities Commission to explore sex discrimination in the recruitment process over a two-year period between 1983 and 1985. This research concentrated on the observation of selection practices in forty-five private-sector organizations, representing five separate industries across the north-west of England (see Collinson, 1988b; 1988c).

In seeking to make sense of this data, our analysis was originally inspired by Burrell's (1984) argument that management has always been concerned to protect production by eliminating any manifestations of sexuality from the organization. He suggests that from the industrial revolution onwards, sexual activity within capitalist organizations has been treated as incompatible with and disruptive of production. Accordingly, the suppression of sexuality, either by eradication or containment has always been an identifiable managerial strategy which has developed alongside the emergence of modern bureaucratic organization. In particular, the commodification and standardization of time and of labour which evolved through the industrial revolution to facilitate capital accumulation was crucial in facilitating what Burrell terms 'the desexualization of labour' (1984:99). The decline in the domestic mode of production and the transfer of the workforce into the factory enabled the exercise of tighter workforce discipline. Consequently, 'sex had its place but not within the walls of the factory' (Burrell, 1984:108).

Burrell also emphasizes that management's concern to desexualize organizations has not always been successful. He cites a variety of examples of men's and women's resistance to desexualization where their involvement in sexual relations expresses a 'demand not to be controlled' (1984:102).

Initially, this historical and broad-ranging examination of workplace sexuality and power seemed to make a valuable and plausible contribution to the data we had collected in contemporary workplaces. Certainly the segregation of men and women at work had been justified by some managers in the research on the grounds that it would eliminate the possibility of any 'hanky panky' between the sexes (see also Game and Pringle, 1983:85). Moreover, some recruiters had expressed their commitment to desexualizing the labour process by excluding women from certain jobs such as insurance sales (see Collinson, 1988b). Here women's presence was perceived to be an unnecessary 'distraction' from the business of selling.

And yet the majority of our data on sexuality in organizations could not be fully explained from this perspective. For in many cases management did not appear to be primarily concerned to desexualize the labour process. Equally, the manifestations of sexuality present in the data could not be neatly interpreted as forms of resistance to the process of desexualization. Rather, the evidence overwhelmingly tended to highlight the persistence and dominance of conventional forms of *men's* sexuality within organizations. We therefore came to the conclusion that an exclusive focus on management control and labour resistance neglected a full consideration of the male-dominated nature of organizations (Hakim, 1979) and the way that men's definitions and practices concerning sexuality continue to pervade contemporary organizations. In short, the persistence and privileging (Brittan, 1989) of men's sexuality in organizations did not fit easily within the management control–labour resistance paradigm.

Alternatively, Hearn's (1985) analysis of the way that men in organizational positions of both domination and subordination may draw on sexuality to sustain or reinforce their power, was more relevant to the data presented in this chapter. He documents four main types of sexual behaviour in which men can indulge: horseplay, the exploitation of sexuality, sexual harassment and mutual sexuality. Each category is illustrated with examples that demonstrate a link between men's sexuality and organizational power. So, for example, Hearn interprets men's involvement in horseplay within 'macho' heterosexual workplace cultures as an expression of male power in the face of other men, management and dehumanizing work experiences. Equally, women's sexuality can be exploited both by workers in their preoccupation with pornographic literature and explicit discussions about sexuality, and by managers who use attractive secretaries in order to further their business dealings (see also Chapter 10 of this volume). In addition, Hearn suggests that the sexual harassment of women can act as a powerful form of economic protection and exclusion from men's territory. Finally, he argues that mutual sexuality and actual romances most often involve a power differential in which the man is in a higher organizational position than the woman (see also Quinn, 1977).

These four categories of horseplay, exploitation, harassment and mutual sexuality can be found in the following case studies of men's sexuality in the workplace. Drawing on detailed qualitative material, the research findings examine the dominance and management of men's (hetero)sexuality within contemporary organizations. The evidence demonstrates the pervasiveness of men's sexuality and the way that the managements of these organizations tended either to be blind to, tolerate or even accept traditional forms of men's sexuality.

The accounts recorded confirm the validity of the gender-differentiated discourses surrounding sexuality outlined by Hollway (1984). Men in positions of both power and subordination within these organizations were found to invest in what Hollway has termed 'the male sexual drive' and 'female have/hold' discourses. In brief, the former refers to the taken-for-granted way in which men's sexuality is assumed to be biologically driven, 'natural' and 'out of control'. Men are deemed to be 'sexually incontinent' (Hollway, 1984:232), whilst women are seen as the *objects* of sexuality who precipitate men's natural urges. The latter discourse emphasizes marriage, monogamy and the family. Here women are the *subjects* of the discourse in their concern to attract and keep a man. Whilst married women are considered to be almost asexual, underneath this idea is the belief that female desire is potentially 'rabid and dangerous' (Hollway, 1984:232). The emphasis on family life and women's relationship with husband and children is viewed as the means by which their sexuality is controlled.

The following empirical analysis concentrates on three different organizational settings that are characterized by contrasting degrees of sex segregation (Hakim, 1979). The first case study highlights the pervasiveness of men's preoccupation with sexuality in the all-male shop-floor context of a lorry-producing factory. The second example discusses men's sexuality in a 'white-collar' trade union which is overwhelmingly, but not exclusively, male dominated. The third case study is drawn from a major UK insurance company that employs a mixed workforce, in which women are largely confined to subordinate positions. Since the final two illustrations are drawn from the research on recruitment, which was designed to examine specific management and trade union practices, the evidence which emerged from this project was able to go beyond a narrow focus on men's *accounts* about sexuality to which the shop-floor study is inevitably limited. Although the latter is in itself valuable, what men say about their own and women's sexuality, particularly in the company of other men, and how they actually engage in sexual relations, may diverge considerably (Brittan, 1989). Accordingly this discrepancy between discourse and practice is largely overcome in the second two case studies where organizational practices are fully observed and placed alongside participants' accounts.

The empirical data will now be presented in the three organizational settings. Focusing on horseplay, sexual harassment and mutual sexuality, respectively, these studies illustrate the pervasiveness and dominance of men's sexuality in the workplace. They also illustrate the complex interrelationships which can emerge between men's definitions of male and female sexuality, and other organizational practices such as shop-floor resistance, the internal politics of trade unions, and workplace 'fiddles'.

Men's sexuality on the shop floor

The research on the shop floor concentrated on the components division of the lorry-producing factory. This particular division employed an exclusively male workforce of 250, the vast majority of whom were classified as skilled engineers. Interviews with over sixty of these workers were conducted on a regular basis and were supplemented by non-participant observation. A recurrent finding of this project was the extent to which discourses about men's sexuality characterized everyday life and interaction on the shop floor.

Within the components division, masculine sexual prowess was a pervasive topic. Mediated through bravado and joking relations (see Collinson, 1988a), a stereotypical image of self, which was assertive, independent, powerful and sexually insatiable was constructed and protected through the men's discourses about sexuality. By contrast, women were dismissed as passive, dependent and only interested in catching a man. Clearly, these discourses contributed to a form of male unity on the shop floor and constituted a powerful pressure, to which all workers were required to conform.

Photos of female nudes could be found on most shop-floor walls in the division. Many of these had been supplied by the 'Porn King' who maintained a large 'sex library' of magazines for shop-floor edification. The men's discourse of 'macho' sexuality was characterized by profuse swearing, masculine bravado and highly explicit joking relations. Proud boasts and comments such as the following were part of the daily fabric of shop-floor interaction.

'I've had many a jump at the local train station.'

'Men come from the womb and spend the rest of their lives trying to get back in.'

'You'll never win with women because they're sitting on a goldmine. They'll always have the power.'

'At school I was very shy. I went red if girls talked to me. If they talk to me now, I'll shag them!'

'You should see the new barmaid in the "Coach and Horses", but you should see the cunt that's fucking it!'

Such statements confirmed to manual workers and their colleagues who and what they were, i.e. tough, autonomous and invulnerable men who simply expressed their predatory nature in an obsessive but joking preoccupation with sexual matters. It was considered 'normal' and 'natural' for men to talk explicitly about sexuality. Failure to participate raised serious questions about the deviants' masculinity. Newcomers were soon initiated into the groups' central values through ritualized ceremonies which were overtly sexual in content. For example, Pancake Tuesday was celebrated by 'greasing the bollocks' of the apprentices with emulsion and then 'locking them in the shithouse, bollock naked'. The lads had to 'take it', in order to survive on the shop floor. Similarly, the story of one young lad who entered the company with 'diplomas galore' was often proudly recited, 'They had a french letter on his back by ten o'clock. They had him singing and dancing in the loo with the pretext of practising for a pantomime . . . we soon brought him round to our way of thinking.'

Two primary and typical forms of men's sexuality, related to the conventional male life cycle, permeated shop-floor discourse. Younger men tended to display a fetishization of sexuality and a reduction of women to sexual objects. This was exemplified by the 'sexploitative' mentality of 23-year-old 'Boris'. Much of his shop-floor contact was spent embellishing his infamous reputation as a self-defined 'superstud'. He maintained a 'sex diary' which listed all of his past 'conquests'. Concerned to 'trap females' Boris graded out of ten the 'performance' of his twenty 'victims'. A 'scientific analysis' revealed that, the older the woman (especially if married), the higher she was graded. Boris proudly boasted of his escapades and the 'carpet burns on me knees'. But his exaggerated accounts of sexual exploits were received with disbelief and ridicule. A recurrent comment by Ernie was, 'He's a Don Juan is Boris. . . . When he's had Juan he's Don!!'[1]

Older manual workers often prioritized their domestic power as the family breadwinner. Accordingly, they treated work primarily as a means of securing an income. This role of the provider invariably constituted a crucial element of a more mature form of masculine self-respect, as one worker indicated, 'I think you should be useful with your life. I love family responsibility. I would have ten kids, if I could afford them. It's easy to have kids, but it takes a man to bring them up.'

Here the men's sexuality and sense of identity tended to be expressed less in terms of sexual conquest and more with regard to their domestic power and authority. Many workers claimed that they kept their wages secret from their wife, as one stated, 'A lot of blokes in here do tip,[2] but I don't think a woman should see your wage packet. It's a matter of understanding in our house. She understands I am in command.' The emphasis of the shop-floor discourse on sexuality had therefore shifted from 'trapping' to 'tipping', from sexuality to domestic power. As one older worker explained, 'At eighteen I thought they were good for screwing, now I realise they've other uses.' One male self-identity, as sexually rampant, was superseded by another, that of the responsible and powerful family breadwinner.

What united these two discourses, however, was the men's insistence on their power over women and on their masculine autonomy and independence which could be expressed in manual labour. Underlying these discourses was the workers' defensive preoccupation with masculine identity. This concern was reinforced by the conditions of shop-floor experience, which threatened workers' sense of dignity. Of all company employees, those on the shop floor worked the longest hours in the most insecure and tightly controlled jobs, enjoyed the worst canteen and car park facilities and the poorest holiday, pension and sickness provision. These conditions confirmed to shop-floor workers that they were the least valued and most easily disposable of employees. Hence the experience of manual work generated a problem of identity for the men (see also Sennett and Cobb, 1977).

'Dirty Bar' displayed how manual workers typically dealt with this degrading experience. He emphasized how manual work was the essence of masculinity, 'Fellas on the shop floor are genuine. They're the salt of the earth, but they're all twats and nancy boys in th'offices.'

The male workers perceived their own culture to be a symbol of freedom and autonomy, which contrasted with the more reserved work conditions and character of the office staff. The uncompromising banter of the shop floor, which was permeated by uninhibited swearing, mutual ridicule, displays of sexuality and 'pranks', was contrasted, exaggerated and elevated above the middle-class politeness, cleanliness and more restrained demeanour of the offices. Ironically, when compared to others, the subordinated world of the shop floor came to be seen as a free space in which the 'true self' could be expressed; as another worker put it, 'You can have a load of fun on the shop floor, but in the offices, they're not the type to have a laff and a joke. You can't say "you fucking twat!" in the offices.'

In a similar way, the shop-floor culture reflected and reinforced the sense of 'us and them' in relations with management. The perceived conformism and inability to make decisions of managers, nicknamed 'the yes men', also led to them being ridiculed as effeminate. On one occasion, as a result of a workforce 'go slow', a significant shortfall occurred on management's projected production levels. This stimulated the axle shop steward to joke, '[The production manager] will have a baby when he sees these figures.'

These discourses facilitated manual workers' self-differentiation from, and antagonism to, both white-collar staff and managers. The preoccupation with masculine sexuality therefore reflected the men's concern to deny their subordinate hierarchical position within the organization.

And yet, despite the men's insistence on the power, autonomy and unity of their all-male shop-floor world, the precariousness of these cultural discourses surrounding sexuality was revealed at the end of the research, when closure of the components plant was announced with the loss of 153 jobs. Rather than reinforcing the men's solidarity to fight (at the minimum) for improved redundancy payments, this decision merely exacerbated the fragmentation of the workforce. Against the advice of the trade union, the workers voted to accept the lump-sum package without a fight. Ultimately, in this company, the pervasive concern to differentiate a highly masculine sense of self from the organization through joking and discourses surrounding sexuality was shown to contradict the reality of organizational power and managerial control.

Other research on male-dominated shop floors has revealed a similar investment by respondents in male sexual drive discourses as an expression of resistance and as a precarious form of masculine unity (e.g. Willis, 1977; Cockburn, 1983; Hearn, 1985; Fine, 1987; Gray, 1987). Together these studies illustrate that in the absence of women workers, discourses concerning men's sexuality are likely to pervade the workplace. The first case study presented here in particular suggests that the men's emphasis on sexuality constituted an attempt to deny their subordinate position within the organization. Equally, the evidence indicates that so long as women were excluded from the shop floor, men's discourses about sexuality, their initiation ceremonies, practical jokes and banter, and displays of 'pin ups' and other pornographic literature were tacitly accepted by managers who could see no major incompatibility between these demonstrations of masculinity and production. Insofar as the men's preoccupation with sexuality reflected and reinforced their elevation and celebration of manual work as an expression of personal power and significance, then the discourse deflected resistance away from the organizational hierarchy. Even though the shop-floor preoccupation with sexuality consumed a great deal of workers' time and energy, which could be disruptive to production not least in generating conflict and squabbling between the workers (see Collinson, 1988a), management accepted that these expressions of men's sexuality were a natural and inevitable part of the male-dominated workplace. This case study suggests that men's articulation of a sexual drive discourse was therefore treated as unproblematic by management, who were happy to contain it within the shop-floor environs.

If you can't stand the heat, get out of the kitchen

The following case study again illustrates the way in which men can seek to use sexuality as a means of enhancing or sustaining their power and status within organizations. Moreover it displays how those in authority may treat this expression of men's sexuality as unproblematic. The case focuses on the internal workings of a 'white-collar' trade union which, although not an exclusively male arena as in the previous example, is heavily dominated by men. Whilst women constitute almost half of the union membership, they have been largely absent from senior positions. The following account explores the impact on one specific company division of the wider trade union when a female area representative was elected on to the division's previously all-male executive committee. This body was responsible for negotiations and consisted of the five senior officials of the union, who were accountable to an Area Council. The council met bi-monthly and comprised thirty area representatives drawn from the company's nationwide structure. In addition to the five senior officials, this company division of the union also employed three seconded representatives who, as full-time officials, dealt with local matters arising within their allotted areas.

Sue became the first woman to be elected to the division's executive committee, following her major involvement in union work, since her election as an area representative in 1983.[3] For example, she was willing to travel to London regularly for union meetings despite living 200 miles away. Although staying in hotels was particularly inconvenient because she was divorced with two children in their early teens, the support of neighbours enabled her to continue trade union work which she found interesting and rewarding.

As the first ever female member of the executive, Sue experienced initial problems with both union colleagues and senior managers who had never before had to 'deal with' the presence of a woman in such a senior position. She continued to ignore their over-sensitivity to her presence, their sexual innuendos, joking and sexist 'compliments', such as 'How pleasant it is to have Sue here brightening up the office.' . . . 'Your hair smells very nice today, Sue.'

Many of these comments were disregarded by Sue as she concentrated on developing her 'credibility' on the executive committee. However when accusations were made about her sexuality in relation to other members of the executive committee, she considered these too serious to ignore. Sue's refusal to disregard these accusations generated a major controversy which gripped the union for several weeks.

During a union conference, a conversation took place in the men's toilets between a member of another division of the trade union and the assistant secretary of Sue's division. The former asked the latter whether, 'the rumours are true that you are screwing Sue Fleming?' He stated that this rumour was rife within the whole union and that the Chairman [sic] of the division was reputed to be 'screwing her too'. Within the other company divisions of the union, the topic had come to be known as 'the three in a bed saga'. When the assistant secretary enquired who was spreading the rumour, he was told that it was a seconded representative (Bill) within the division.

A meeting was then called by the assistant secretary at which he confronted the seconded representative with this accusation in front of the Chairman and Sue. Bill confirmed his responsibility for the rumour and added, 'Well we've all been wondering about you three and all these nights in hotels.' On being asked by Sue why this should be said, Bill replied, 'Why not? How else could you have got into that position on the executive?'

This remark generated extensive acrimony between the assistant secretary and the seconded representative. Refusing to discuss the matter further, Bill then left the meeting, whereupon he immediately complained to a senior official of the parent union about the 'antagonistic' way that he had been treated by the assistant secretary. This accusation was treated seriously by the senior union official, who then interviewed all concerned about the incident. When Sue protested that he seemed much more concerned about the seconded representative's accusations than about the original reason for the meeting or that Bill had *admitted* to spreading malicious rumours, she was told by the official,

> 'Now I don't know whether the rumours are true or false, but you've got to be able to take it girl. It's all round the union and has been ever since I took over. It's not going to change. So if you can't take it, I'd advise you to get out of the trade union movement. If you can't stand the heat, get out of the kitchen!'

In response, Sue reminded the official of the trade union's formal and public commitment on equal opportunities and then stated,

> 'You should be supporting women who have to move in male circles which is very difficult at the best of times. So even though I've conducted myself above reproach, just because I know their assertions are not true,

then I should allow them to say anything they want about me? They can't just be allowed to do anything they like.'

Sue received no support and indeed some antagonism from senior officials of the union, who insisted that she must accept and accommodate to the male-dominated culture. Consequently Sue contacted her solicitor, who advised her that the matter was serious enough to justify the following formal letter requesting an apology and retraction.

Solicitor's letter sent by Sue
Dear Sir,
> We act for Mrs Fleming, who has told us of the personalities and circumstances concerning malicious rumours about our Client.
>
> In the presence of witnesses it seems you have admitted passing remarks to the effect that our Client's purpose in attending union meetings at hotels is to enable her to sleep with the Chairman or Assistant Secretary.
>
> Our Client has had no intimate relationship with either of these men and has a serious interest in her union work.
>
> The remarks are quite clearly defamatory and form the basis of an actionable slander. They were made in the presence of reliable witnesses.
>
> Unless we hear from you within 10 days with satisfactory proposals, proceedings will be issued and served against you without further notice.

Yours faithfully,

As this deadline approached, considerable informal pressure was placed on Sue by senior union officials, firstly to withdraw her letter and then secondly to accept a verbal rather than a written apology. She was warned that should the matter go to court, Sue could well lose, the result of which might be the loss of her job with the company. With two children to support this was clearly a serious threat. Even the assistant secretary who had instigated the first meeting attempted to moderate Sue's demands and to convince her to accept a verbal apology. However, Sue resisted these pressures. Ultimately, rather than go to court the seconded representative and the union officials arranged to produce a written apology. A meeting was scheduled at which the following letter was passed to Sue, whilst she in turn gave a written assurance that she would not pursue the case further.

Letter of retraction
Dear Mrs Fleming,

I retract the incorrect statement I have made about there being any intimate relationship between yourself and the Chairman and the Assistant Secretary, and apologize for the anxiety this has caused you.

I undertake also, not to repeat any such statements in the future, but ask you to note that I cannot be held liable if it comes to your notice after the date hereof, that such incorrect statements are being made by any other person or persons.

Yours sincerely,

And yet the episode did not finish there.

Close union friends of Bill believed that he had been unfairly attacked and that Sue's use of solicitors' letters was an extreme and 'over the top' reaction incompatible with trade union principles. In particular, the Deputy Chairman [sic] of the division prolonged the dispute by writing a letter to the Chairman expressing his concern at 'Mrs Fleming's use of solicitors against her brothers in her own division'. Sue also received the following anonymous letter sent to her home address.

Anonymous letter

You are aware that the President and your fellow colleagues want you out of the Union.

The Company want lunatic feminists off the Executive. They have told me.

You should resign prior to the AGM.

The Deputy Chairman then sent a second letter to the Chairman complaining about Mrs Fleming's behaviour which, this time, he also circulated to the Area Council. At this point, Sue realized that she would have to stand for the post of Deputy Chairman in the coming elections at the Annual General Meeting. This was because, having confirmed in writing that she would not discuss the matter further, Sue was still being attacked by senior members of the division who appeared to be seeking to discredit her and to force her off the executive committee. Hence she had no choice but to stand for election to the position of the person attacking her.

Whilst the Deputy Chairman built his whole campaign for re-election around the foregoing issues, Sue dealt exclusively with matters related to the trade union and its members. The result was that Sue won the election with a clear majority.[4] As a consequence, the Deputy Chairman resigned his position on the executive and stormed out of the meeting in frustration. Given the council's support for Sue the seconded rep's position had become untenable. Soon after the Annual General Meeting, Bill resigned his full-time union post and returned to his job working in the company.

This case illustrates the problems women can face when entering traditional male domains. The pervasive nature of the male sexual drive discourse within this 'white-collar' trade union was perpetuated in particular by the informal discussions which always took place in the bar after the formal union business had been completed (see also Chapter 9 of this volume). The evidence demonstrates how a woman's commitment to her union work can be redefined and dismissed within the men's discourse as merely the outcome of the manipulation of her sexuality. In addition, the severe difficulties that women face in resisting such attacks is also revealed. Sue's refusal to accept the persistence of these rumours was criticized by union colleagues and senior officials who clearly believed that she should accommodate to the male-dominated culture. Extensive pressure was placed on Sue to withdraw her demand and, even after she received the letter of retraction, criticism from senior male colleagues continued.

Hence the case study highlights the deep-seated nature of the male sexual drive discourse and the way it can be used to try to exclude or subordinate women. These findings support DiTomaso's argument (in Chapter 5 of this volume, p. 71) that where women enter male-dominated areas, men may use sexuality to maintain their dominant position. Accordingly, men's focus on sexuality is 'as much an exercise of power as it is of sex'.

Fiddling flexitime

The previous two case studies examined how sexuality can be used by men in order to establish or sustain power and status within organizations. Conversely, the final case study illustrates how hierarchical power can be drawn on to facilitate a sexual relationship. The research material focuses on a main branch of a major UK insurance company which employed a mixed workforce. Firstly, it explores the way in which a supervisor conducted his affair with a female clerk. Secondly, it then examines the managerial response when this relationship begins to impact negatively on the organization.

Chris was an experienced supervisor (Grade 9) in the Fire and Accident Department whose technical underwriting skills were highly valued by his superiors. He supervised one section within the department which consisted of himself and six female clerks (graded 3 to 7). Chris was also heavily involved in the organization of the branch Sports and Social Club, which required a great deal of his company time. In addition, he ran a tuck shop during working hours and spent a considerable amount of time and money betting on horse races. He had a reputation as a highly sociable person who was very popular, particularly with male colleagues.

Married with two children, he was also considered to be a 'ladies' man'. This was primarily because of his long-standing affair with a Grade 7 clerk, 'Pat', who worked in another section of the department. Their relationship had always been conducted with great confidence and in the full gaze of colleagues and supervisors working in the open-plan offices. The turbulent nature of the affair was well known throughout the department. This was largely because Chris tended to subscribe to a male sexual drive discourse, which from time to time antagonized Pat, who was concerned to develop a deeper relationship.

Management had consistently ignored the relationship even though a substantial amount of both Chris and Pat's working time and energy was devoted to each other. However, just when Chris was about to be promoted to Assistant Superintendent (Grade 11), his relationship with Pat spilled over into his work life in such a serious way that it could no longer be ignored by his superiors. Chris was accused by his section of defrauding the flexitime system in order to claim hours not worked for both Pat and himself.

On entering or leaving the building, all employees were required to 'clock on' and 'off'. Staff had to be present during 'core time' (i.e. 10.00 a.m. until 4 p.m.) but otherwise had discretion over 'working time' (i.e. 8.00 a.m. until 6 p.m.). At the end of every month, each person's hours were accumulated and matched against a set figure of prescribed basic hours for that period (calculated on the basis of seven hours per working day). Whilst staff were not allowed to go more than ten hours below this figure, 'excess hours' could be used in lieu of a flexiday. Hence, by working longer hours, a spare day's holiday could be accumulated.

However, although Chris and Pat had spent a considerable amount of time away from work, having days off together, and arriving late and leaving early, they always tended to be 'in credit' when the monthly hours were calculated. Chris's section became increasingly suspicious that he was 'fiddling' his and Pat's clock. For example, it was rumoured that on the days when Pat was absent, Chris would switch her clock on for half a day. Moreover, that Chris often 'forgot' to stop his clock during the lunch break was well known to his section, the whole department and other

The Domination of Men's Sexuality 105

supervisors. It was suspected in the department that Chris and Pat were accumulating excess hours in order to enable them to spend more time together during the day. As a result, Chris's section decided to check the clock reading against his recording of the monthly hours' total on the summary sheet before it was formally submitted to the Deputy Superintendent. This revealed that Chris had added five and six hours to his and Pat's records respectively. When the women in the section complained to Chris, his response was highly aggressive and dismissive. As a result of the ensuing acrimony the issue came to the attention of senior management, who had no alternative but to investigate further by interviewing all those involved.

After their initial enquiries, the two male branch managers were quite prepared to accept Chris's version of events. Chris had quickly admitted his falsification of hours worked. However, he insisted that this was merely a means of 'flushing out jealousy and resentment' and 'bringing to a head' a whole series of 'malicious rumours and insinuations' about both his past abuse of flexitime and his relationship with Pat. He stated that although the erroneous figures were recorded on the summary sheets, which members of the section had seen, the correct figures had actually been submitted to the Superintendent. Chris complained that he was being 'victimized' by his section, and that the women's accusations were the result of their jealousy concerning his relationship with Pat. He claimed that there was 'a campaign against Pat and myself'. The two managers were prepared to accept Chris's version of events, although in their formal report they added that Chris had 'misjudged the effect of his relationship with Pat Smith on other members of the staff'.

Nevertheless, at a meeting arranged to 'air the matter and get it out of the way', the all-female section became incensed that Chris's accusations of victimization were being taken seriously by management. Two important points were raised. Firstly, why had Chris become so abusive when challenged by the section? During this meeting he had made no attempt to explain the reasons for his actions or to confront their suspicions and resolve the matter once and for all. In addition, *after* this acrimonious meeting, Chris was observed walking out of the office with the file containing the month's summary sheets which had been on the Deputy Superintendent's desk awaiting his attention. This suggested that only after being accused of falsification had Chris gone to amend the formal records. These points finally convinced management that Chris's accusations of his section's jealousy were unfounded and were merely a smoke-screen designed to camouflage his deliberate falsification. Before receiving written statements from two of the women that Chris had been seen leaving the office with the file, the male managers had been prepared to accept the supervisor's claim that his all-female section were jealous of his relationship with Pat.

Yet even after establishing Chris's culpability, local management still sought to minimize his punishment. Defrauding the flexitime system usually resulted in automatic dismissal. Instead, they recommended to corporate personnel that Chris should:

1 not be considered for promotion to Assistant Superintendent;
2 be issued a final warning for twelve months;
3 be transferred to another branch into a Fire and Security Surveyor vacancy (equivalent grade).

A supporting letter from the branch manager emphasized Chris's 'long and outstanding service' and that, ' I do feel his stupid actions may have been influenced by the stress and strains of the heavy workloads of the past year or so.' The manager added, 'Mr Brown has been naive beyond belief, but in a strange way one can understand his illogical thinking and actions that have led to this unhappy situation.'

Corporate personnel rejected this 'plea of mitigation', arguing that demotion to Grade 7 was the minimum punishment that could be accepted. Local management had to implement the head office decision. However, at the formal disciplinary meeting in March, the branch manager outlined the company decision but then assured Chris, 'Setbacks do happen, but you should not regard a tragic mistake as ruining a promising career. . . . There is a fresh path to be trodden if you are prepared to follow it and we will do all we can to assist you.'

After Chris had accepted the disciplinary terms, the branch manager stated, 'I am delighted to hear this. I will now go on record to say if you perform as I know you can, I would seriously consider you for promotion to a supervisor's position even within the twelve months warning period.' He merely added, 'Can I refer to Mrs Smith? She will not be in your department and I would suggest that it would be in yours and her best interests to keep your friendship away from the work situation. In that way there should be fewer problems.'

While Chris was allowed to return to the Fire and Accident Department, Pat was transferred to the Marketing Department. This outcome reinforces the findings of other research which suggests that women are more likely than men to suffer the consequences of affairs in organizations (Quinn, 1977). Moreover, remaining true to his recorded statement, the branch manager promoted Chris to a supervisor's position within the twelve months warning period.

In sum, the case study demonstrates how a male supervisor abused his hierarchical power in order to facilitate a sexual relationship. It also reveals how management were prepared, firstly to tolerate the disruptive effects of the affair, secondly to accept the supervisor's initial definition of 'the problem' as an expression of female jealousy, and finally to resist taking any action against the supervisor when faced with incontrovertible evidence of his misconduct. This case study thereby reinforces Gutek's argument (Chapter 4 of this volume) that men's sexuality is often treated as unproblematic by those in positions of power within contemporary organizations.

Conclusion

This chapter has drawn on detailed empirical studies from the UK engineering and insurance industries and from the trade union movement to examine the way in which men's sexuality can be reproduced in organizational practices. Revealing how men's sexuality is routinely privileged and embedded within particular organizational practices, the empirical material demonstrates that an adequate understanding of organization sexuality requires its location within specific contexts and practices. Similarly, the data also indicate that a thorough explication of organizational practices, such as those discussed, of control, resistance, union politics and 'fiddling' may well necessitate an analytical sensitivity to sexuality. Whether in the engineering company where women were entirely absent, the trade union which was highly male dominated or the insurance company which employed a mixed workforce, the findings suggest that men's sexuality and organizational power are inextricably linked.

In the first case study, manual workers subscribed to a male sexual drive discourse which was designed to establish their sense of power, dignity and masculine identity in conditions of its erosion. The men's preoccupation with sexuality as an expression of personal power, significance and autonomy reflected their concern to resist management control and the organizational status system and to deny the reality of their subordination within the organization. The second case study also illustrated how men may draw on sexuality as a means of maintaining power and control within organizations. In this example, attempts were made to discredit and undermine the commitment of the first female executive member of the trade union. The very presence of a woman in a relatively senior position was treated as problematic by colleagues, who, in turn, promulgated rumours about her sexual life that were entirely unfounded. The men's association and indeed conflation of 'woman' with 'sexuality' demonstrates how male-dominated labour organizations can be characterized by assumptions and practices which seek to discredit and exclude women. In contrast to the foregoing studies, the final example highlights how a supervisor sought to manipulate his hierarchical position in order to sustain a sexual relationship. Moreover, even when the supervisor's abuse of his position was challenged and exposed, management adopted a protective approach towards him.

Together the three case studies provide detailed evidence of how men may seek to secure themselves and their identity by drawing on conventional forms of masculine sexuality and organizational power. They illustrate how the domination of men's discourses and practices about sexuality can reflect and reproduce the male-dominated nature of contemporary organizations. Equally, they show how management may treat these expressions of men's sexuality as largely unproblematic.

The evidence thus provides some support for the argument that a structure of patriarchy in addition to the capitalist pressure to commodify and control labour is a necessary analytical prerequisite for the understanding of how power and sexuality are reproduced in organizations (Walby, 1986). Yet this is not to argue for an analytically separate system of patriarchy. For a recognition of the consistent and structural character of male domination in contemporary organizations must also acknowledge the way in which capitalist and patriarchal power and inequalities, whilst possibly in tension, are nevertheless *interwoven* in the same organizational practices (Connell, 1987).

Moreover, it is important to avoid an overly deterministic analysis of male and managerial power within organizations. This is firstly because such an approach neglects the possible contradictory consequences for men of their attempts to establish or retain power, identity and control in organizations. The case studies demonstrate that men's preoccupation with maintaining gender and hierarchical identity through discourses about sexuality on the shop floor, in the trade union and in the office generated counter productive consequences for themselves, not least in terms of job loss (i.e. redundancy and resignation) and demotion. Secondly, an overly deterministic analysis neglects the agency of women in organizations (Collinson, 1988c). As other writers have argued (Hearn and Parkin, 1987; Mills, Chapter 2 of this volume), women are not merely passive objects of men's attempts to maintain organizational and personal control. Women do recognize and resist some of the contradictions of men's conventional expressions of sexuality and power within organizations.

The two final case studies, in particular, provided strong evidence of women's resistance to the patriarchal assumptions of men's and women's sexuality. The women's resistance was constructed in the face of extensive pressure from managers and male colleagues to discontinue their action. In each case the women were labelled 'troublemakers' by those whom they were resisting. Whilst in both instances the original organizational 'problem' was initiated by men's preoccupation with sexuality, it was subsequently redefined as a reflection of women's inability to adjust to men's discourses and practices about sexuality. Yet, despite this pressure, the women were not only willing to pursue their grievance, but were also effective in challenging men's patriarchal assumptions.

The findings thus reveal the capacity of women's oppositional practices to challenge the contradictory nature of conventional discourses and practices concerning male and female sexuality. The patriarchal nature of organizations often renders women's resistance invisible and ineffective. However, these studies caution against the neglect of women's agency and resistance and thereby challenge overly deterministic analyses of men's sexuality and managerial power in contemporary organizations.

Notes

Thanks to Jeff Hearn, Deborah Sheppard, Peta Tancred-Sheriff and Gibson Burrell for their helpful comments on an earlier version of this chapter.

1. Given the sexual reputation of the original 'Don Juan', this joke contains a particularly subtle *double entendre*, reinforced by the local accent in use. The second part could thus be heard as follows: ' . . . when he's had one he's done!!'

2. Tipping was a cultural term used on the shop floor to describe the process of giving wages to 'the wife'.

3. In order to ensure confidentiality and anonymity, all names used in the text are pseudonyms.

4. This result reveals that a majority of men on the area council supported Sue.

7
Private Experiences in the Public Domain: Sexuality and Residential Care Organizations

Wendy Parkin

> Although these next two chapters are, like the last three, concerned with sexuality in the workplace their focus is as much on the absence of or ambiguity around sexuality as its overt display. Both also deal with the complex interplay of private experiences, some sexual, some not, in the public domain. This chapter discusses such questions in a particular type of organization, namely those providing residential care, operating in the 'intermediate zone', between the public domain and the private domain. Special emphasis is placed on the importance of ambiguities – both sexual and organizational – in such organizations.

The central theme of this chapter is that sexuality is an ever-present issue for workers and residents within residential care organizations, yet is notably absent from staff meeting agendas, training programmes, organizational policies, rules and guidelines. As such this theme links with previous analysis of the supposed, yet false, separation of 'sex' and 'work', brought together in the concept of 'organization sexuality' (Hearn and Parkin, 1987). This chapter explores the significance of sexuality in the context of a research study of residential care organizations. The study has involved interviews and discussions with residential care workers, residential managers and about forty CQSW (Certificate of Qualification in Social Work) students, with whom I had direct contact over a three-year period, who had undertaken a three-and-a-half-month assessed placement in a residential establishment. The anomalous position of residential 'homes' both within large welfare bureaucracies, and between the public organizational world of paid work and the private world of the family, is recognized. The powerlessness of the client groups, the low status of the workers, the 'semi-professional' status of social work, and the operation of generic powers (Hearn and Parkin, 1987) will be addressed.

The organizational settings under examination are residential organizations providing full-time service delivery of care to vulnerable client groups such as children in care, frail elderly people, mentally handicapped, mentally ill, and disabled people who cannot live independently. These client groups need 24-hour care, many permanently and, although medical needs can be met, the prime focus of the establishment is care provision not medical treatment.[1] Such establishments are run by local authorities, voluntary organizations, and the private sector. While local authority care is the prime focus of the research, some examples are also drawn from the voluntary sector.

Sexuality and residential care organizations: case material

'Service delivery of care' entails people living in close proximity to each other: residents with residents, residents with staff, staff with staff. An important aspect of this proximity is the intimacy of touch. This occurs in the meeting of basic needs for washing, toileting, dressing and feeding; and in the giving and receiving of 'comfort'. A certain level of intimacy follows from the inevitable closeness of people living in small units, sharing group tasks and leisure activities. While this is part and parcel of the routine of the establishment, it can also have implicit connotations of sexuality, as, for example, when rotations of duties are drawn up to ensure that frail elderly female residents are only bathed by female staff, but male residents can be attended to by both male and female staff. Touch is part of the work of certain 'people organizations', such as social work settings and particularly residential units. Touch is also often highly ambiguous in organizational settings; it can be interpreted sexually; it can also be harassment (Hearn and Parkin, 1987: 105–6). Where children are being cared for, a further issue is the alerting of all children and young people to the dangers of some forms of touching through 'Childline' campaigns and publicity. Thus, some male students and male residential workers reported that they would be reluctant to get close to a crying girl in order to comfort her, especially if she was alone. Even more restrictions were seen on male members of staff holding boys to comfort them. As Keith White writes with respect to the care of adolescents:

> What is not perhaps realised by those who have not experienced the group care situation first hand is how much of daily living and planning revolves around the issue of sexual behaviour, taboos and fears. Any member of staff at any time is worried about being alone with a child. (1987:54)

112 The Sexuality of Organization

Similarly, a male student on placement in an adolescent unit for girls stated:

> Girls would sit on my knee. I was aware at all times of sexuality, it was always on my mind. I asked myself whether it had gone beyond the father-figure/child relationship. Sometimes I sensed it had. The children had no guidelines and they would deliberately create a situation. There were no groups to discuss sexuality, it was never made public or 'put on the table' but it was always felt as powerful and influential.

This issue is not confined to units for children. There is also intimacy of touch in old people's homes. Thus workers in this study discussed the issue of men who had erections, who 'flirted' with female staff and wanted particular members of staff to attend to their bodily needs. In this context of close proximity and the carrying out of necessary personal tasks in the residential setting, it is not surprising that sexuality is an ever-present issue. Lower-level staff and students in this study all reported a large amount of informal discussion on the subject within units. Student groups eagerly took the opportunity to discuss these problems and ambiguities.

This contrasted markedly with the 'deafening silence' from senior staff, management and training units on the issue and the lack of explicit basic rules and guidelines. White suggested:

> we would expect a good deal of information, research and reports on the subject [of sexuality]. Instead it is one of the most neglected areas of residential care. It occurs, of course, after scandals like Kincora[2] but not in more routine assessments or descriptions. For example, the DHSS[3] Inspection of Community Homes barely mentions it. The main concern is with contraception and contraceptive advice. The concomitants of sexual experience, aggression and violence, have received much more attention, . . . but sex is the poor relation. It is a classic case of the literature and the policy-makers being completely out of touch with the realities at grass-roots level. (1987:53)

Similarly in my study, a supervisor advised a male student not to go into the girls' bedrooms 'for your own and the girls' protection' but did not spell this out any further as an issue of sexuality; this was given as informal advice rather than as formalized rules and guidelines with explanations. Elsewhere, implicit rules were reflected in separate wings for male and female residents; statements about how and in what circumstances residents could be in opposite wings; staff rotas which ensured that male staff were not on duty alone; and instances where male staff members could not take boys on outings. Within these implicit rules and unclear guidelines on behaviour could be read an awareness of sexuality, and an assumption of heterosexuality, as well as a recognition of the number of sexual issues which the staff had to deal with daily. Staff in different establishments worked with: children who had been sexually abused in their families; people with need for contraceptive advice; women who menstruated, suffered from pre-menstrual tension, and dysmenorrhoea; adolescents who were pregnant and wanted abortions; handicapped people who masturbated; disabled and old people who wanted sexual satisfaction and privacy. Thus there is a combination of overt sexual need and expression, implicit recognition of sexuality through allocation of space, rotation of duties and informal supervision, but no explicit, laid down rules of conduct.

The only exception found in this study of about forty organizations was a respite care unit for mentally handicapped children, where a paper was circulated to staff members on how to deal with sexual behaviour of residents particularly with reference to masturbation (Beard et al., n.d.). At first sight the instructions, including legal aspects, appeared to be a management document, but the officer-in-charge of the unit said not, for it had been drawn up by the staff members themselves. It recognized the issue of sexuality, and began the formulation of guidelines for practice. The guidelines not only dealt with this issue but gave explicit information about what staff could, or could not, do in respect of residents. For example, it explained that it is illegal to teach residents how to masturbate. This contrasted with a similar unit, where the staff response to sexuality was to see it as the responsibility of the children's parents, and staff response to masturbating young people was to say 'if you *must* do that then go to your bedroom'. These tensions may be exacerbated in work with the mentally handicapped. The description of people with mental handicap as having a 'mental age' of, say, nine years, ignores development in other abilities and feelings, such as adult sexuality.

Students and staff recognized that living in close proximity with residents continually raised issues of sexuality, which contrasted starkly with the lack of formal guidelines, rules and procedures on the subject. Some commentators, such as Coley and Marler (1987:79–80), suggest that '(t)raining for staff, together with written policies and guidelines, can help professionals to make an appropriate response . . .'. In the absence of guidelines, along with the hidden nature of sexuality, it is not surprising that instances of sexual relationships between staff and residents do occur but are not always formally known within the establishment or organization (Davis, 1980). In some cases sexual scandals do come to light in residential settings. Following the Kincora scandal, where three male staff sexually assaulted resident boys, the Hughes Report

(1986) brought to light offences in other residential establishments. White commented how:

> Among other things the affair demonstrated how difficult it is to get facts on sexuality if you are outside a residential setting; how the media and the public react when something goes wrong in care; how sexuality has dominated and will dominate (in a different sense) the daily experience of care for most adolescents in care. (1987:63)

Recent publicity about sexual activity between male staff and children in Birmingham children's homes gives further evidence of the sexual abuse of residents by those in power over them, and supposedly caring for them. Paradoxically, part of the problem is that there are difficulties for staff within residential establishments getting their voices heard. In Birmingham two female staff at a children's home had 'shared concerns' with management in April 1986, and again the following March. It was not until October 1987 that specific complaints were made and the senior officer was suspended after he had taken, without explanation, boys and girls to his office on their own for hours on end. With no guidelines in existence, there was a prolonged failure by managers to deal with the problems; the officer-in-charge was allowed to resign the day before he was due to face disciplinary hearings. At another home five staff received pay-offs totalling £18,500 when they quit before disciplinary hearings into allegations of physical abuse of boys and girls (*The Guardian*, 1988; *Community Care*, 1988; *Social Work Today*, 1988). The response of management was as follows:

> We have also considered the need for a swift response to complaints. A new leaflet outlining the complaints procedure for all client groups is now being issued. But we felt children in care had a different set of requirements. For them, a handbook entitled *Questions and Answers* is in preparation with a section on how to make a complaint – to the director if necessary, using a tear-off sheet. (*Social Work Today*, 1988:3)

The complaints procedure, arising out of the scandal, continues to avoid the fact that the central issues were sexuality and abuse of power. A tear-off sheet is no use to powerless clients, some of whom can't read or write. If staff have difficulties in being heard, it seems unlikely that residents' views will be taken seriously. The reluctance of managers to acknowledge sexual abuse of children in residential establishments seems to parallel the reluctance to acknowledge its presence in families and act upon it.

Another aspect of the failure to protect clients is in establishments where residents are responsible adults and sexual relationships take place with staff. In both the following cases disciplinary action was taken, but only implicitly about sexuality. The explicit reason was 'unprofessional conduct'. A worker in a hostel for mentally ill people was sacked for having an affair with a resident even though 'the philosophy of the hostel was that we treated residents as equals and it was encouraged that we should develop personal relationships there. *But there was absolutely no code of guidance from management as to how far these relationships should go*' (Sharron, 1983; my emphasis). The response of the area manager was to say that: 'the Department's code of conduct did not specify behaviour concerning personal relationships but that whether the people involved are adults or children they are in the care of the department and we expect social workers to behave in a controlled professional manner.'

In another case an officer-in-charge of a progressive home for physically handicapped adults was sacked for failing to put a stop to a love affair between a 23-year-old wheelchair-bound temporary resident and a care assistant (Boseley, 1983). Again there was no written policy, with 'professionalism' and the 'dependent nature of the client' as the reasons given for dismissal.

These examples again highlight the lack of organizational policies as well as giving insight into the sexualization of the work setting. This may fuel speculation and rumour about sexual activities in residential settings. At the same time there may be ambivalence amongst staff and managers, as these establishments are where people live and where they presumably should be able to pursue private activity, such as sexuality, without interference. Many of these units are called homes and efforts are made by staff to make them as 'homelike' as possible. Yet these 'homes' are located in organizations and open to public scrutiny. As Murphy (1988) states:

> public concern can overrule legally acceptable situations where care and control of certain groups are paramount. . . . There would be public outcry and families could be enraged if sexual activity was allowed to take place in an establishment even if the participants were over the age of consent. The 'normal' controls of separate families and residences do not operate and people are thrown together and expected to mirror a family morality within an institution. The morality of staff within establishments is paramount also. Although mimicking the family model staff are expected to maintain a distance from each other and their charges in the name of 'professionalism'.

Here we may note that sexuality is seen as both private and public, both personal and political. In some residential organizations there is not only sexual exploitation of residents but also the sexual harassment of staff. Within the Birmingham situation referred to earlier, male senior colleagues were alleged to have intimidated homes staff, with eight women staff quitting during the eighteen months of complaints. One woman said that four of the women resigned and four transferred to other jobs, some lower paid. Most of the women's careers suffered as a result. A year on, one was still unemployed; another was on long-term sick leave because of high blood pressure brought on by the strain (*The Guardian*, 1988).

Another case which exemplifies the issue of men's sexual harassment of women within these workplaces is that of an unqualified female residential care worker in a unit run by a husband and wife team. There was a very high turnover of female care staff in this unit. A cycle of victimization occurred, with the husband arranging rotas so that he would be on duty with targeted female staff. Complaints to higher male managers appeared to be fed back to the husband and wife team, resulting in further victimization. One employee made a long statement about incidents and how she had tried to deal with them and failed. She was asked if she was prepared to give evidence and she agreed to this only to find her statement had 'disappeared'. Management knew about the high staff turnover and the reasons for it, yet chose not to act. This went on for twelve years. The grievances never got to a decision, and management appeared to prefer to replace female care assistants than dismiss the officer. The domestic staff knew of the situation and spoke about it in rumour, nods and winks, wanting to keep their jobs. Residents also knew about the harassment of staff but were frightened to make their voices heard, lest they were victimized themselves. When the couple left the establishment the management response was to change procedures to say they would never again employ a married couple in a residential setting (also see Chapter 6).

The final case material in this section highlights the implications of homophobia. Some students expressed strong personal feelings when male/male sexual relationships were discussed whether between children, adults, or children and adults. This can be understood in the context of an analysis of homophobia, 'the fear of feelings of love for members of one's own sex, and therefore the hatred of those feelings in others' (Taylor, 1986). Another example was implicit discrimination against a 'male homosexual' who was on the domestic staff and who asked to take a boy on an outing. The refusal was on the grounds that he was not a member of the care staff though this had not prevented female members of the domestic staff from taking children out. It was assumed by some staff members that his homosexuality rather than his domestic status was the real reason for the refusal. Another example was the reluctance of staff members to accept adult males wishing to live together if physically or mentally handicapped.

This section has drawn upon a selection of case material available to illustrate the variety and complexity of the issues. The following section considers some of the issues arising from the case material within its societal context.

Case material in its societal context

In this section discussion of the case material is broadened to explore some reasons for the omission of sexuality from organizational guidelines and decision-making processes. This entails attention to the false dualism of the public/private divide, and an exploration of the ambiguous 'intermediate zone' where the public and private domains overlap and merge. Within residential care institutions, often called 'homes', themselves within the intermediate zone, there are elements of both the public world of work and the private world of the family, even though organizational regimes and structures are often comparable to those of total institutions. In such settings the protection and condoning of oppressive men's sexuality is all the more powerful because of the ambiguous organizational position and the vulnerability of residents and many staff.

In listening, over three years, to students and residential workers talk about sexuality, it appears to be an area of major grievance and difficulty which seldom reaches a point of decision making about rules and procedures because the issue fails to reach the management decision-making processes. The example cited earlier (Beard et al., n.d.) of the staff themselves drawing up rules and guidelines represented a staff initiative to circumvent this; this, however, was unusual. In nearly all the establishments issues around sexuality continued to be grievances for staff and residents alike, with both powerless to have them heard officially. This non-decision-making process operates as a form of power when more influential groups 'mobilize bias' to keep issues from reaching the public agenda (Bachrach and Baratz, 1962; 1963) within essentially male-dominated decision-making processes. Sexuality is seen as a personal and private activity taking place in the private world of the family or in residential units designated 'homes'. It is seen as neither a political nor a public issue, for the politicization of sexuality, for example in explicit policies and guidelines, would be an acknowledgement that sexuality is in the public world of work and cannot be designated solely as a private issue (Hearn and Parkin, 1987).

The public/private divide is increasingly recognized as a useful analytical division in studying gender issues (e.g. Ardener, 1978). The public world of work, mainly organizationally based and relatively politicized, is compared with the private and personal world of the family. Clark and Lange (1979:xiv) also describe two spheres of life:

> Sphere A is the sphere of the 'productive' or 'political' activity, of 'public' life and the sphere of reason. Sphere B is that of women, is that of 'non-productive', 'non-political', 'merely reproductive', 'private', 'natural', and emotional activity. . . .
> There are several important dissimilarities between Spheres A and B. For one thing, whereas a minority of males . . . control by means of rules and ownership the vast majority of both the males and females remaining, the control of females by other females is minimal, and control by females of males is virtually non-existent.

This duality is analytically important in exploring male domination, especially men's double domination, as they dominate in the private world of the family and in the public world of work; moreover, the public dominates the private.

Within society male domination is perpetuated at many levels:

— the public over the private (Elshtain, 1981; Stacey and Price, 1981);
— production over reproduction (O'Brien, 1981; Hearn, 1987);
— paid work over domestic and unpaid work;
— the labour market for men over the dual labour markets for women, who are part of the 'reserve army of labour' (e.g. Barron and Norris, 1976; Bruegel, 1979);
— the 'work role' of men over the 'dual roles' or 'triple roles' of women as paid workers, domestic child carers and carers of the elderly and infirm.

Within organizations male domination is also perpetuated at many levels:

— men predominating in positions of power, authority and leadership and holding high-status, highly paid posts, over women in low-status, low-paid positions with little authority, power and influence;
— men as intellectual workers over women as manual workers (Willis, 1977);
— men as professionals over women as semi-professionals (Simpson and Simpson, 1969);
— men as manual workers in non-domestic trades over women as manual workers in domestic trades (e.g. Lupton, 1963);
— men as full-time permanent workers over women as part-time and temporary workers;

- men in 'central', non-boundary roles over women in 'boundary roles', whom men interview and select;
- men as registered unemployed over women not registered as unemployed;
- men's heterosexuality over women's sexuality, men's gayness, and lesbianism: this domination being both a basis and a reinforcement of the oppressions within all the above.

Historically many women's tasks, for example the production of goods, health care, midwifery, education, have moved from the home and become organizationally based (Ehrenreich and English, 1979). Health and welfare bureaucracies have not only taken over traditional roles but have also become part of state intervention into family life. The devaluing of the domestic role of women both within the family and within organizations has been well researched and documented. As Clark and Lange state:

> if reproductive labours had been seen to be as socially necessary as productive labour, then it would have been impossible to argue that it was rightfully done for nothing and it would have been equally impossible to argue that women were rightfully regarded as inferior because of the 'natural' character of the labour they were constrained to perform . . . this different relationship is not rooted in nature at all, but in convention. . . . Precisely because this difference is in fact conventional we must now re-examine our history to show why the division of labour between the sexes emerged as it did, and how this arrangement served to maintain a system in which both women and reproductive labours were condemned to dependent servility. (1979:xi)

The public/private divide and the gender division of labour, specifically the devaluing of women's work, is seen within welfare bureaucracies. Howe (1986) and Finch and Groves (1982) demonstrate this division of labour within the personal social services, and show the predominance of women in low-status jobs and low-paid jobs, particularly the untrained residential sector and the routine care of the elderly and mentally handicapped people. This division of labour reflects the role of women as part of the 'reserve army of labour' as are black workers also found in low-paid, low-status jobs. The student groups on placement in the residential sector continually recognized that they were working in settings where the majority of staff were women, and were undervalued. Often the women had no formal training, and their opportunities for secondment on to formal training courses were low. The jobs were predominantly seen as 'care' work and domestic work. The language used was that of the domestic rather than the organizational world, with people designated as 'cooks', 'care assistants', 'house parents', 'aunties', and 'uncles', within units called 'homes'. This can partly be explained through the preceding analysis of the public/private divide and gender division of labour. These residential units occupy an anomalous position across the public/private divide. The establishments are frequently called 'homes' with the connotation of the private realm, but they are located firmly within large welfare bureaucratic organizations. Not only is there the prevalence of bureaucratic decision making over professional decision making; the power of professionals over semi-professionals; the power of trained semi-professionals over untrained care workers. There is also the ambiguity surrounding the 'designation' of the organization itself.

Stacey and Davies suggest that:

> It did seem inadequate to talk simply of tasks being removed from the domestic arena, for as we have seen, the family is not detached from society. Its members move to and fro between the domains, increasingly the women as well as the men. In this context the notion of some kind of ambiguous zone where the concepts and values of the public domain mingled and conflicted with the values of the domestic domain seemed to have some explanatory potential. . . . There are consequences where work occurs in both domains (always, or almost always women's work) in the depression of wages for the work in the public domain. Work which straddles the domains tends to be denigrated in public domain terms. (1983:13–14)

Stacey and Davies's concept of the 'intermediate zone' is useful for analysing the ambiguity of the residential setting and its terminology. If the residential setting straddles the public and private domains, sitting uneasily between the two, then it is possible to see how the issue of sexuality reflects this ambiguity. It offers an added dimension of understanding why issues of sexuality are not on management agendas.

These residential units are usually themselves part of large welfare bureaucracies. Within these, rational bureaucratic decision making prevails, implicitly equating masculinity with rationality and controlling ambiguous organizational settings, such as 'homes', within which women predominate in routine caring roles. Within these 'homes', sexual activity is more clearly an issue because of the close proximity in which people live. Not only is sexuality seen as irrational and unpredictable: women also have been seen in these terms (Broverman et al., 1981). It could thus be argued that in addition to the ambiguous intermediate zone is a designation of residential settings as 'irrational' zones, inhabited by women, and arenas for sexuality, which thus do not fit into rational bureaucratic decision-making processes. Therefore issues of sexuality have to be reframed and redefined in terms of, for example, 'unprofessional conduct'. It could also be argued that in the intermediate zone men can also have ambiguous roles. They can exercise male power as they would in a family setting, having power over women and children directly, and also exercise the power by being employed in the public domain. In this intermediate zone of residential work is the interface of the double domination of the public over the private, as described earlier. In the residential setting men can have an arena for sexual exploitation, which can be called private or public; the ambiguous nature of such settings could be one explanation for the slowness of sexual abuse of minors or sexual harassment of staff reaching the status of an official complaint. In the private world of the family, rules and procedures about sexuality are not usually explicitly drawn up, even though sexual abuse of children within the family is a rapidly growing area of concern. Residential settings are not only obvious arenas for sexuality, but are also arenas for the abuse and exploitation of vulnerable workers and residents.

Residential units often have much in common with total institutions (Goffman, 1961) and 'people processing organizations' (Hasenfeld, 1972), where individuals have to comply with an institutional regime. Within the 'totality', people's whole lives are under observation, including their sexuality. One care worker described an elderly couple who were married and requested a double room within the residential home. This request was granted; however, staff looked in on them every hour throughout the night in the 'interests of their health'. The reason given was fear of heart attack; the more likely reason would seem to be surveillance of their sexuality in a total institution setting. One person living alone in their own home would not be surveyed for this sort of risk, let alone a couple. Another example was from a hostel for mentally handicapped young adults, where all bedroom doors had to be kept open all night: epilepsy was used as an excuse even though only two of the residents suffered from epilepsy. Another instance was of older physically handicapped married adults having to ask staff to take them to the privacy of their own rooms because of their own immobility. They had to endure jokes and innuendoes about their wish for privacy. Perhaps the ultimate is a nursing home for young physically handicapped adults where closed circuit television in each room enabled one staff member to survey all the residents (cf. Foucault, 1977 on Bentham's panopticon).

The designation of residential establishments as 'homes' seems, at first sight, far removed from that of total institutions. White (1987) describes two alternative models of care for adolescents, the 'family' model and the 'school' model. In the 'family' model he described problems arising around the issue of sexuality when sibling/parent roles are part of the designation as a family but the residents are not related to each other, or to the staff, and family taboos on sexual relationships cannot be assumed. In the 'school' model the remoteness of many of the institutions was described as leading to closer resident/resident relationships, and homosexual activity arising out of need for human warmth and contact. However, in terms of sexuality, this division is of limited value as both models lack clear policy statements from managers and present potentially problematic relationships, whether resident/resident, resident/staff or staff/staff. In this study, it became suddenly obvious that it isn't a matter of one model or another, but of the 'home' model overlapping with the 'total institution' model. As soon as this was recognized, that the designation of 'home' blurred with features of 'totality', it became clear that this opened up a further dimension to the control and exploitation of vulnerable, powerless and dependent residents. It may also explain why a range of grievances, from both residents and staff, especially around sexuality, fail to reach management agendas and the decision-making processes.

When discussing this analysis with a former officer-in-charge of a children's residential home, the latter began to realize the implications of his going to view the home for the first time and remarking that the geography of the building was no good for surveillance. This exemplifies the blurring of 'home' and 'totality'; he admitted that his changed philosophy of running the home arose from the impossibility of surveillance in that setting rather than a recognition that this was a 'home' unit where client and staff grievances should be heard and acted upon.

In the ambiguous intermediate zone the question of why issues of sexuality and sexual exploitation fail to reach formal decision-making processes could be seen as a mobilization of bias. This operates when essentially male-dominated decision-making processes protect oppressive men's sexuality, condoned and accepted in both the public and private realms. A further analysis is the recognition that men and their sexuality dominate in this intermediate zone also, and their power in this zone is enhanced, rather than diminished, by the units operating as total institutions.

There thus exists this blurred, ambiguous, intermediate zone of organizational life where the public domain incorporates and scrutinizes private and personal experiences, which thus cease to be private. Designation as a 'home' can lead to a false assumption that personal issues, such as sexuality, can remain private and that residents generally need not be open to rules and scrutiny from outside. However, those holding power in these establishments can continue to incorporate elements of family life in the name of care for the individual and respect for privacy, while at the same time incorporating elements of totality, as people are processed, controlled and observed. The power wielded in the privacy of families can combine with the power wielded in a total setting to give an extra dimension to the issue of power particular to these settings. The exercise of generic powers has been recognized in the male domination of the private realm and the public realm and the double male domination resulting from the domination of the public realm over the private, plus the way these existing powers are underpinned by the male sexual narrative (Hearn and Parkin, 1987). In residential establishments there is the recognition of the exercise of generic powers within both the private realm and the public; there is the recognition of how these powers are underpinned by the male sexual narrative, and the further dimension of the ambiguousness of the organizational setting as neither public nor private but both at the same time. Researching the issue of sexuality within these establishments and its exclusion from policies and guidelines has led to the recognition of the sexual politics of sexuality in settings which are neither public nor private but can be defined as both.

Conclusion

This study arose from the recognition that sexuality was a topic for both residents and staff in residential establishments set up to care for a number of vulnerable groups of people. There was little training on issues of sexuality and seldom any formal organizational rules, guidelines or procedures from management for staff and residents. Many rules and guidelines were implicitly about sexuality, and information from managers and senior staff to newcomers was usually gained informally and accidentally. Service delivery in residential units takes place in an ambiguous organizational setting, straddling the public and private realms, but the ambiguity of this intermediate zone increases the potential for exploitation. Many establishments give high standards of care to residents with the minimum of exploitation but the study has highlighted the exploitative nature of the *setting itself*, beyond the control of individual units and staff. Sexuality is an obvious issue there, as people have intimate physical needs; in addition the close proximity of people through group living might lead one to assume there would be guidelines and policies. Their absence in research has opened up several new questions and analyses, but the most forceful has been the recognition of the way the 'home' model has combined and blurred with the 'total institution' model within an intermediate zone which incorporates elements of both public and private realms. This effective merging can enable different models of decision making to operate within different regimes of power, to be used by those in positions of power, as is convenient to them: some matters being dealt with by public realm rules, some by private realm rules. The deceptive terminology of the 'family unit' can distract from the recognition of the totality of the control and surveillance there, and can be a way of avoiding questions of how power is exercised within the units.

Sexuality is a crucial question in residential care organizations, as this private issue is now firmly within the public domain, yet this would appear to be denied when sexuality does not feature in public domain agendas and decisions. Exploitation of sexuality is a public issue within organizations, which straddle the public and the private, which are neither public nor private yet which incorporate elements of both, so that power may be exerted through either the public or the private mode, or through moving between the two, or through both modes together.

Notes

My first acknowledgement is to the anonymous people who live in residential establishments, who formed the basis of this study, but who are invisible, unnamed, and who frequently have no voice. My second acknowledgement is to the students on the CQSW Course at Huddersfield Polytechnic, residential staff and managers, who have contributed their experience. Thanks are also due to the staff at 18 Carlton Close, Hemsworth, West Yorkshire, UK, for permission to quote from their staff document; to Jeff Hearn, Sue Jones, Deborah Sheppard and Peta Tancred-Sheriff for reading drafts and for their encouragement; and to Sue Moody for her willingness to type at short notice and speedily produce very accurate copy.

1. Service delivery of health care in a medical setting is distinct, even though some of the same issues around sexuality are likely to be present. A training manual on sexuality in health care settings has recently been produced by Sue Kilroe and Ron Wiener (1988).

2. Kincora was a boys' hostel in East Belfast where three male members of care staff were involved in sexual assaults against resident boys.

3. Department of Health and Social Security, the British government ministry that has since been divided into the Departments of Health, and of Social Security.

8
Private Experiences in the Public Domain: Lesbians in Organizations

Marny Hall

> While the last chapter dealt with a particular type of organization, this deals with lesbians, in a variety of organizational settings. Lesbians are liable to experience double jeopardy, in terms of their gender as women, and in terms of their sexuality. This study used naturalistic interviews of thirteen lesbians to explore their private experiences in the public domain. The picture that emerges is complex and often ambiguous, particularly around the decision process of disclosure/non-disclosure of their lesbianism, and the development of coping strategies in the organizational world.

Organizations and homosexuality

Organization sexuality thrives on indirection. By masquerading as sign and symbol, as informal and formal exchange, and by changing disguises frequently and fluidly, such 'orgexuality' (Hearn and Parkin, 1987:131) manages to remain subliminal and avoid censure in a theoretically inimical environment. Eroticism, not easily consigned to the margins of consciousness, however, violates the norms which rule that the organization must *appear* to be a sexless, rational realm.

An obvious and intense flirtation between two heterosexual colleagues may not elicit actual censure until the two are discovered *in flagrante delicto* in the staff lounge. In contrast, the person known to be homosexual must do nothing in particular in order to be perceived in terms of excessive eroticism. This role spillover (see Chapter 4) or, more aptly, role suffusion, may bring into consciousness the previously subliminal homosexuality which threads certain apparently innocent homosocial exchanges. Newly self-conscious, the actors may be too inhibited to interact spontaneously. Within the shadowy word of organization sexuality, then, homosexuality must remain within the darkest penumbra, sealed away from any illuminating awareness.

There is an even more compelling reason – historically rooted – for antagonism between homosexuality and organizations. The same social and economic paroxysms that transformed the agrarian family into the highly gendered and private domestic arrangement of the late nineteenth century, also spawned the category of 'homosexuality' (D'Emilio and Freedman, 1988). Indeed, by serving as repository for all the impulses which conflicted with the new emphasis on gender differences and sexual 'normalcy', the homosexual, with its indeterminate gender and abnormal sex practices, buttressed the new family.

This entwined definitional lineage of family, and antifamily, i.e. homosexuality, place both squarely in an affective realm. This realm competes with the organization – the turn-of-the-century factory as well as the contemporary corporation – for the time and allegiance of the worker. As well as acting as nemesis to the organization, however, the family also serves as complement, providing continuity, and the rest and recreation workers need to be productive. The gay lifestyle is not perceived to be stable or to offer the same restoratives. In addition, unlike the heterosexual whose entrance into the organization marks his or her exit from familial roles, the homosexual, definitionally conscripted for the social/sexual projections of the dominant culture, cannot exit from affectivity, any more than s/he can avoid the sentence of never-ending eroticism. And affectivity, unlike eroticism, is truly unassimilable by the organization, provisionally tolerable only if it remains within the confines of the very separate institution of family.

Double jeopardy: the case of lesbians

Lesbians in particular not only contribute as symbol to this transgression of organizational culture, but their presence also violates the precepts of the organization on a more personal level. Hegel posited a dialectic between self and other. It was through an exchange of comparisons and interactive explorations that one synthesized one's self, one's personal identity (Hegel, 1949). Psychologists, explicating women's psychology, have gendered this concept, and located it developmentally in infancy and childhood. According to Chodorow (1978), it is the male's definition of differentness vis-a-vis his primary love object – the mother – that accounts for his firm sense of self. Women, for better or worse, forfeit this degree of self-definition, because for them mother represents not difference but similarity. If one considers the role of women in institutions, e.g. the organization, it would seem that this process of male individuation, reputedly a stage-specific event, is, instead, a never-ending psycho-social process.

At the same time women must prove their own credibility in organizations in which they are, in every sense, incredible; they must not overtly (by being too masculine in dress or behaviour – see Chapter 9) deny males the 'other' they require for their continuing process of self-definition. Rather than analysing the elements in this narrative-building dialogue – how much of it is erotic, where the erotic merges with or parts from particular signs and symbols, roles and statuses, etc. – it is important to note how frequently the narrative must, because of slight changes in context, switch tones or modalities. The boss interacts very differently with his secretary in the inner sanctum of his office than he does when she is the designated note taker at a board meeting. When he encounters her again, at lunch, on the company jogging track, there is yet another tonal shift.

The sheer weight of dominant cultural attributions lesbians must carry, if their orientation is known, renders them unavailable for the myriad and quickly shifting micro-projections necessary to maintain and elaborate the male narrative of self. Because her identity is dense with specific meaning, the lesbian cannot be the protean 'other' who can at one moment be perceived as coy, at another motherly, at another seductive and available, and at yet another moment self-contained and competent. Although women, to varying degrees, collude in, or refrain from, this male narrational process, they are forbidden to contradict it by citing an opposing reality. Except to those males who, by particularly strenuous imaginative exertions, can incorporate it into their personal narratives, lesbianism constitutes, *ipso facto*, an opposing reality – a defiance of the mandate to occupy the role of 'other'. The penalty for this mutiny is, within the organization, at the very least, a forfeiture of good will; at the most retaliation, harassment and the loss of one's job. If lesbians did not intuitively apprehend the perilousness of their situation, and their consequent need for secrecy, the data collected over the last decade would make it evident. A survey distributed at a 1980 meeting of career-oriented lesbians in San Francisco, California revealed that 38 (78 percent) of the 51 women responding to the questionnaire felt that disclosing their lesbianism would be a problem; 22 (45 percent) felt they would not have the same job security; 18 (38 percent) thought they were unlikely to be treated as equals, and 25 (54 percent) thought they would lose customers or clients (Hall, 1981). In a 1986 national survey of 216 lesbians, employers and supervisors headed the list of individuals from whom it was most important to keep information about one's sexual orientation (Wendell, 1988).

The results of two surveys of lesbians who worked in a variety of settings – one conducted by the Lesbian Employment Rights group (LER) in 1984 (Taylor, 1986) and the other by Blumstein and Schwartz in 1983 – suggest that lesbians' disclosure anxiety is engendered – at least in part – by instances of discrimination. One hundred and fifty-one of the 171 lesbians polled by LER had experienced one or more types of anti-lesbianism at work. A third of the approximately 1500 lesbians polled by Blumstein and Schwartz reported having problems on the job because they were known or suspected to be gay. The degree of fear of disclosure, and the experienced consequences of such disclosure would, presumably, be even more pronounced among an exclusively corporate lesbian group. In 1982, David Cox, a management consultant and author, polled 1000 top and middle managers from thirteen major US corporations about their attitudes on a range of issues – homosexuality among them. Half of these executives felt that being gay had a 'very negative' impact on promotion possibilities within their companies.

Lesbians and corporations: a conundrum

Despite the biases of corporations towards lesbians, as documented above (also see Chapter 1:24) and lesbians' well founded apprehension about their reception in the workplace, lesbians continue to be well represented at all corporate levels. Their ubiquitous presence suggests that they have developed certain ways of protecting themselves in an inhospitable corporate culture – ways to manage a secret that would discredit them, while simultaneously embracing, at least in theory, the self-disclosing stance advocated by the gay rights movement.

In order to explore these coping strategies, I interviewed thirteen lesbian respondents in their homes, over lunch in restaurants, and in their offices. The taped interviews lasted between forty and seventy minutes each. Four interviewees held lower or middle management positions. Four worked in technical jobs; three had clerical jobs; one was in sales and one was in personnel. All worked in corporations employing more than one hundred people. Except for one woman who was 22, all the respondents fell between the ages of 27 and 40. Two interviewees had been at their companies for ten years, one had been at her job for seven years; the remaining eleven had been at their companies for one and a half to four years.[1]

Method of enquiry
My embeddedness in the lesbian community – personally, socially and professionally – as well as my gay-affirmative politics precluded an 'objective' method of data gathering or analysis. Instead I employed a naturalistic mode of enquiry. Such an approach, because it emphasizes the multiple, constructed, context-bound nature of reality and acknowledges the intersubjectivity of interviewer and interviewee (Merleau-Ponty, 1962), was most consonant with my values as a lesbian and feminist.

This approach led me to call friends who had worked in corporations or who knew other lesbians who had had corporate experience. In addition I began attending meetings of lesbian business and professional organizations. Through this networking process I met a number of lesbians who worked in corporations. I lunched with several of them individually and then met with a group of lesbians and gay employees who worked for the same corporation. The general themes that emerged during these meetings and discussions formed the basis for the interview questions I devised. The questions were open ended and designed to evoke the ways in which the respondents experienced their lesbianism at work. Afterwards I listened to the tapes, distilled themes and integrated them into a descriptive statement of the experience (Giorgi, 1975).

The lesbian corporate experience

The danger of disclosure
Constantly occurring in the work setting were experiences that triggered the women's awareness of their lesbianism. Anti-gay jokes, or comments presuming heterosexuality, such as 'Why don't you get married? . . . you're almost twenty eight', stimulated an awareness of being different. Because the revelation of one's lesbianism could have serious consequences, these women were constantly preoccupied with concealing that aspect of their lives. Sometimes concealment occurred as automatically as retinal adjustment to light change. At other times, it was deliberate and felt more stressful. Whether automatic or deliberate, the process of concealment called for constant attention to every nuance of social interaction. The background buzz of assumptions became centrally important for the lesbian because it signalled where vigilance was necessary or where she could relax and 'be herself'. The workplace reality for the lesbian, therefore, was one of heightened awareness and sensitivity toward the usually hidden matrices of behaviour, values and attitudes in self and others.

The respondents had been convinced that disclosure would be dangerous in several ways. Those who had not experienced discrimination directly by losing a job or missing a promotion had experienced it in the homophobic attitudes of co-workers. After the assassination of gay San Francisco City Council member Harvey Milk in 1978, one woman's boss said, 'Good . . . things needed to be cleaned up.' One lesbian, not known to be homosexual, was warned by a well-meaning co-worker to stay away from another co-worker who wore a 'dyke' pin. Other respondents experienced direct discrimination against lesbians and gays. One woman knew two lesbians who were fired for being open at work, while another respondent lost a coveted project because the supervisor was told she was lesbian and he refused to work with her.

Dangers of non-disclosure
Accompanying the need for protective secrecy was a 'state-of-siege' mentality, a feeling of 'us and them'. Often the feeling associated with these states was anxiety or anger, or both, sometimes in the form of intellectual distance: 'I don't fit in, and I don't necessarily want to'; 'They're so ignorant'; 'You just have to see where they're coming from.'

Even if a subject's lesbianism continued to be a well kept secret, it was perceived as a disadvantage that caused lesbians to receive 'unfair treatment'. No matter how long they had lived with their partners, lesbians couldn't tap corporate benefits, such as 'family' health insurance or travel bonuses which included spouses. One woman, who had lived with her lover for seven years, had earned enough sales points for a company-sponsored trip to Hawaii; however, she had to go alone. There were no family allowances for lesbians who were relocated and whose partners chose to accompany them. Nor could lesbians play the management game, because they would never have the requisite opposite-sexed spouse and a country club membership in the suburbs.

Being secretive created inner conflicts: 'I wanted to come out, but I just couldn't', as well as constant anxiety about discovery: 'If my bosses knew, they'd find a way to get rid of me'; 'In the case of my supervisees, sometimes it gets emotional, and they might hug me. What would go through their minds if they knew I was a lesbian?'

Several women felt that their lesbianism, because it was invisible, was less of a hindrance than their gender, which they could not disguise. Being a woman was seen as a major disadvantage in the corporate world: 'As a woman, I'm generally assumed to be incompetent whereas the men are assumed to be competent unless proven otherwise.'

Their lesbianism reinforced separation between work and leisure. Some respondents contended that this was congruent with their needs: 'I am a private person anyway. Even if I weren't gay, I wouldn't want to mix work with my life outside work.' For the others the discontinuity was a source of frustration and anger: 'These guys go home and their friends are the same people they see all day. For me, coming to work is bowing out of my world completely and going into theirs.'

The respondents felt conflict between the need or expectation to be open and friendly and their realization that if they were to share the ordinary events of their day-to-day lives they would show that they were different from everyone else. One way to avoid this was simply to avoid heterosexual co-workers. Several respondents said they tried to keep out of personal situations: 'I maintain a professional air and shy away from those issues. I never socialize with them.' Another common strategy to cope with this need for deceit was to dissociate oneself from part of one's behaviour. In the same interview, respondents would talk about ways of concealing their lesbianism while stating firmly, 'I don't hide my gayness.' The use of this form of dissociation spared respondents the knowledge – and attendant self-reproach – about their own deceptiveness and, at the same time, protected them from the anxiety and risks of revelation.

Several comments indicated that at times the respondents experienced their lesbianism as a source of strength. 'Because I am gay, I have more confidence'; and 'There's a feeling of camaraderie with other lesbians at work.'

At times, being misapprehended enhanced their status. Because one woman's partner was invisible to management, she was presumed to be unmarried and mobile, and was therefore offered special training in another city. Another woman in a non-traditional job felt that because she was seen as masculine, she was given more challenging job assignments than some of her counterparts who were seen as feminine.

Even though the non-disclosure of their homosexuality was crucial, several respondents felt the secret was not always within their control. For example, one woman was showing a friend from work the plans of the new house she and her lover had bought. Pointing out the main bedroom, she accidentally said, 'This is where we sleep.' She was appalled to have revealed the intimate nature of her relationship. Other respondents felt they revealed their lesbianism through their physical appearance. A lesbian who wore jeans to a clerical job said, 'The way I dress I was in a way forcing it down their throats.' Another woman said, 'At the time they started suspecting, I made a mistake and cut my hair short. That was the tip-off.'

Many of the interviewees said their homosexuality had been revealed inadvertently. In one instance, a woman was featured in the business section of her home-town newspaper when she became the 300th member to join a local gay business organization. She had been assured, falsely, by the photographer who covered the event that the story would appear only in gay publications. Another woman said her co-workers found out about her when her lover, wearing jeans and short hair, stopped by her office one day to drop something off. These accidental disclosures generated embarrassment and fear and were perceived by respondents as an 'Oh no!' experience. Even when these near-calamities did not trigger the expected dire consequences, the incidents themselves were remembered vividly.

Disclosure options
Certain respondents did choose to disclose their lesbianism. Friendship with a co-worker was the primary impetus: 'We'd gotten very close and she shared a lot about her personal life. She kept talking about some gay friends of hers who tended to keep to themselves and exclude her . . . how disappointed she felt. I thought she was trying to let me know it was OK to come out.' Another impetus for disclosure was feeling misunderstood, depersonalized or victimized. One woman said, 'They sit there every day and make cracks about gays. I don't say anything. One day I'm just going to yell "Surprise! I'm one of them."'

Even if respondents wanted to come out on such occasions, they usually didn't. Instead they suppressed or translated the impulse into an act that revealed anger, but not their lesbianism. After listening to several co-workers complain about the recent political appointment of an open lesbian, 'Isn't it terrible . . . all the fruits running around', the respondent went to a nearby storeroom and started noisily sorting and heaving boxes. 'I hadn't said what I wanted to', she said, 'but at least we had the cleanest storeroom in the company by the end of the afternoon.' Some respondents made an art of transforming their feelings in hostile situations, taking pride in how well the act went. When one woman heard anti-gay comments, she simply asked if the person being discussed did a good job. 'That usually shuts them up', she said. She asked the same performance-oriented question when co-workers commented about Blacks or other devalued groups. Thus she managed to defend gays without seeming like a gay rights advocate, a reputation she felt would have been damaging. Instead she appeared liberal. Suppression or transformation took many forms. Some lesbians didn't respond to comments, changed the subject, misrepresented themselves, brought 'dates' to office functions, and even had separate house-warming parties for heterosexual co-workers and lesbian friends.

For some respondents, concealment of their homosexuality was automatic and caused no discomfort. Others felt uncomfortable; and some were extremely distressed at what they saw as self-betrayal. One woman said, 'I'd just come back from a gay rights march . . . and yet in that situation with those people I worked with, I couldn't say anything . . . It was extremely upsetting.'

Effects of disclosure
When, at particular times, certain respondents chose to reveal their lesbianism, the disclosures had the qualities of both premeditation and impulsiveness. Describing this, one respondent said, 'I'd thought about it for a long time, but I didn't know when or if I was going to tell her. . . . Then one night we had a few drinks and it just came out.' Usually the respondent carefully chose the person to whom she was disclosing herself. Often the disclosure and the reaction were anti-climactic: 'I don't know how she felt. . . . She didn't say much.' Or 'He said when I told him, "I knew it . . . I just wondered if you cared enough to tell me."' Or 'Nobody seems to think it's as important as I do.'

Disclosure had the paradoxical effect of magnifying the problem of concealment because now one or more others were included in keeping the secret. After an initial release, these women experienced increased tension because of the greater possibility of inadvertent disclosure. The new heterosexual confidante didn't have the same investment in secrecy as did the lesbian involved and had nothing to lose – and perhaps something to gain – by passing on the woman's secret. And respondents had the additional worry of implicating their friends. If their lesbianism became known widely, their lovers or friends who worked in the same company might also be labelled as lesbians.

One woman considered that the revelation of her lesbianism was part of her growth process. She felt it was her mission to educate people. Rather than sharing a secret, she intended to widen horizons. She said,

> I like to come out in a way that's natural . . . in an undercurrent way that doesn't call attention to me . . . [It] just reinforces that we are everywhere. . . . Like the gay riots where people are talking about 'those

gays!' I just said, 'yes, it's true that we don't have to express our anger that way.'

When respondents came out to co-workers whom they suspected were also homosexual, the exchange was more of a ritual. Respondents would 'have a sixth sense' about someone else's orientation and begin to drop hints about gay bars, restaurants or cultural events that would be meaningful only to other gays and lesbians. Such remarks would often make an actual announcement unnecessary.

Conversely, some respondents made a point of staying away from co-workers who seemed too openly gay. One woman, describing the unwanted attention of another lesbian in the same company, said:

> She had masculine traits . . . the way she walked . . . the way she talked . . . and she was very open about being gay . . . and she talked about her female lover . . . I got to know her . . . I don't remember how . . . but it got to the point where she came to visit me in my office . . . and I was very uncomfortable . . . because of her image. I guess the first couple of times she came to visit, I visited. Finally I just explained that I was very busy.

Concealment did not necessarily stop in the case of respondents who were known to be lesbian. To maintain a low profile, many of the interviewees avoided conversations that would have highlighted their lesbianism. One respondent said, 'Even if it would be appropriate to add something about my lover because of the turn in the conversation, I don't because I don't feel comfortable derailing the conversation. I don't want to be a curiosity.' Another respondent said, 'Everyone knew we were lovers. We didn't dance together even though other people were. I just didn't want to cause any social discomfort.'

Disclosure and promotions

Though no respondent thought her homosexuality had any impact on work performance, most felt their future options were limited by their lesbianism. They could advance to a certain level but not beyond because they could not project the necessary corporate image. Some seemed not to care; several said, 'I'm not ambitious'; some were resigned: 'I've definitely settled for less.' Others aimed for careers outside the business world, where their lesbianism wouldn't be an obstacle. Several planned to go into business for themselves or to become freelance consultants. Still others took refuge in technical areas in which they had little interaction with co-workers.

Most respondents felt hopeless about creating changes in their organizations. The task seemed overwhelming. When the hypothetical situation of working in a mostly gay company was posed to interviewees, their responses were often accompanied by sighs, postural shifts and, occasionally, some rueful cackling at being asked to consider what seemed a preposterous proposition. They would, they said, aspire to higher jobs, expect to be more successful, feel more relaxed, more 'like themselves'. Afterwards, several said they were surprised at their answers, shocked to find that a reversal of the usual hierarchy would make such a difference.[2]

Coping strategies

Karr (1978), McConaghy (1967), and Morin (1975) have established experimentally the presence of adverse feelings toward individuals assumed to be homosexual. Additionally, in Karr's experiment, individuals who labelled others as homosexual were frequently regarded positively by observers. Given such a strongly charged atmosphere, we can expect women who define themselves as lesbian in this culture to have developed strategies to manoeuvre in inimical environments in which any deviation from male, heterosexual norms results in less status, less opportunity, loss of co-workers' esteem, ostracism, harassment and/or firing.

A group tends to develop its own strategies. Women, for example, have 'felt constrained to begin in areas of specialization for which they could claim special insight or ability'. Consequently they have been overly represented in personnel departments – the 'relational' sectors of the organization – and underrepresented in the technical departments (Warner et al., 1982:227). An additional strategy has been to seek mentors (McLane, 1980). According to Cheek, a Black strategy has been to 'shine 'em on . . . don't let the white man know what you really feel and think' (1976:16). Similarly, from the analysis of the interviews it can be concluded that lesbian employees have developed strategies for dealing specifically with homophobia in the workplace.

The neuterized/neutralized strategy
Femaleness is the discredited and visible side of one's lesbianism. Consequently if gender can be minimized, lesbianism is less likely to come into focus. Computer-related jobs were particularly popular. One can speculate that, because they combine the masculine aspects of technology with the female tradition of keyboard work, computers effectively de-gender their programmers. Consequently sexuality and sexual preference questions are neutralized.

In a related strategy, women who are perceived as masculine can tap positive qualities attributed to males. In a corporation, the advantages occasioned by such perceptions may outweigh, or at least balance, the disadvantages of being seen as 'unfeminine'.

Non-disclosure strategies
One can infer the pervasive anxiety about disclosure from the extent to which all lesbians, even those who have come out, continue to use non-disclosure as a strategy. The intense observation of details that escape others is part of the non-disclosure strategy. Bateson writes that we are surrounded by an infinitude of detail and possible observations. The differences between a floor tile and a ceiling tile, or two people's hair styles, do not necessarily constitute information. Information, according to Bateson, is 'a difference which makes a difference' (1972:453).

For most heterosexuals, subtle cues are not as important as they are for the lesbian who feels herself to be in an unsafe environment in which a person's wedding ring, interest in a professional football team, or use of personal pronouns constitute a real difference. From these bits of information the lesbian can construct a hypothesis that will guide her behaviour.

Strategies that balance non-disclosure
All forms of non-disclosure, whether the occasional substitute of 'he' for 'she' when describing a weekend outing with a lover or the complete fabrication of a heterosexual life, leave a lesbian in a difficult moral position. Not only is she denying what she knows to be true, but she is also ignoring the strong exhortations of the lesbian community to come out. In the foreword to *Out of the Closets*, for instance, Jay and Young state that their book is written 'in the hope that one day ALL gay people will be out of the closet' (1972:2). The interviewees used a number of strategies to avoid feeling as though they were betraying themselves and their community.

Denial and dissociation Frequently respondents would insist they were not in the closet, and in response to further questioning would contradict themselves, for example, 'No I haven't actually told anyone I'm gay.' They continued to deny, however, that they were being secretive. Others claimed they felt comfortable in the face of homophobic remarks. Though no respondent said it, I speculate that these respondents were using a dissociative strategy; it was not *they* who were being discussed contemptuously. One respondent distinguished between 'dykey women', and gays who 'handled their gayness discreetly'. The dichotomization between good and bad gays is another dissociative strategy.

Avoidance Several respondents simply avoided personal situations at work. Some regretted the absence of social interactions with co-workers. Others said they did not want to get close to co-workers because they had nothing in common with them.

Distraction Respondents purposefully cultivated images that conveyed differentness – a feminist, a liberal – in order to distract from the more discreditable identification of lesbian. Unfavourable self-assessments about being duplicitous could thus be balanced by principled stand-taking.

Token disclosure While concealing the true nature of their relationships, some respondents let it be known that they had done something with 'a room-mate'. This was a partial disclosure since their room-mates were also their lovers. Similarly, after Harvey Milk's assassination, one woman asked a homophobic job supervisor for time off to go to the funeral of a friend. She did not mention that the 'friend' was Milk. In response to an anti-gay joke, one lesbian said, 'You'd better get yourself some new 'material', revealing her irritation, but not her gay identity.

The most common partial-disclosure strategy was simply to disclose their homosexuality only to certain people they felt they could trust. Because this information could leak, such a partial disclosure often set off a new round of strategies to find out if one's secret had been more widely revealed.

All of these balancing strategies seemed to restore to some degree respondents' threatened sense of integrity.

Implications and conclusions

Rather like a horse that finds itself simultaneously reined in and spurred on, corporate lesbians are caught in a crossfire of conflicting cultural and subcultural imperatives. The strategies lesbians used to manoeuvre their ways through this thicket of contradictions reveals that the old reductionist notion of 'coming out' is not an act, but rather a never-ending and labyrinthine process of decision and indecision, of nuanced and calculated presentations as well as impulsive and inadvertent revelations – a process, in short, as shifting as the contexts in which it occurs.

Is there, one might ask, a position beyond strategy, of simply acting naturally as one respondent claimed she did? Upon examination, the 'natural' stance is simply another ploy, an 'as-if' strategy in which the respondent acted as if she were entitled to the same social prerogatives, could count on the same good will assumed by her heterosexual co-workers. According to Goffman, this sort of 'open' strategy thrusts a new career upon the stigmatized person, 'that of representing [her] category. [She] finds [herself] too eminent to avoid being presented by [her] own as an instance of them' (1963:26). And, one might add, or tokenized by heterosexual co-workers.

And so the final irony for those who are thoroughly, consistently and extensively open at work is that they are effectively shorn of the authenticity and individuality they sought by this 'naturalness'. As Laing writes, 'lonely and painful . . . to be misunderstood, but to be correctly understood is also to be in danger of being engulfed, when the "understanding" occurs within a framework that one had hoped to break out of' (1970:76). And Goffman notes, 'There may be no "authentic" solution at all' (1963:124).

The rare lesbian who reveals her orientation, and who survives the consequences of violating the gendered expectations which structure the organization succumbs, then, to the organization in another way. Stylized out of existence, she forfeits her private mutinies, cannot mobilize the resistance necessary to shield her individuality from engulfment by the collective purpose of the organization. Homogenized, the token corporate lesbian becomes the consummate 'organization (wo)man'.

Notes

1. The lesbian interview data cited in this chapter first appeared in an article entitled 'The Lesbian Corporate Experience', published in *The Journal of Homosexuality* 12 (3/4), May 1986.

2. The ideal working conditions envisioned by the respondents when they pictured themselves working independently of heterosexuals, may, in fact, be just as elusive in a predominantly gay corporation. Just such an organization, an all-lesbian auto repair shop, dissolved because of unresolvable disputes between labour and management. One can conclude that the focus on the gay/straight organizational schism may mask and distract from more profound and inequitable distinctions indigenous to capitalist systems.

9
Organizations, Power and Sexuality: the Image and Self-image of Women Managers

Deborah L. Sheppard

> These last two chapters build on and bring together many of the insights already discussed at length. Thus although power is one of the major themes throughout the book, in these two studies patriarchal relations of power and subordination are at the centre of the stage. Both chapters draw on interviews, with both women and men, to stress the importance of methodological questions and the social construction of knowledge within feminist research. This next chapter focuses on the predicaments and strategies of women managers, facing the contradictory demands of being a woman and being a manager. Lesbian managers may have an especially complicated set of demands on their everyday actions. Thus, like the previous chapter, this study is concerned with the way women's self-presentations may be simultaneously gendered, sexual, organizational and, indeed, often precarious. As such, sexuality and the social construction of organizational power are intensely interrelated.

Sexuality, gender and social science

Sexuality and gender tend to be treated as 'special topics' in social science research. This approach reflects an epistemology which views the social world as empirically bounded and knowable as a series of interrelated sub-units of a larger social system. One consequence of this approach is its taken-for-granted quality with regard to social structure: the social world is seen as existing prior to consciousness and is received as such by the individual. This militates against revealing the constructed, processual quality of what is experienced as external structure.

Another consequence is the removal of sexuality and gender from the ongoing context of everyday life. Once defined and bounded as organizational 'topics' or 'problems', they become invisible as intrinsic parts of organizational structure. One of the major contributions of feminist scholarship has been the recovery of gender from its invisible status within the 'presumed neutrality of science' (Gilligan, 1982:6). However, to the extent that this recovery process is based on the epistemological assumptions just described, an understanding of gender as an essential component in the ongoing construction and interpretation of organizational reality remains neglected. This research is premised on the notion of 'taking gender seriously' (Morgan, 1981). Such an approach reveals the gendered basis of the taken-for-granted world. Organizations are not genderless in and of themselves, but in fact reflect and contribute to the prevailing societal gender structure.

This discussion is based on ongoing research examining the gendered basis of organizational culture. The material presented here is derived from in-depth interviews conducted with thirty-four women and sixteen men in managerial and professional organizational positions in Canada. These interviews begin to reveal the ways in which women formulate their organizational experiences with reference to their gender identity. They indicate how women learn to manage their sexuality and gender as a necessary component of organizational membership. Further, the data suggest that management of sexuality and gender is an essential part of the construction and enactment of organizational power. 'Gender' is used here to mean the process of constructing and assigning psychological, cultural, sociological, economic and political meanings based on perceptions of femaleness and maleness. 'Sexuality' can be understood within the context of gender as the process of incorporating eroticism, reproduction and physiological differences within an interpretive framework of psychological, cultural, sociological, economic and political meanings. Both gender and sexuality are processes of construction and attribution of meaning rather than static properties. The meaningfulness of both gender and sexuality is profoundly embedded in the ongoing process of social construction and self-definition and cannot be understood apart from an analysis of power (see Chapter 2 in this volume).

Organizational roles and statuses have traditionally been gendered; i.e. certain positions have been considered appropriate to, and filled by, women or men. This gendered aspect is located within a larger patriarchal social world which is hierarchically based, with men occupying positions of dominance over women, men, young people and minority group members. The taken-for-granted assumptions about this gender-based power structure start to be confronted by the growing presence of women in what have traditionally been male positions. Crossing this traditional boundary, defined by assumptions of gender dominance and subordination, potentially heightens awareness of gender and sexuality for organizational members. The question of gender in relation to organizational structure and power has been viewed largely in terms of barriers to women's organizational participation and comparisons of women's and men's organizational performance and characteristics (e.g. Moss and Fonda, 1980; Bernadin, 1982; Hoiberg, 1982; Kahn-Hut et al., 1982; Wallace, 1982; Voydanoff, 1984). Similarly, to the extent to which sexuality in organizations has even been considered, this has been largely with regard to sexual harassment and control of sexuality (Burrell, 1984). The growing body of literature suggests that women and men experience organizational life differently, whether compared within or between status levels. While such research has been essential in illuminating issues related to gender, it has focused primarily on behaviour and perceptions within a presupposed organizational structure. The construction of organizational reality through ongoing interpretation and interaction in relation to gender and sexuality has been explored very little (Hearn and Parkin, 1987).

Looking at gender differences
As part of the push towards equality of opportunity for women, a major emphasis of feminist scholarly research has been the examination of differences and similarities in gender capacity and performance. The implicit assumption has been that evidence of difference was ideological and discriminatory; women and men are unequally valued (e.g. Greenglass, 1982:256). This needed to be strongly confronted with clear evidence of women's capacity to participate on an equal footing with men. There have also been assumptions that the presence of women would serve to transform authoritarian organizational cultures into 'androgynous' settings in which both women and men would be able to exhibit female and male behaviours (Sargent, 1983). At the same time, we can see a growing recognition of continuing differences of experience of women and men that is of a different order than a discussion of innate tendencies or capacities. Under the tremendous pressures for acceptance and conformity necessary to success at work in our social world, which are heightened greatly for women in a male-dominated environment, the differences in the ways in which women and men may formulate their experiences are generally not readily apparent. While women continue to demonstrate their capacity for succeeding at 'men's work' and often excelling at it, we are realizing that under the surface of achievement, women are experiencing a work reality that differs from that of men in many ways.

The organizational research that has explicitly dealt with the issue of gender suggests that women and men experience organizational life differently. Female secretaries and male bosses have different experiences and give different interpretations of 'organization', and so do women and men managers who occupy similar hierarchical positions. Popular literature has reflected these gender differences in the appearance over the last ten or so years of magazines and books specifically addressed to women's experiences in the workforce and in managing both work and family. Studies such as *Men and Women of the Corporation* (Kanter, 1977) and *The Managerial Woman* (Hennig and Jardim, 1977) give accounts of different ways in which the organizational experience is constructed and interpreted according to gender. Beyond the organizational literature, there is a growing body of work suggesting that there are important differences between women and men in terms of perceptions of dominance, power and morality (e.g. Chodorow, 1971; Miller, 1976; Gilligan, 1982).

The question of investigating the world of subjective experience raises epistemological and methodological issues that bear on the problem of sexism in research. An approach premised on positivism (the dominant paradigm in the social sciences) assumes a world which is knowable to an observer who searches for patterns and regularities based on previously defined concepts and categories. Much of the emphasis of feminist scholarship has been to reveal the prevalence of male experience and interpretation as normative and as exclusive of much of women's experience. While there has been debate about the implications of searching for gender differences rather than similarities (Eichler, 1980), the interrelationship of the dominance of positivistic social science and a male normative standard must be addressed.

The notion of organizational structure as an objective, empirical and genderless reality is itself a gendered notion. In a structure where male dominance is taken for granted, the assumption of the invisibility of gender can be understood as an ideological position. It masks the extent to which organizational politics are premised on the dominance of one set of definitions and assumptions that are essentially gender based. The connection between language, symbolism and other aspects of organizational culture, and the gendered basis of organizational power, has been suggested (e.g. Riley, 1983). Feminist research continues to demonstrate the pervasiveness of patriarchal relations of power and subordination in all facets of our social life. It is within this broader social context that organizations are enacted and experienced, and our analysis of organizational power must search for and reveal this fundamental relationship.

Gender and organizational power

My research explores the different ways in which definitions of femaleness and maleness, and the ambiguity and punitive potential of perceptions of sexuality (i.e. eroticism) are used to define and maintain organizational power relations. Using a 'snowball' sampling method, in-depth interviews have been conducted with two different samples of Canadian managers and professionals: one sample with fifteen women who work in ten large public and private organizations, and the second with nineteen women and sixteen men in twenty-nine organizations. The first study focused on women exclusively and was of a more exploratory nature; the second included both women and men, but the respondents from both samples resembled each other in terms of organizational position. The respondents were asked a variety of open-ended questions about perceptions of organizational life and about how their work fitted in with their personal and family lives. While none of the questions explicitly dealt with sexuality, several addressed the issue of gender, and the responses to the questions as a whole suggest a number of ways in which sexuality is used to promote and maintain existing arrangements of power and control within organizations.

The sample of fifteen women was asked (among other questions) 'Do women and men have different organizational lives, in your experience?' The sample of thirty-five managers was asked (among other questions) 'Are you ever aware of gender as a factor at work?' and 'What impact, if any, do you think the growing number of working women is having on your organization?' In response to the first question, all fifteen women in the first sample said there were differences; two qualified their answers by saying that individual differences were often more significant than gender differences. These women perceive themselves and other women to be confronting constantly the dualistic experience of being 'feminine' and 'businesslike' at the same time, while they do not perceive men experiencing the same contradiction between their gender and work identities. (For an analysis of 'sex-role spillover' of female social–sexual characteristics to the workplace, see Gutek (1985) and Chapter 4 of this volume.)

In the second sample, both women and men generally answered affirmatively when asked if gender were ever a factor at work. This factor had somewhat different meanings for women and men respondents. Fifteen of the nineteen women answered that they were aware of gender, four qualified their responses to some degree, and one (the most senior woman interviewed) said gender was never a factor because she 'ignored' it. The women's responses ranged from seeing gender as a factor present at all times in all situations, to being a factor emerging in relation to male domination of positions of power and limitations on women's advancement opportunities, to being an issue that emerges only occasionally.

Among the sixteen men, nine stated clearly that gender was a factor, four answered in an indirect or qualified manner, and three answered negatively. Awareness of gender was expressed in a number of ways, including perception of the absence of women at decision-making or policy levels; perception of women as having different abilities or behaviours from men, some of which can produce managerial problems (such as parental leave); belief that the presence of women necessitated changes in their own behaviour; and the perceived consequences, usually negative, of affirmative action programmes.

The striking feature of female and male perceptions of gender and sexuality is the focus by both groups on femaleness rather than maleness. Femaleness is in varying degrees a problem primarily for women, and secondarily for men. Maleness remains embedded in the organizational cultural context and as such is not experienced as problematic (see Gutek, 1985 and Chapter 4 of this volume). Certain kinds of male behaviour may be experienced as problematic by women, but challenging the gendered basis of such behaviour may lead to challenging the prevailing organizational norms and structure. Since women managers and professionals presumably desire success and acceptance within that normative system, their definition of the situation shifts to a focus on their own gender identity.

Strategies of managing gender
For women 'immigrants' moving into male-dominated culture (Franklin, 1985), learning how to manage the world of the organization necessarily implies learning how to redefine and manage 'femaleness'. This management of women's gender self-presentation takes place within a context of a male-defined set of norms and expectations. Women moving into traditionally male positions formulate their experiences in such a way as to suggest that for them 'organizational' learning is in many ways coterminous with 'male' learning.

What unifies the accounts of the women respondents is the apparent reference to strategies of gender management. Deliberate behaviours were seen as needed to balance the conflicting statuses of 'female' and 'manager' and such strategies were seen as necessary for organizational success. This status conflict is heightened by their sense of marginality, of being always potentially or actually seen as different and on the periphery. The themes of isolation and marginality which emerge from the data create an image of managerial women as high-wire artists. They live in the spotlight, highly visible, and they are very much alone up there on the corporate tightrope.

There is a profound ambivalence in this position. On the one hand, these women experience positive, often heady, feelings of success and accomplishment at having arrived in the world of male status and power. On the other hand, their high-profile position creates feelings of discomfort and caution. It can be gratifying and exciting to have all eyes focused on oneself, but very uncomfortable to feel that one may not have been told all one needs to know to stay up on the high wire, that one's own ability may not be enough to guarantee success, and that there may be no safety net in the case of unpredictable winds of adversity.

The use of strategies for handling the ambivalence and lack of definition of the situation may not be deliberate or even conscious. A number of women respondents initially stated that gender was not a factor for them at work and that being female was not important. Subsequently they described a variety of strategies including dress, language and relationships with peers and superiors, although they didn't particularly identify them as strategies related to being female. Almost all respondents are aware of gender as a factor that plays an ongoing role in shaping their organizational experience, although they formulate this experience in different ways. They share a perception of gender as a *managed status*: being a woman in a male-dominated environment demands handling one's gender in particular ways, and this process is done with reference to one's interpretation of the prevailing power structure in the organization. Without constant vigilance regarding gender (and sexual) self-presentation, these women perceive that they run the risk of not being taken seriously, not being heard, and not receiving necessary information – in other words, of not being able to participate fully in the organizational system.

These strategies seem to form a continuum. At one end is acceptance of the organizational status quo vis-a-vis male dominance, and at the other is a rejection or challenging of this status quo. There are a range of such strategies, which seem to vary with type of organizational setting, rank within the organizational hierarchy, presence of other women, characteristics of the particular organizational culture, and the personalities and biographies of individual women. This discussion will focus on two such strategies, which emerged most clearly from the interview data. This is not an exhaustive analysis of such strategies, however, and broader or more diverse samples would probably reveal other methods of gender and sexual management related to organizational culture and structure.

Blending in and claiming a rightful place
The strategy used by most respondents is one of 'blending in' to the existing organizational culture. The desire to blend in is expressed in terms of wanting to soften the excluding rigidity with which women believe themselves to be perceived by their male peers. The blending depends on a very careful management of being 'feminine enough' (i.e. in terms of appearance, self-presentation, etc.) so that conventional rules and expectations of gender behaviour can be maintained by the men in the situation, while simultaneously being 'businesslike enough' (i.e. rational, competent, instrumental, impersonal – in other words, stereotypically masculine) so that the issue of gender and sexuality are apparently minimized in the work context. This strategy attempts to conform to the prevailing expectations and comfort levels of male co-workers and bosses, and explains problems such as discrimination or harassment as the responsibility of the individual woman to manage herself more effectively even when discrimination is acknowledged.

A less commonly used strategy involves a general acceptance of organizational goals but with an articulated critique of male dominance and a claim to a 'rightful place' in the organization. This strategy shows less reluctance to challenge prevailing gender assumptions, and defines problematic situations as structurally rather than individually based. Women who share this view are less likely to deliberately accommodate to a perceived need to make men more comfortable as part of a larger strategy to improve or protect their organizational position.

While the 'blending' strategy sees the achievement of an understated femininity as reducing the threat to male normality, the 'rightful place' strategy stresses a need to be on guard against the possible exploitation that comes from being seen as feminine. One respondent articulated this view in the following way:

> I'm very conscious when I go to company functions with a male that I not be on the passenger seat, that I should be driving, that he doesn't hold the door for me. . . . It's a sign of weakness. . . . You're afraid of your facade being dropped, that they say, you see, she really is a girl underneath, . . . she would really like us to dominate her. . . . It's

almost like you don't want to show an ounce of femininity or vulnerability at all.

Strategies of gender management are based on assumptions of sexual orientation. The prevailing assumption is one of heterosexuality. Thus for lesbian women, a fundamental aspect of dealing with sexual and gender self-presentation is the decision of whether or not to be self-disclosing, what sort of information should be disclosed and to whom. Hall (1986 and Chapter 8 of this volume) refers to several 'balancing strategies' used by lesbians. These strategies are attempts to come to terms with the contradictions of a positive self-identification with the lesbian community and a need for feelings of 'sameness' versus the fear of homophobia and hostility of a male heterosexual organizational culture. Thus the problems of interpreting and acting on understandings of being 'feminine', 'businesslike', 'not sexy' are exacerbated for lesbians who, in Hall's words, must also deal with 'the extremely complex process of managing discrediting information about oneself' (Hall, 1986:74).

Precariousness of strategies
A central theme to emerge from the interviews is the precariousness of managing personal boundaries related to sexuality and gender. This is due in part to the high visibility that results from women's under-representation (Kanter, 1977), but also to the ambiguity caused by a lack of precedents or current 'rules' governing organizational identity vis-a-vis sexuality and gender. The higher visibility of women can be experienced as advantageous but may also create vulnerability. As the respondent quoted above stated, 'When things are going well, you can really shine more than any male would in your position. But when you fall, it's very visible, and probably a lot of people are happy that you fall on your face.' High visibility seems to heighten the perception of women as sexual, beyond even an increased awareness of their gender. In this situation, being defined as 'sexual' tends to take precedence over being seen as 'organizational'. This poses a dilemma. There is ambiguity about being seen as 'female': femaleness embodies sexuality which must be contained, but being seen as 'unfemale', i.e. not sexually attractive or available to men (for example a lesbian) still means that a woman is perceived primarily in sexual terms.

The balance between being feminine and being businesslike is maintained with varying degrees of success depending on the situational efficacy of a particular strategy. However, women perceive themselves as being constantly vulnerable to unpredictable violations of the balance. They perceive that this violation comes from men's giving greater salience to women's sexuality or femininity in certain situations, and they also perceive themselves as generally needing to take responsibility for having triggered such violations.

The danger of appearing too feminine or too masculine means possible loss of credibility. The need to be seen as 'credible' was expressed many times by the women interviewed (see the second case study discussed in Chapter 6). The problem for women is in judging where the line falls between the two. A number of women discussed in some detail the care with which they dress for work as a way of establishing credibility as 'serious' managers. Hair colour and style, amount of make-up and jewellery were seen as part of an overall style of self-presentation. The need to manage appearance in this way seems to vary somewhat among industries or organizations, but nevertheless produces a recognizable style (e.g. Harragan, 1977:336–47). One respondent, who in discussing this style said that it is always preferable to 'err on the side of conservatism' when it comes to appearance, claims that a 'corporate women's culture' exists within her own organization, and that one way of recognizing cultural members is that 'we all look alike'. But there is clearly a perceived need to keep this mirroring limited and controlled. A woman who does not appear to be or to act 'feminine' enough (the criteria for which change between organizations and over time) may find herself perceived as 'too masculine'. Such a definition is negative and may result in the use of labels that are seen as punitive, such as 'lesbian' or 'castrating bitch'. (Homophobia, with use of labels such as 'fag', is a powerful means of controlling male behaviour as well.)

The adoption of a kind of uniform of dress and behaviour may help women feel a sense of power. The perceived need to appear more powerful in order to enhance organizational mobility means selectively borrowing masculine traits or modes of appearance. The padded suit shoulders, the understated colours, the tailored, conservative styling all mimic male dress, and attempt to confer on women the same kind of status that men have. Presumably just as padded shoulders give men an appearance of largeness and, by implication, more authority, so should this manner of dressing benefit women's appearance of power.

The area of appearance seems to be one where women feel they can most easily exert some control over how they will be responded to, and it is the area of behaviour that is the most clearly articulated. For example, one woman bought an expensive business suit which she wears when I don't want anyone to think I'm a woman, you know, when I just want to be part of the woodwork. . . . So I wear this beige suit with sort of a white blouse and it's very well cut and it looks expensive, and I look appropriate and it's perfect, it's great. I just fade right away. . . .

By choosing a particular way of dressing, she hopes to avoid the problem of high visibility. If she is successful, however, she 'fades away' so that she becomes invisible not only in terms of gender but as a person. Thus she must always be anticipating the impact she may be having on other people. This impact also clearly varies from one situation to the next. In addition, the informal rules and guidelines about the appropriateness of appearance keep shifting, which helps explain the continued appearance of books and magazines which tell women how to dress and behave at work.

This aspect of managing gender and sexuality extends to body language and speech. One woman described in considerable detail how she has learned to change her body language when doing presentations to groups of men so that she no longer paces, uses a pointer or puts her hands in her skirt or jacket pockets (all of which she cites as characteristic of men and as connoting personal authority). While her inclination was to behave in this assertive manner, she now stands still, uses overhead projections instead of blackboard and pointer, holds her hands by her sides, and addresses her audience in a controlled, low-pitched voice using inclusive questions in the first-person plural instead of declarative statements in the first-person singular. She acknowledged that such self-consciousness requires considerable attention and energy that men do not have to expend. However, based on her earlier experience, she felt that she would not be able to hold the men's attention if she used mannerisms that were not gender appropriate, even if they were appropriate to her organizational position and authority.

Desexualization of the person
The need for women to desexualize themselves while maintaining some requisite level of overt 'femininity' produces deliberate techniques of dressing, speaking and acting aimed at minimizing any potential suggestion of eroticism. These techniques of desexualization are also related to organizational status. There is a perceived need for women managers to establish difference between themselves and women secretaries and clerks. The boss–secretary relationship has become imbued with the suggestion of sexuality in a variety of ways (see Chapter 10 of this volume). It becomes very important for women managers not to become perceived in the same sexualized way, as this would risk their power and authority and they would not be 'taken seriously'. The current magazines

aimed at working women have been promoting a somewhat greater range of clothing style, and several respondents objected to tailored suits as 'too masculine'. The distinction between 'feminine' and 'businesslike' may shift somewhat, but the very nature of this changeability becomes a problem for women. Images in popular culture and the standards of acceptability in a particular organizational culture may be in conflict, and women must be attentive to these shifts so as to avoid an inadvertent crossing of the fine line.

Despite the highly sexualized images of women that pervade the rest of social life, the respondents indicated that this was not a dimension of themselves that was permissible in the organization. One woman wears suits and blouses with long sleeves and high necks in order to 'do nothing to provoke or to play on my sexuality . . . I enjoy being a woman but I don't want to use it.' A number of respondents referred to techniques to de-emphasize their breasts, including wearing high-necked blouses, avoiding sweaters, and wearing tailored jackets. A book on 'dressing for success' advises 'There's only one lingerie rule for the businesswoman: Wear bras that hold your breasts in place and hide your nipples' (Molloy, 1977:99). Padded shoulders '. . . do more than increase the size of a woman's presence when she is seated . . . They also detract from the size of her bust' (Scollard, 1983:49). Another book specifies ways in which women should handle leaving a business group in order to go to the bathroom, generally involving reference to phone calls to be made: 'She never refers to her bodily habits, her gender, or any personal need' (Scollard, 1983:81). The same author cautions against ever being seen purchasing a sanitary napkin in the women's bathroom, since this could lead to a manager's behaviour being attributed to her menstrual cycle (1983:148).

The popular literature giving advice to women in corporations devotes considerable detail to controlling female sexuality. The focus is on creating an appearance of wealth and status which convey authority and power, while deemphasizing sexuality. In one such author's view, '. . . dressing to succeed in business and dressing to be sexually attractive are almost mutually exclusive' (Molloy, 1977:21). This extends beyond the physical self to a broader notion of personal space. Thus he suggests that for office decor, 'any painting should be sexless. A painting of a cavalry charge or a steam locomotive would probably be too masculine: a watercolour of a meadow with a lot of pastels might be too feminine. Hang only neuter art' (1977:99).

This desexualization is generally perceived as a necessary protective strategy, but is also presented as one which leads to greater rewards. The loss of stereotypically feminine sexuality is seen as a trade-up for a more highly valued characteristic: 'The successful woman is discovering what men have long known: success in itself is very sexy. Power is sexy' (Scollard, 1983:4–9). For men, organizational success produces organizational, financial and personal power (see Gould, 1974 for a discussion of the relationship between masculine success and financial success). This definition of success ('power is sexy') is touted as available to women by containing and controlling feminine sexuality. The 'sexy' aspects of power for women are not sexual in fact, but reflect a kind of desexualized quasi-masculine demeanour and appearance, as well as a male-defined definition of organizational success.

Despite assumptions of a desexualized organizational norm and their often elaborate strategies to conform to it, women are subject to being seen as sexual *rather* than as managerial. A woman manager described an incident in which, upon successful completion of an arduous department auditing procedure, the male vice-president with whom she had been working commented upon leaving, 'You know, you're a real sexy broad.' This respondent felt that this comment was not only highly inappropriate, but also so unexpected that she found herself completely incapable of knowing how, or if, to respond. In a half-joking manner, she attempted to explain his behaviour by attributing it to her having worn a red silk dress (see Chapter 4, p. 62). In other words, despite her criticism of the administrator's remark, she still felt that it could have been something she had done that had triggered his reaction (i.e. she implied that a red dress had a symbolic sexual connotation). She clearly had not anticipated his reaction, which underscores the unpredictability of her situation – she never knows when such a remark, based on her gender rather than on her work performance, is likely to be made. In fact, a woman in this position doesn't need to do or say anything to bring about such a response; her mere presence is enough. Nevertheless, she may continue to attempt to contain such threats by blaming herself on some level. In a situation of relative powerlessness, she will exert control at the only level perceived as accessible: her own behaviour.

Pregnancy: the emphasis on and denial of female sexuality
Pregnancy is a highly sexualized status but with ambivalent and often negative attributions. It calls attention to women's sexual and reproductive uniqueness while revealing the incompatibility and often hostility with which pregnant women are regarded in organizational life. Several women expressed concern about how they would be treated by their male colleagues when they eventually

became pregnant. They worried that they would no longer be seen as 'serious' organizational members because the perceived demands of childbearing and child-rearing would be seen as incompatible with organizational responsibilities. Other research has shown that selection and promotion of women reflect widespread adherence to unsubstantiated beliefs that all women will leave to have children and that pregnancy leads to more organizational wastage than any other factor (Homans, 1987:91).

Pregnancy is clearly understood as a threat to whatever claims to organizational power a woman may make. One book of advice for women acknowledges that corporations have been prejudiced against pregnant women in considering them unattractive and readily firing them or keeping them away from work so as to be out of sight. Rather than criticizing this attitude as discriminatory or unfair, the author suggests that the best strategy for handling pregnancy is to minimize it as much as possible. A number of tips are listed on 'Maintaining Power Throughout Pregnancy and Childbirth', concerning the management of male resentment and concern (Scollard, 1983). The need to 'maintain power' implies that pregnancy, if not strategized for, will inherently produce a loss of power. For example, the pregnant executive is advised to take no more than six weeks off, because 'she understands that men regard post-pregnancy time as goof-off time' (Scollard, 1983:158). The assumption that needs of childbearing and child-rearing should be tailored to fit the demands of the organization is generally not questioned by women who follow a strategy of 'blending in', although they may voice dismay and resentment at the lack of understanding of their situation by male peers. Organizational and governmental policies concerning parental leave vary widely, and the women in both samples expressed a range of decisions concerning how they had handled absence from work related to childbearing.

Pregnancy and women's family responsibilities are seen by men managers generally as being problems experienced on an individual level. One man talked about the problems of handling the 'loss' of a woman plant manager for two parental leaves of four months each within three years, and perceived this as causing a dilemma for both the individual and the organization. He acknowledged that while absence due to illness would create the same management problem, he found that he applied a different standard to pregnancy.

The presence of greater numbers of women may alter this perception (Kanter, 1977). Another male manager in a social service organization whose professional staff were mostly women had ongoing problems in handling requests by his staff to work part time or to keep their positions available (the legislation in his jurisdiction requires that positions be held available for up to two years of unpaid parental leave). His perspective on the problem was quite different from the other manager quoted earlier, as he experienced this as an organizational rather than an individual problem. He expressed frustration with the fact that the husbands of his female staff were never the ones to accommodate to family demands; thus his women-dominated organization suffered.

Sexualized social contexts
The assumption of the asexual quality of organizational culture is belied by the overtly sexual character of many social contexts which form part of organizational life. These contexts are often sex segregated, and conventional sex-role norms dictate the exclusion or limitation of women's participation. Women respondents mentioned bars, taverns, strip joints, fishing trips, hockey, golf and ball games and even bathrooms as places from which they are in varying degrees excluded but where they know that important organizational information is exchanged and decisions made. Being fully included may appear to indicate acceptance by male peers, but when inclusion means participation in activities which are not appropriate or acceptable for women, the significance of this apparent acceptance becomes questionable.

This is particularly evident in relation to overtly sexualized activities. One respondent used a strategy whereby she made herself 'unprim . . . there was never a topic you couldn't discuss, or language you couldn't use, or places where I [wouldn't] go. . . . ' A result of this strategy was to be included in male activities, which once involved attending a strip club with seven men. This resulted in discomfort for her, since she found that it required her to adopt the prevailing male sexual definition of the situation. This meant viewing the women strippers in an objectified and sexually explicit way, as though she were a man. Because she saw the woman as her counterpart, she experienced considerable conflict resulting from her desire to be included and accepted by her male peers which also meant participating in her own objectification.

Inclusion in the male organizational culture in fact may heighten rather than reduce differences. When a woman attended an otherwise all-male sales conference at a country resort, some of the men played a prank involving stealing personal items from the participants' rooms. The break-in made her feel very vulnerable, and she was acutely embarrassed at having to retrieve her toiletries, including sanitary napkins, in the presence of the others. Her sexuality was displayed in a public setting in a way she experienced as embarrassing. While the prank was viewed negatively by most of the men, her reaction (she cried, felt threatened and was angry) was seen to be extreme, and served as evidence that she 'couldn't take a joke', in the words of her boss.

This illustrates the kind of dilemma that can be created by strategies which attempt to neutralize gender identity in situations where women expect that aspects of their femaleness should be recognized. The respondent felt that the men who broke into her room should have understood the particular vulnerability and risk experienced by women when travelling. Yet such recognition would have served to exclude her from the informal culture, with ramifications for further exclusion at a more formal level. The respondent used the strategy of claiming her place at work, and this example illustrates the risks inherent in this strategy: a more assertive claim of the right to full organizational participation probably results in a re-affirmation of the status quo by male power holders, who use sexuality as an enforcement mechanism.

Punitive use of sexuality
Managerial and professional women in male-dominated environments are vulnerable to having their organizational status overridden by their sexual identity, regardless of how scrupulously they manage their sexuality and gender. Women's sexuality is available to be used as a method of control through humiliation or discomfort. A woman can be subject to criticism for being 'too sexy' or 'not sexy enough' for having violated an organizational or a gender norm. A woman may be seen in terms of her sexual characteristics, a status that can be justified as complimentary when confronted, and which therefore seeks to blame the woman who questions the appropriateness or desirability of such a categorization. Being seen in this light reduces her from organizational participant to sexual object. The prevailing definition of the situation does not allow her to be both sexual and organizational at the same time.

A woman who is not responsive to sexual overtures or whose organizational behaviour is defined as unfeminine may be labelled as lesbian. Given the prevalence of homophobic attitudes, such a label is likely to be experienced as punitive. In the estimation of an 'advice book' author, it is an unwise strategy for lesbians to disclose their orientation 'since many corporate men are even more threatened by a gay woman than an obviously gay man' (Scollard, 1983:106). For women managers who are lesbian and who are fearful of public disclosure because of anticipated harassment or discrimination, their sexual orientation needs to be managed along with the fact of being female (see Chapter 8). The need to maintain an image of sexual neutrality or heterosexuality in order to 'blend in' and protect oneself from stigmatization contributes to a sense of alienation and separation. A more assertive strategy, which involves disclosing lesbian status in order to discourage men from making sexual advances, may also be problematic. One advice book for women managers that mentions problems faced by lesbian managers warns that such a strategy when used by young women can have the effect of encouraging the 'redblooded' men to regard this as a challenge and to thus increase their sexualization of the woman in question (Harragan, 1977:365).

In the same way, a woman may be derided by being labelled as sexually unattractive. A respondent discussed how social functions where alcohol is consumed often produce this type of punitiveness. She described how 'people will get really bombed and attack you viciously . . . coming out and finally saying, "you know, sometimes I wonder if we took up a collection and got you laid more often you would still work until nine o'clock at night"'. This example shows the use of sexuality to denigrate a woman manager's work performance. The same respondent, who 'claimed her rightful place' as a gender management strategy, reported a number of such punitive incidents. Even when the harassing nature of such behaviour was apparent to the other men in the situation, her reaction was more prominently attended to than the behaviour itself. The more confronting or assertive a woman is perceived to be, the more vulnerable she seems to this type of sexualized punitiveness (see the discussion of the second case study in Chapter 6).

Many of the respondents, both women and men, perceived women as needing to work harder than men for the same recognition, but this violates 'rate-busting' norms governing commitment of time and energy at work. Such norms are not apparently based on gender. However, being female puts women in the way of norm violation. Sexuality can then be used to call attention to or punish such violations, and reassert the dominance of the status quo. It is not clear how frequently such instances of sexual punitiveness occur, as sexual innuendoes are often emotionally charged and their interpretation or disclosure are not necessarily forthcoming from respondents. The tendency for women to take responsibility for controlling the occurrence of such behaviour means that reporting it is an indication of failure on their part.

Conclusions

What are the implications for women's lives when they begin to enter the male culture of the organization in other than stereotypic female roles? Women are faced with a dilemma: their gender and sexual identity need to be somehow transformed in order to enable them to participate in the male-defined organizational world. While a number of women respondents see themselves as successful and confident, they also acknowledge the continued existence of discrimination and double standards applied to women. They have developed strategies which allow them to maintain personal distance from such problems, saying that solutions lie with individuals rather than with the organizational structure, that sexism is a 'fact of life' and that women need to 'laugh off' sexual politics. This approach seems characteristic of the majority of women in these samples. Some see this as a demanding or unfair process; others accept it pragmatically as a means to a valued end. This strategy can be critically understood as a form of false consciousness, in that women are actively participating in a process which compromises and devalues aspects of their core identity.

Strategies which are more assertive or insistent raise gender (which is to say, femaleness) to a level of awareness that is challenging or threatening to the (male) status quo. Insistence on gender equity involves taking less individual blame for what is understood as a structural phenomenon. Some women express perceptions of inequity more directly. They express more anger and direct their analysis of discrimination to organizational and societal factors. Such an analysis lays the blame outside oneself, but also fosters feelings of powerlessness and alienation.

Despite the lack of overt recognition of sexuality as part of organizational culture, its presence and significance are attested to by the ongoing strategizing by women to control others' perception of them as sexual persons. Regardless of the type of strategy women consciously or unconsciously adopt to handle what they come to experience as the problem of being female, sexuality is a common link that reveals the precariousness of gender management. Women who feel that they have successfully 'blended in' are aware that they may unpredictably be seen as sexual rather than as organizational. Women who feel that they must always be vigilant in protecting their position against discrimination find that sexuality is used as a punitive means of controlling their behaviour. Sexuality is thus available to be used as a means of asserting prevailing organizational power relations and definitions by reducing women to a devalued organizational status.

Note

This research was funded by the Social Sciences and Humanities Research Council of Canada, Grants Nos. 482-83-1012 and 4885-0009, and was conducted while I was Assistant Professor in the Department of Sociology and Anthropology, Concordia University, Montreal, Quebec, Canada. I would like to thank Jeff Hearn, Peta Tancred-Sherrif, Albert Mills, Barbara Gutek and Rosemary Pringle for their comments on an earlier version of this chapter, and Peggy Fothergill and Cheryl Storey for their assistance in conducting the research.

10
Bureaucracy, Rationality and Sexuality: The Case of Secretaries

Rosemary Pringle

> The theme of sexuality and power is continued in this last chapter. In this case, however, the study is of women in less powerful organizational positions, namely secretaries. Interviews with some 300 people, including 'pairs' of bosses and secretaries, provide the basis for a discussion of the complex interplay of bureaucracy, rationality and sexuality, pleasure and power. Using feminist, psychoanalytic and postmodernist theory, this chapter explores the multiple meanings of the boss–secretary relationship, in such terms as, 'compulsory heterosexuality', 'family roles', the master–slave relationship and sadomasochism. The boss–secretary relationship is in many ways the paradigm case of sexual/gender relations between men and women in organizations.

Sex is like paperclips in the office: commonplace, useful, underestimated, ubiquitous. Hardly appreciated until it goes wrong. It is the cement in every working relationship. It has little to do with sweating bosses cuddling their secretaries behind closed doors. . . . It is more adult, more complicated, more of a weapon. (Jones, 1972:12)

Pleasure and power do not cancel or turn back against one another; they seek out, overlap, reinforce one another. They are linked together by complex mechanisms and devices of excitation and incitement. (Foucault, 1979:48)

No one seriously believes that secretaries spend much time on the bosses' knee. Actual sexual interactions are the exception rather than the norm and, jokes aside, the centrality of work to the boss–secretary relationship is generally conceded. Yet the sexual possibilities colour the way in which the relationship is seen. Outside of the sex industry itself it is the most sexualized of all workplace relationships. Even if the cruder representations are discounted, the relationship is seen to be oozing with sexuality which is suppressed, sublimated or given limited expression in flirtation and flattery. It bases itself on personal rapport (some bosses say 'chemistry'), involves a degree of intimacy, day-to-day familiarity and shared secrets unusual for any but lovers or close friends, and is capable of generating intense feelings of loyalty, dependency and personal commitment.

This chapter considers the implications of the boss–secretary relationship for an understanding of the wider operations of power in organizations. It draws on a larger study of secretaries, carried out in Sydney between 1984 and 1987, which included interviews with some 300 people in a variety of organizations, large and small, public and private (Game and Pringle, 1986; Pringle, 1989). We interviewed 'pairs' of bosses and secretaries, as well as a range of managerial, clerical and administrative workers with whom secretaries work. I shall use some of this material to argue that the boss–secretary relation, rather than being out of step with modern bureaucratic structures, is the most visible aspect of a pattern of domination based on desire and sexuality. Far from being an exception, it vividly illustrates the workings of modern bureaucracies. Gender and sexuality are central not only in the boss–secretary relation but in *all* workplace power relations.

As theorized by Weber, bureaucracy 'has a "rational" character: rules, means, ends, and matter-of-factness dominate its bearing . . . . The march of bureaucracy has destroyed structures of domination which had no rational character, in the special sense of the term' (Gerth and Mills, 1958:244). According to Weber's 'ideal type', bureaucracies are based on impersonality, functional specialization, a hierarchy of authority and the impartial application of rules. There are well defined duties for each specialized position and recruitment takes place on criteria of demonstrated knowledge and competence. Authority is held in the context of strict rules and regulations and graded hierarchically with the supervision of lower offices by higher ones. Authority established by rules stands in contrast to the 'regulation of relationships through individual privileges and bestowals of favour' which characterized traditional structures. Above all there is a separation of the public world of rationality and efficiency from the private sphere of emotional and personal life.

Secretaries seem to contradict every one of these criteria. By having direct access to the powerful, they are outside the hierarchy of authority. Far from being specialized, they can be called upon to do just about anything, and there may be considerable overlap between their work and that of their boss. In bringing to bear the emotional, personal and sexual, they represent the opposite of 'rationality' and should, in Weber's terms, have been eliminated a long time ago. How then are we to explain the continued existence of this least 'bureaucratic' of relationships? The obvious answer is to say that Weber had it wrong, or that his 'ideal type' was never intended to have any empirical existence. The limits of his theory have already been clearly shown in more than half a century of organization studies. Nevertheless Weber's version retains enormous ideological power. People's views of how organizations actually do work and how they 'ought' to work are still filtered through Weber and the theory becomes in some sense, a self-fulfilling prophecy. Equal employment opportunity and affirmative action plans, for example, emphasize the importance of excluding 'private' considerations and insist on the impersonal application of rules. Weber still sets the terms of the dominant discourse on power and organizations. Whatever modifications or even radical revisions might need to be made to the theory it is assumed there is a core of truth to it and this makes it difficult to move outside it.

For Weber bureaucracy is progressive in that it breaks down the old patriarchal structures and removes the arbitrary power held by fathers and masters in traditional society. He has been given a favourable reading by some feminists because he does appear to provide a basis for understanding the breakdown of patriarchal relations. Rosabeth Moss Kanter uses a Weberian framework for one of the few feminist organization studies to have been carried out. She argues that secretaries represent a bureaucratic anomaly. She explains the 'intrusion' of the personal and the sexual as a remnant of traditional forms of domination. The boss–secretary relationship is, she argues, 'the most striking instance of the retention of patrimony within the bureaucracy' (1977:73). It is patrimonial in that

> bosses make demands at their own discretion and arbitrarily; choose secretaries on grounds that enhance their own personal status rather than meeting organizational efficiency tests; expect personal services with limits negotiated privately; exact loyalty and make the secretary a part of their private retinue, moving when they move . . .

The implication here is that secretarial work should be 'rationalized', made to fit the bureaucratic pattern. Kanter explicitly denies the relevance of gender as a separate category of analysis. She argues that what look like sex differences are really power differences and that 'power wipes out sex' (1977:201). In this framework the problem for secretaries is that they lack power; they are caught up in an old-fashioned patriarchal relationship that is out of kilter with 'modern' business practices. The question then becomes how can individual secretaries remove themselves from these backwaters and place themselves on the management ladder?

In order to prioritize questions of gender and sexuality the 'core of truth' in Weber needs to be deconstructed. I am not concerned here with how far he was 'right' or 'wrong' but with the ways in which the discourse positions men and women, bosses and secretaries. Weber's account of 'rationality' can be read in gender terms as a commentary on the construction of a particular kind of masculinity based on the exclusion of the personal, the sexual and the feminine from any definition of 'rationality'.[1] His distinction between traditionalism, which is patriarchal, and the rational legal order of the modern world parallels the debate between patriarchalists and contract theorists in liberal political theory. Pateman (1988) has demonstrated that liberal contract theory actually retained key patriarchal assumptions. It can similarly be argued that the rational–legal or bureaucratic form, while it presents itself as gender neutral, in fact constitutes a new kind of patriarchal structure. The apparent neutrality of rules and goals disguises the class and gender interests served by them.

What is striking in the interviews we carried out is the use of family metaphors to describe workplace relations. Despite the ideology that public and private are separate, workplaces do not actually manage to exclude the personal or sexual, and sexuality and family symbolism are an important part of modern authority structures. But the family is no longer a protagonist so much as a site of intervention and supervision. Barrett and McIntosh (1982:31) point to the ways in which the society as a whole has been familialized. The media, advertising and popular culture are saturated in familial ideology which provides a dominant set of social meanings in contemporary capitalist society. It is in and through the family that sexuality is constituted and we come to recognize ourselves as gendered subjects.

'Rationality' requires as a condition of its existence the simultaneous creation of the realm of the personal, the emotional, the sexual, the 'irrational'. Bureaucracy creates the illusion of ordered rationality but could not exist unless the other side were there too. Masculine rationality is constructed in opposition to the feminine, as a denial of the feminine, but does not exist without it. Rather than existing in separate social spaces, public and private occur simultaneously within one social space. To treat the personal dimension as a relic of past forms is entirely to overlook the appearance of new forms of power and control based around the construction of sexuality. Theorists of bureaucracy have long recognized that the personal intrudes into the workplace all the time; even that it is necessary to have an informal arrangement alongside the formal structure to motivate people and to make things actually work. Far from being a limitation on bureaucracy there is some evidence that informal relations and unofficial practices often contribute to efficient operations (Blau and Meyer, 1971:25). It is also possible that detachment is required only in those relationships that are involved in the transaction of official business (Blau and Meyer, 1971:37). The 'human relations' theorists have shown that people want more from their work than just pay and that the existence of cohesive bonds between co-workers is a prerequisite for high morale and optimum performance (Rose, 1975:Part 3).

In these accounts the existence of 'the personal' in the workplace is seen as consistent with bureaucratic organization and even as supportive of it. Yet the personal is still seen as separate from bureaucracy proper (it 'intrudes'), and sexuality, it will be noted, rarely gets a mention at all. We need an account of power and authority in the workplace that not only makes central the personal and the sexual, but questions the dichotomies between formal/informal and public/private.

Rather than thinking in terms of one 'ideal type' of organization as characteristically modern it might be more useful to consider a range of different types. Part of the problem with the Weberian approach is the attribution of goals or purposes to the organization. This avoids the issue of the specific and possibly conflicting interests of the individuals or groups who are the actors in organizational settings. Silverman (1970) suggests that the 'structures' of organizations are a good deal less solid and permanent than is often suggested; that they should be seen as the transient outcomes of the actions and interactions of individuals and groups pursuing their own ends with whatever resources are available to them. This shifts the analysis away from the relation between formal and informal structures and opens up new ways of understanding power relations in organizations.

The boss–secretary relation, then, need not be seen as an anomalous piece of traditionalism, or an incursion of the private sphere, but rather as a site of strategies of power in which sexuality is an important though by no means the only dimension. Far from being marginal to the workplace, sexuality is everywhere. It is alluded to in dress and self-presentation, in jokes and gossip, looks and flirtations, secret affairs and dalliances, in fantasy, and in the range of coercive behaviours that we now call sexual harassment. Rather than being exceptional in its sexualization, the boss–secretary relation should be seen as an important nodal point for the organization of sexuality and pleasure.

Sex at work is very much on display. It is undoubtedly true that for both men and women sexual fantasies and interactions are a way of killing time, of giving a sense of adventure, of livening up an otherwise boring day. As Michael Korda put it, 'the amount of sexual energy circulating in any office is awe-inspiring, and given the slightest sanction and opportunity it bursts out' (1972:108). Marcuse was one of the first to recognize the pervasiveness of sexuality in the workplace and to theorize it. He recognized that it was not just an instance of incomplete repression but was encouraged as a means of gratification in otherwise boring jobs. If open-plan offices are about surveillance they are also, he suggests, about controlled sex.

Marcuse introduced the concept of 'repressive desublimation' to explain how people were being integrated into a system which 'in its sweeping rationality, which propels efficiency and growth, is itself irrational' (1968:12). He pointed to the ways in which

> without ceasing to be an instrument of labour, the body is allowed to exhibit its sexual features in the everyday work world and in work relations . . . . The sexy office and sales girls, the handsome, virile junior executive and floor worker are highly marketable commodities, and the possession of suitable mistresses . . . facilitates the career of even the less exalted ranks in the business community . . . . Sex is integrated into work and public relations and is thus made susceptible to (controlled) satisfaction. . . . But no matter how controlled . . . it is also gratifying to the managed individuals . . . . Pleasure, thus adjusted, generates submission. (1968:70–1)

The difficulty with this analysis is that it is entirely gender blind. It presumes that men and women are equally oppressed and ignores the fact that it is women who are required to market sexual attractiveness to men. As MacKinnon remarks 'when gender – women and men – is discussed, sexuality per se is left to be inferred. Symmetrically, when sexuality is discussed, gender tends to be glossed over, as if sexuality means the same thing for women as it does for men' (1979:21).

Feminism and sexuality

Discourses about the separation of sex and work make more sense from men's perspectives than they do from women's. For women the two obviously go together. As Kay Daniels points out this is true not just in the 'extreme' case of prostitution (work for women, leisure for men) but across the board (1984:12–13). Women are constantly aware of sexual power structures and the need to put up barriers against men. Though they enjoy male company and male jokes they are careful to limit their participation and to make it clear to men 'how far they can go.' Secretaries often choose their jobs on the basis of avoiding further experiences of sexual harassment. One head office I visited, nicknamed the 'twenty five year club' because of the length of time most of the managers had been there, was regarded as something of a refuge. If there was no sexual excitement on the sixteenth floor, at least there was no danger.

The term 'sexual harassment' only came into the language around 1976. It has quickly become recognized as a central feature of gender inequalities at work and covered by anti-discrimination legislation. Yet it is often still dismissed either as trivial and isolated or as universal 'natural' behaviour. Most women I asked about it feel that they are responsible for controlling men's behaviour, that women should be able to deal with unwanted advances and preferably avoid getting into the situation in the first place. Yet many said they had experienced sexual harassment and had even left jobs because of it. Feminists have insisted that sexual harassment is not only an individual problem but part of an organized expression of male power. Sexual harassment functions particularly to keep women out of non-traditional occupations and to reinforce their secondary status in the workplace. Gutek and Dunwoody (1987) have pointed out that even non-harassing sexual behaviour has negative consequences for women. The office affair can have detrimental effects on a woman's credibility as well as her career. Many women say they are not flattered by sexual overtures at work and experience even complimentary remarks as insulting. Men on the other hand report virtually no work-related consequences of sexual behaviour and the majority are flattered by sexual overtures from women. Blatant male sexual advances go largely unnoticed because 'organizational man', goal oriented, rational, competitive, is not perceived in explicitly sexual terms. It is ironic that women are perceived as using sex to their advantage, for they are much less likely to initiate sexual encounters and more likely to be hurt by sex at work.

The gender division of labour is mediated by gender constructions that in numerous aspects bear on sexuality. Rich's notion of 'compulsory heterosexuality' (1984) can be applied here for the sexual 'normality' of daily life in the office is relentlessly heterosexual. This takes place in concrete social practices ranging from managerial policies through to everyday informal conversations (Hearn and Parkin, 1987:94–5). It involves the domination of men's heterosexuality over women's heterosexuality and the subordination of all other forms of sexuality. It was striking how few homosexuals, either bosses or secretaries, we turned up in our workplace visits. This was despite the fact that half of the interviews were carried out by homosexuals who offered cues that it was 'safe' to talk about the subject. Those we did talk to were nearly all volunteers who had been contacted via other 'non-work' channels. Very few were 'out' at work in any more than a limited way. Where they were it was either in a 'creative' area where it was acceptable, or they were treated by the rest of the office as the tame pervert. The only lesbian secretary who was completely open about her sexuality was a woman who had been married and had children and could thus claim to have paid her dues to 'normality'. She said, 'I think I'm good PR for lesbians . . . because I'm so bloody ordinary. You know, I've been married, I've had children, I own a house, I own a car. I'm Ms Middleclass Suburbia!' Another secretary told me that she deliberately chose temporary work so that she could move on before having to face the chit-chat over morning tea about private life.

In naming and theorizing sexual harassment feminists have drawn attention to the centrality of sexuality in workplace organization. However, they have largely restricted sexuality to its coercive dimensions. Radical feminists have emphasized sexual aggression and violence as the basis of men's power. If women experience pleasure it is treated as 'coerced caring' (MacKinnon, 1979:54–5). In these accounts either virtually all heterosexual activity may be labelled as sexual harassment or a line has to be drawn between what is harassment and what is 'acceptable'. The identification of some activities as 'sexual harassment' may legitimate and obscure other forms of male power. But men control women not only through rape or through forcing them to do what they want to do, but through definitions of pleasure and selfhood.

At this point the argument becomes complicated for it is not clear where 'male power' begins and ends, whether women are in all cases 'victims' or whether they too can exercise sexual power. It is hard to know what a 'free' choice would be. Rather than being yanked screaming into 'compulsory heterosexuality', most women actively seek it out and find pleasure in it. Rich seems to assume some underlying bond with the mother that would be free to develop, flowing into 'lesbian continuum'. But women may choose heterosexuality precisely to get away from the constraints of the mother/daughter relationship. If mothers were not held uniquely responsible for child care the intensity and ambivalence of the mother/daughter bond might actually lessen. Indeed it might be less likely that we would experience any pressure to 'choose' between heterosexuality and homosexuality or that 'lesbian continuum' would be set up in contrast to 'compulsory heterosexuality'. We might see a construction of sexuality that did not prioritize men over women, heterosexuality over homosexuality, intercourse over other sexual acts.

While it has opened up discussion of sexuality and power in the workplace, sexual harassment is not an adequate way of conceptualizing the issues. The more sophisticated analyses of power and pleasure deriving from cultural analysis have still to be applied to work. Opposition to sexual harassment is only one component of a sexual politics in the workplace. It needs to be supplemented with analyses of the ways in which sexual pleasure might be used to disrupt male rationality and to empower women. Merely to attempt to drive sexuality from the workplace leaves the ideology of separate spheres effectively unchallenged.

Feminists differ in their attitudes to sexuality. While some have concentrated on its coercive aspects – rape, incest, domestic violence, paedophilia, sexual harassment and so on – others have argued that the priority given to danger and coercion has led to a marginalization of female pleasure (Vance, (1984). Lynne Segal (1987) and Gayle Rubin (1984) take a more libertarian position. Segal simply wants a return to the early 1970s concern with sexual pleasure, claiming that sexuality has been over-emphasized and that men's sexual domination is based on their social and economic power and not the reverse. Rubin, drawing on Foucault, points to the tendency in our culture to treat sex with suspicion, to sanction certain kinds of sexual activity and to create a hierarchy of sexual values. She challenges this by siding with the sexual minorities, aiming to replace the notion of a single universal ideal sexuality with a pluralistic sexual ethics. The difficulty with both of these positions is that they risk falling into an essentialism that takes any sexual desire as somehow authentic. They avoid any critical examination of the material basis of consent and historical shifts in sexual power.

On another tack, difference theorists celebrate the multiplicity of identities and pleasures based on the female body which they contrast with the one-dimensional, instrumental and abstract culture of the male. This enables them to develop a rhetoric of pleasure which completely bypasses current realities. Silverman (1984) argues that female sexuality has been constructed by the interaction of (male) discourse with the female body. She analyses the master–slave pornography of the *Story of O* (Réage, 1965) to show the ways in which discourse quite literally maps meaning on to bodies. Women will not challenge the symbolic order from 'outside', she argues, but by altering their relation to discourse.

Challenging discourse involves an exploration of what it means to be sexual subjects rather than objects. Given the difficulties and long-term nature of this process it is important to accept female sexuality as it is currently constituted. Rather than assuming that secretaries are always the pathetic victims of sexual harassment it might be possible to consider the power and pleasure they currently get in their interactions with people and raise the question of how they can get what they want on their own terms. As Barbara Creed (1984) pointed out in her analysis of Mills and Boon, even here, in what is regarded as romantic trash, and despite the sexist stereotypes, we can find opportunities to subvert the existing order, for example by giving women control of the gaze.

Sexuality as discourse

Sexuality in the workplace is not simply repressed or sublimated or subjected to controlled expression. It is actively produced in a range of discourses and interactions. Modern Western societies have accumulated a vast network of discourses on sex and pleasure. We expect to find pleasure in self-improvement in both our work and non-work activities. Purposive activity operates not through the denial of pleasure but by its promise: we will become desirable. Foucault is particularly concerned with the processes by which individuals come to think of themselves as 'sexual subjects'. Sex has become not merely another object of knowledge but the basis of 'identity'. The greater the valorization of the individual as the ideal subject, the greater the demand for techniques of individual training and retraining. The emphasis on individual choice is consonant with the maximizing of disciplinary controls. 'Controls' operate not to repress but to prolong, intensify and refine the possibilities of pleasure.

This is not as far from Weber as it might seem. Where Weber treated sex as outside 'rationality' Foucault looks at the ways in which sex came under the control of 'sexuality' operating through techniques of power. For Foucault power relations are always rational in the sense that they are 'imbued, through and through, with calculation' (1979:95) and they follow a series of aims and objectives. Both see rationalization as characteristic of modern life; but whereas Weber (and Marcuse) see it as a global historical process, and one based on a distinction between public and private, Foucault is concerned with specific rationalities and cuts right across the public/private division. For Weber and Marcuse the dominance of instrumental reason is a general process to which the whole society is assumed to be uniformly and inexorably subject. Where they are pessimistic about the future Foucault stresses that resistance is ever present. This could be taken to mean that since resistance is already inbuilt in the exercise of power we are therefore doomed to defeat. But if this is so, why does he call so persistently for resistance to domination and prefer struggle over submission? While resistance and struggle are intrinsic to the exercise of power, people also act as subjects whose actions are to some extent freely chosen from a set of alternative possibilities.

The double-sidedness of 'resistance' strikes many chords when considering the situation of secretaries. Secretaries have been variously represented as sell-outs, as victims, stooges of management, or as potential bearers of a proletarian consciousness based on their deskilling and reduction in status. But it is not at all clear that they should be placed on one of two sides. In foucauldian terms the situation is more fluid:

> Instead there is a plurality of resistances, each of them a special case: resistances that are possible, necessary, improbable; others that are spontaneous, savage, solitary, concerted, rampant, or violent; still others that are quick to compromise, interested, or sacrificial; . . . the points, knots, or focuses of resistance are spread over time and space at varying densities, at times mobilizing groups or individuals in a definitive way, inflaming certain points of the body, certain moments in life, certain types of behaviour. . . . (Foucault, 1979:96)

If we accept that a series of discourses on sexuality underpin bureaucratic control it is possible to see secretaries not as a pre-bureaucratic relic but as the most visible aspect of a structure of domination based on desire and sexuality. Far from being victims they necessarily engage in forms of resistance. This does not mean that they constitute a revolutionary group but neither are they automatically inscribed within existing power relations.

Foucauldian accounts of power sit rather uneasily with accounts that emphasize the structures of class and gender. In radical feminist thought power is an expression of male interests and refers to an overall structure of male domination. Foucault's account of power is counterposed to any binary opposition between rulers and ruled. Though he underplays the significance of gender he does provide the basis for developing a more dynamic and fluid conception of power relations between men and women. 'Male power' is not simply and unilaterally imposed on women – gender relations are a process involving strategies and counter-strategies of power.

Sexuality and the family

Secretaries may be symbolically placed as office wives, mothers or daughters,[2] and may participate in these constructions or find ways of resisting. Bosses frequently try to break down divisions between home and work, either by asking their secretaries to do 'non-work' tasks or by intruding on their non-work lives. One boss had his secretary do all his grocery shopping and even go home and take his washing off the line! Bosses often control their secretaries by having a detailed knowledge of their personal lives: of their families, boyfriends, future plans. This knowledge is usually very one way. In some cases they spend a lot of social time together, talk about their personal problems over a drink, chat about their families. On the strength of this he may then be able to ask her to work incredibly long hours and organize her whole life around the job. Many bosses sought to stretch the limits of the working day, demanding long overtime for no additional pay. This was presented as pleasurable, a sign that the job was interesting and challenging, evidence that the secretary was part of management rather than a mere worker, a superior sort of person to the nine-to-fivers.

Male bosses can decide for themselves the extent to which they will keep home and work, their public and private lives separate. Secretaries do not have this luxury. Male bosses go into their secretaries' offices unannounced, assume the right to pronounce on their clothes and appearance, have them doing housework and personal chores, expect them to do overtime at short notice and ring them at home. Secretaries would rarely ring bosses at home (unless specifically asked to) or intrude on their privacy. Indeed their task as gatekeepers is to protect that privacy. On the other hand men 'invade' women's private space all the time and women have to defend it. The sexual metaphor is apt.

It is notorious that bosses do not like disciplining secretaries. They do not like overt conflict in the relationship and prefer their secretaries to work largely unsupervised. Hence they worry a lot about getting the 'right' person. Even where the boss knows nothing about his secretary's life outside work, family criteria are frequently used in the selection process. Some avoid divorcees or women with young children; others like young married women who have been taught by their husbands how to please men; others go for women from large families because they are thought to have learnt 'discipline', or for women who dress in a way that indicates commitment and efficiency. Having made the choice, the establishment of symbolic family and/or sexual dimensions is frequently used to overcome the 'discipline' problem.

One boss was particularly concerned to 'desexualize' the boss–secretary relationship and argued that sex has no rightful place in the office. He saw any acknowledgement of sexual attraction as undermining his authority and was wary of women using their sexual wiles to gain advantages. He placed himself above those men who need to seek sexual solace in the workplace.

> If there was ever a waste of time in life it was shorthand . . . I think that shorthand is a device invented by managers who feel lonely and want to sit with a lady and talk to her a little bit and give them a cup of tea. It is a sort of sexual fantasy I think, shorthand . . . and I think it should be banned. I don't think anybody should be allowed to learn shorthand.

The topic of sexual harassment provided him with another opportunity to display his humour and assert his (sexual) superiority. He recalled two cases: 'One of them I think was a mammary mauler and I think the other was a posterior pincher. Obviously the mammary glands have got more importance than the posterior because he was transferred and the other guy just became an office joke.'

Despite his refusal to interact personally in the office, he stressed the importance of family situations in making his initial choice. He avoids secretaries with young children, believing that women should stay at home and look after them. He had no compunction in saying he preferred women no older than 40 or 45: 'because they do tend to become a bit domesticated at that age . . . . Well their thoughts are around their husband and the home and the grandchildren, or their children . . . and they really seem to lose interest in business matters when they get to about forty five.'

He talked at length and amusingly about the selection process, turning the joke on to himself:

> Two secretaries back the specification was that she must be a non-smoker, must live within four miles of the office and not be divorced . . . . Well, I thought that if she was divorced then she is probably neurotic and I don't want her taking it out on me . . . . But it is actually difficult to know which are the better secretaries . . . the single girls, the married ladies or the divorced ones . . . . This particular one fulfilled everything. . . . Then she took up smoking, then she moved out to Manly and then she got a divorce.

Master–slave is an important model for boss–secretary relations but it is not the only one. Gendered subjectivity is produced in a number of contradictory discourses which make available different positions and different powers for men and women. Following Wendy Hollway's example (1984), we might identify three discourses on bosses and secretaries which construct different subject positions. The first, the master–slave discourse, clearly sets up the boss as subject and secretary as object. The latter may take a number of forms including subordinate wife, devoted spinster, attractive mistress. Because these positions are not equally available to men and women all sorts of difficulties arise when women take up the subject or men the object position. Male bosses fear that if they have a male secretary they will have to give him recognition – and he may then not be a secretary. Secretaries may feel that a female boss is not powerful or prestigious enough to give them the recognition they seek. Even if she is they may not feel the safety in merging with the powerful that they feel with men, because they cannot trust her to set the boundaries.

Parallel to master–slave is a mother–son discourse which places the secretary in the subject position as mother, dragon or dominating wife, and the man is the object. She insists that he needs her and regards him as a helpless little boy that has to be looked after. He may complain about being mothered or simply deny that it is happening or that he is dependent on her. Often it is not denied so much as trivialized. He may concede he is dependent in a limited way but insist that she is replaceable.[3]

Often in the interview men would agree that 'office wife' was an appropriate way to describe their secretaries, while the secretary would insist that 'mother' was more accurate. The secretary may exercise a lot of power through setting up as 'second in command' and insisting that everything go through her. Difficulties often arise where the boss is a woman: the two may be rivals for the position of mother, and the secretary is in danger of losing out and becoming the daughter. Secretaries are ambivalent about mothering women. The difference between mothering sons and daughters is reproduced here. They tend to think the latter should learn to do things for themselves and hence are reluctant to do as much for women bosses, who should do their own secretarial work. The relationship works best where one or other is acknowledged as mother.

Third there is a discourse of reciprocity–equality. This is supposedly gender neutral with no fixed subject and object positions. The secretary works *with* rather than *for* the boss, and they operate as a 'team'. This is the 'modern' form, often accentuated by the fact that the secretaries work for a number of people and not just one. Even in this situation remnants of the one-to-one relation are preserved by both parties. 'The boss' is differentiated from the others she 'works for' and is the only one to receive personal services. In turn she expects his protection and support. To the extent that bosses and secretaries are already positioned by the other two discourses it is hard to ignore gender here. While secretaries like to believe in reciprocity the relation is usually very one way.

Richard is a senior advertising executive, in his mid-30s, married with young children. Stephanie is in her late 20s and is single. On the face of it they do not have a 'master–slave' relationship. They see themselves as much more modern. The relationship is couched in terms of equality and reciprocity. Yet as he talks it becomes clear that the 'team' approach is interwoven with others. Richard wants control and he has numerous strategies for gaining it. They rarely operate through coercion but rather out of his 'caring' for her. This is possible because of the emphasis placed on the personal relationship, the joking and socializing and the breaking down of the division between home and work. He is able to define what gives her pleasure and self-esteem and insist that he knows what is 'best' for her.

The extent of the demand that is placed on Stephanie is both acknowledged and denied. Richard claims that it works on a 'swings and roundabouts' basis. If there is nothing happening she can take time off. She agrees that it's 'give and take'. But 'give and take' hardly seems to fit the situation described. Not only does Stephanie put in 70–80 hours a week, working overtime at short notice and with no additional pay. She is placed in a position where it is virtually impossible to have a social life, let alone a domestic life. In exchange she is allowed to have the occasional day off or a long lunch.

Although he talks the language of reciprocity, Richard sees her as being there primarily to meet *his* needs: to anticipate, protect and provide emotional support. It is a very gentle version of master–slave: she recognizes him without any reciprocal right for recognition. It is crucial to him that she experiences pleasure as evidence that she does these things because she cares and is not merely obeying because she is paid to do so. That she does so voluntarily obscures from both of them the underlying dynamic. This kind of misrecognition is very common amongst secretaries who have a lot vested in believing that they have a reciprocal relationship with their boss. That there is 'give and take' is an indication that they are respected as autonomous beings. To maintain this belief they have to deny the extent to which bosses withhold that recognition and treat secretaries essentially as extensions of themselves.

Her 'minding' activities stretch much further than he is prepared to admit. She reveals, for example, how she gets together with his wife to organize the most basic everyday tasks:

> . . . his wife writes him notes so I check through his briefcase to make sure he does everything that Jan's asked him to do. . . . She will ring up and say, listen, make sure he does this. . . . Between us we plot and plan his dentists and doctors because he doesn't want to know about it. . .

The Case of Secretaries 173

For Richard to disclose this would be to admit a degree of dependence that could threaten his autonomy and take away his sense of mastery. What enters here is another discourse in which he is actually object rather than subject. I have called this the mother–son discourse yet this suggests that Stephanie exercises more power than she does. She is positioned as more servile than 'mother' or 'wife'. 'Nanny' might be the better term, if a trifle archaic, for it conveys a servant who is being paid to carry out this task. (Nanny–naughty little boy who needs punishment, fits quite comfortably into the theme of emotional sadomasochism.)

If male managers use sexuality and family relations to establish their control over secretaries and other staff so too do women managers. But the forms and strategies are rather different. Relations between women bosses and their secretaries are largely organized around narcissism and mother–daughter relationships. Shared taste and style and particularly clothes are often important, as the film *Working Girl* made clear. The kinds of pleasure in coercion that are present with male bosses are notably absent here: power rests on some kind of mutual identification whereby the secretary usually puts herself in the place of the other and therefore 'automatically' does what she wants. Where men may treat their secretaries 'narcissistically' as an extension of themselves, it is in the sense of an appendage; with women it is more like holding up a mirror to each other. It is possible to experience such merging as either pleasurable or dangerous.

A secretary is often able to get some power in relation to male bosses by occupying the position of the 'mother'. But typically women bosses take prior claim to this position, whatever the ages and actual mothering experiences of themselves and their secretaries. This is not surprising since 'mother' is the most powerful symbol available to women. It is central in many women managers' strategies for control, over both secretaries and other staff. Older secretaries, especially the ones who could set themselves up as mother, often find this difficult. In one case the secretary was treated almost as the 'grandmother'. The mothering of the younger woman was heavily emphasized and the relationship was constructed as the adult daughter 'looking after' the ageing mother!

Though sexuality and mother–daughter symbolism are central to the flow of power between women bosses and secretaries the subject of lesbianism is taboo. The fear of such an accusation undoubtedly places limits on the expression of intimacy or affection between women. Where one or other of the women is openly lesbian, the intimacy may be less threatening because a formal barrier has been set up; and the possible sexual meanings of one adult woman 'mothering' another do not have to be suppressed. In one or two cases where the boss was a lesbian, they were turned into a game and the heterosexuality of the secretary was not in any way threatened. She could indulge in role plays and flirtations with the 'deviant' boss. A lesbian secretary who works for a notorious 'tyrant' comments: 'I find it a little bit challenging to be working with a difficult woman . . . to manage to cope with her and learn to get on with her . . . you know, I wouldn't bother with a man.'

They have reached a point where it is possible to joke about each other's sexuality. The boss is curious about lesbian social life and can be teased to 'try it out'. In this way they construct a difference which in a sense marks out territory. A relationship that would have been destructively one-sided has been transformed into something much more equal by the slave's lesbian sexuality. Far from being a handicap, lesbianism has on this occasion been empowering for her.

Gender and sexuality

Central to Foucault's work is the idea that there is no constant human subject or any rational course to history. If there is no human subject then for Foucault there is no gendered subject. Feminist struggles are, like any others, merely immediate responses to local and specific situations. Recent psychoanalytically-informed feminist work would accept the non-rational, non-unitary character of the subject and the idea that masculinity and femininity are not fixed features located exclusively in men and women. Yet we still have to explain the reproduction of systematic gender differences and the relative fixity of gendered subject positions. While it may be the case that masculine and feminine subjects are never fully or permanently constituted there is nonetheless a primary process in which the elements are put into place.

Feminists have drawn on various psychoanalytic perspectives to find ways of combining an account of power as an expression of male interests and a structure of male domination with foucauldian insights into the strategies and counter-strategies of power. Together they enable us to see both how male and female identities are historically produced (primary process) and the ways in which these identities remain in a state of flux. Chodorow (1978) and Benjamin (1984) draw on object relations theory to give an account of masculine and feminine identity. Hollway (1984) and others use a more Lacanian perspective to emphasize the partial and fragile nature of gendered subjectivity, the ways in which it is produced in a series of competing discourses rather than in a single patriarchal ideology and the possibilities of intervention. Silverman (1984) speaks of the discursive 'surplus' which assures the stability of traditional definitions of the female subject across existing discourses and even new ones.

Benjamin (1984) engages directly with the question of the relationship between rationality, gender and sexuality. She argues that violent erotic fantasy can be understood as a response to the increasingly 'rational' character of our culture and the deprivation of nurturance. As the burden of rationality becomes intolerable, erotic fantasy appears as a response to a crisis of male rationality. Eroticism itself is rationalized and coded through the discourses and practices within which it is reproduced. Thus the rational and the irrational permeate each other. Instrumental rationality, while it presents itself as autonomous, and indeed the opposite of the private, is actually embedded in a (masculine) discourse of sado-masochism which structures all our emotional relationships and very particularly the boss–secretary relationship.

Benjamin looks at the devlopment of individual identity in terms of the relation between the need for autonomy and the need for recognition. Rather than finding a balance, in the reciprocal giving of self, we find the genders polarized into subject and object. Men gain autonomy at the price of denying the other's subjectivity and thus denying recognition of the other. Violence is a central part of maintaining their boundaries and denying their need for the other. It is also a way of searching for recognition through attempting to find the other person as an intact being who will set limits. Benjamin suggests that male individuality dovetails with what Western culture has defined as 'rationality'. We have been taken over by impersonal forms of social relation and an urge to control and objectify every living thing. Thus, she suggests, it is hard for any of us, male or female, to satisfy our desires for recognition, transcendence or continuity. These desires were once satisfied by religion and its rituals and by a sense of community. They are now catered for by sexuality and its associated rituals. She looks at the pleasure involved in fantasies and rituals of erotic domination and subordination. While her case study is from pornography (*The Story of O*) she makes it clear that the same tantalizing issues of control and submission flow beneath the surface of *all* sexual relations.

Through his mastery the man can remain in rational control, maintaining his separateness, denying his dependence and enjoying a sense of omnipotence. For the woman, the man's masterful control is a turn-on: it means she can safely lose control and experience a merging. In each case, the pleasure is at the price of denying one side of the self. Violence, whether actual, ritualized or fantasized, is an attempt to break out of the numbing barriers of self, to experience intensity and to come up against the boundaries of the other. Thus, says Benjamin, 'The fantasy, as well as the playing out of rational violence, does offer a controlled form of transcendence, the promise of the real thing' (1984:307). The 'real thing', she believes, is a balance between the opposing impulses for recognition and autonomy. Given that we live in a system in which this is very difficult to achieve, we are locked into a permanent set of games, fantasies, rituals of domination and submission from which we derive a great deal of erotic pleasure. In fantasies of erotic domination the man confirms his identity through the exercise of power over the other. What is important is that the submission be voluntary and that the annihilation of the object be indefinitely deferred. This prolongs the moment of recognition and thus, at least in fantasy, provides partial resolution.

All this talk of sadomasochism will sound extreme to anyone unfamiliar with the debates that have gone on in sexual politics. It may seem crazy that feminists should for a time have been preoccupied with the issue of lesbian sadomasochism, some celebrating it while others raged against it. While perhaps only a tiny minority of people self-consciously practice sadomasochistic rituals, the issue has been a lively one because it raises such fundamental questions about exchanges of power. It involves a recognition that power may inhere in sexuality rather than simply withering away in egalitarian relationships. In pointing to the importance of fantasy it places on the agenda questions about subjectivity and identity. This suggests a highly complex picture of the interplay of power, pleasure and desire.

The archetypal form of S/M is male domination/female submission but there is nothing fixed about this. The games can be played between men or between women and roles can constantly be reversed. We cannot assume that role reversals involve a reversal of power. It may be the ultimate in male power, for example, for a man to play the masochist if he chooses. Neither can we assume that it is the sadist who holds power, for the masochist may control the whole situation. In talking about secretaries we are forced to confront the extent to which power relations at work are organized around a particular form of heterosexuality based on sadomasochistic fantasy.

Sexual games are integral to the play of power at work, and success for women depends on how they negotiate their sexuality. It is often assumed they have only two choices. Either they can desexualize themselves and become 'honorary men' (the beige suit syndrome) or they can stay within femininity and be disempowered.

In fact women moving into management have a variety of strategies based around power and pleasure. These could include ritualized role reversals where, for example, a woman boss employs a male secretary or has an all-male workforce to nurture her, or narcissistic relations with other powerful women, or various ways of playing off men against each other. Clothes are an important means of empowerment. In wearing suits women are not transgressing gender, becoming 'men', but expressing a more masculine, instrumental relation to the body. To dress in this way is to *feel* like a man does, sexually empowered, an actor rather than an object to be looked at. Secretaries may adopt similar strategies to construct more assertive models of femininity. Since discourses have to be reproduced in specific situations there is always room to challenge and modify them. Rather than treating women as the pathetic victims of sexual harassment, it becomes possible to consider the power and pleasure they currently experience and ask how they can operate more on their own terms. The question then is which pleasures, if any, might threaten masculinity or disrupt rationality?

It makes no sense to banish sexuality from the workplace. What needs to be challenged is the way it is treated as an intruder, for this is the basis of the negative representation of women/sexuality/secretaries. It is by making it visible, exposing the masculinity that lurks behind gender-neutrality, asserting women's rights to be subjects rather than objects of sexual discourses, that bureaucracy can be challenged. The emphasis needs to be on processes of change rather than 'correct' or 'incorrect' practices. It is also important to remember that for women pleasure and danger will go on being in some kind of tension with each other, perhaps impossible to separate.

Notes

1. A short discussion of Weber's account of erotic love has recently been provided by Bologh (1987).
2. The prevalence of family symbolism in nursing is analysed in Game and Pringle (1983:Chapter 5).
3. Kanter (1975) describes a variety of paired stereotypes that may be influential in organizational life: macho/seductress; chivalrous knight/helpless maiden; possessive father/pet; tough warrior/nurturant mother.

The Sexuality of Organization: A Postscript

Jeff Hearn, Deborah L. Sheppard, Peta Tancred-Sheriff and Gibson Burrell

Writing, editing and compiling this book has been a social process, and an exciting and enjoyable one, spanning continents, countries, cultures and academic traditions. While 'completing' any written work is always an arbitrary stage, we think it will be useful to draw together in this postscript some of what we have learnt in this process. We will limit ourselves to brief commentaries on four questions: issues and themes; methods of enquiry; theory; and the future.

Issues and themes

When we began to compile this text we were acutely aware of the power and pervasiveness of sexuality in organizations. We were also conscious of the political and academic contribution of the surveys and studies of sexual harassment in many organizations (see Chapters 4 and 5). These starting assumptions have been more than confirmed. We have come to see both the regularity of patterns of domination in organizations and the ever-increasing subtlety of the processes whereby organizations are sexualized. On the first count, most of the chapters give information on the association of organizational domination and sexual domination. Within this theme, a number of comparisons may be made, for example between the experiences of lesbians (Chapter 8), women managers (Chapter 9) and secretaries (Chapter 10). Inevitably this constitutes a further and continuing critique of men's domination of both organizations and sexuality (see Chapter 6). On the second, some of the ways in which organizations are suffused with dominant forms of sexuality are explored in several chapters (especially Chapters 7–10). One of the most important themes to emerge from these latter chapters is the importance of ambiguity in charting the relationship of organizations and sexuality – indeed ambiguity surrounding what is organizational and what is sexual; and even the paradox that what is 'organizational' can become 'sexual' by being 'non-sexual'.

The subtlety of these processes in no way dilutes the patterns of domination just mentioned. On the contrary, it is difficult to overestimate the depth and complexity of the ways in which dominant forms of sexuality are produced and reproduced, not just in the broad structuring of organizations but also in the minutiae of organizations. Accordingly, an emerging theme of this book, and one that needs much more attention in future work, is the nature of the relationships between sexuality, gender and organizational structures. The relationship of gender and organizational structure has in recent years become more fully recognized as an important aspect of organization theory (see Chapters 2 and 3). Even so, gender often remains an encapsulated, separate area of interest in organization theory, not taken on board by malestream theorists in even the most obvious ways. In this respect much organization theory remains pre-scientific. What we and our co-writers in this book are engaged in is an attempt to develop discourse on the relationship of sexuality, gender and organizations. For example, different degrees of hierarchy in organizations are likely to be associated with different forms of sexuality, and moreover heterosexuality, in those organizations. This is because of the general eroticization of dominance (MacKinnon, 1983), and the more specific association of hierarchy and heterosexuality (Zita, 1982). This theme is so pervasive that we should perhaps have named this text *The Heterosexuality of Organization*.

Methods of enquiry

The methods of enquiry adopted in the various chapters have varied considerably – from theoretical analysis to quantitative studies to qualitative and participant observations. We have learnt to appreciate the value of each method, and the way each contributes to the understanding and change of the sexuality of organization. This is not simply to acknowledge a plurality of method, but is a recognition of the need to draw on the range of relevant academic traditions. Thus we would see this collection as part of a rather gradual movement towards interdisciplinarity.

Such a relational perspective is apparent in other ways. An emerging theme of the collection is the development of theory that is 'neither subjective nor objective, neither absolutist nor relativist [that] occupies the middle ground excluded by these oppositional categories' (Grosz, 1987:479). Another relational theme is the continual interrelating of practice and theory, so that the contributions have implications for both theoretical understanding and practical change. And a third is the relation between the focus on sexuality 'itself', and the focus on the connections between sexuality and gender, as well as between sexuality and other social divisions. Sexuality is, in this sense, impossible to isolate: it is not possessed like dress; it exists as and in social relations.

Theory

These methodological and conceptual questions have definite implications for theory and theorizing. The standpoint of this collection is feminist/profeminist; but what that means for the theorizing of the sexuality of organizations remains contested, and in tension. We see sexuality, and its social organization and social control, as fundamental to gender relations in general and patriarchy in particular (MacKinnon, 1982), and thus to organizations. However, the relational perspective of feminist theory and practice suggests it is mistaken to separate sexuality from its (and other) social relations. The various emphases in feminism on the relational (Ferguson, 1988) can be seen as developing in relation to postmodernism, and in counterpoint to modernist traditions. Thus, as Elizabeth Grosz continues: 'feminists will attempt to occupy the impossible, paradoxical position of the middle ground, the ground left uncovered by the oppositional structure – being both subject and object, self and other, reason and passion, mind and body, rather than one or the other' (1987:480).

While male-dominated postmodernism and male postmodernist theorists are frequently genderblind and anti-feminist, some feminists (e.g. Ferguson, 1988; Morris, 1988) see the interaction of feminism and postmodernism as a source of further vitality for feminism. The implications of this latter interaction for the theorizing of organizations, and specifically the sexuality of organization, remain open and diverse. Organizations and organization theories may come to be understood and changed as discourses (Ferguson, 1987). And while there are powerful critiques of discourse theory, feminism, unlike most traditions and certainly most traditions of organization theory, seems able to accept the *sexualization of discourse* – 'that all discourses are produced from and themselves occupy sexually coded positions' (Grosz, 1987:479–80).

Sexuality shares something with postmodernism and feminism, and in a different way profeminism, in its energy, variability and relationality. Organizations, as one of the major social forms of the public domain, and indeed the sexuality of organization, represent powerful areas for the exploration and change of the interrelation of feminism, postmodernism, profeminism and sexuality.

The future

What shape will these interactions take in the future? While we are not in the business of prediction, we do recognize some implications of our work for future practices and policies around the sexuality of organizations. However, as you might expect, the implications are not part of any linear progression; rather they are complex and contradictory. On one hand, we see the likely further desexualization of organizations – the stipulation of 'non-sexual' spaces in some organizations; of employment contracts which proscribe sexual relationships between employees, or between employees and clients – in short the attempt to exlude sexuality from workplace organizations at least (see Chapter 4). On the other, we see the likely further sexualization of organizations – the use of cellular telephone, computer, satellite television and other electronic technologies to suffuse organizations, and the world of consumption around them, with sexuality and sexual imagery; the persistent sexualization of women (Haug et al., 1987), and increasingly of men too, in advertising (Wernick, 1987); the abundance of 'panic sex' (Kroker and Cook, 1988). This apparent contradiction is partly evidence of an increasing separation of sexual activity and sexual representation. Organizational policies are certainly and urgently needed on some aspects of sexuality in some organizations, for example in residential care organizations (see Chapter 7). However, the proceduralization of sexuality in all its aspects is neither possible nor desirable. Furthermore, organizational procedures and controls are likely to lead to a resexualization of that which is proscribed and is held to be 'non-sexual'. Between these historical processes of desexualization and sexualization, of exclusion and suffusion, we recognize the need to make visible the dynamics of sexuality and power in organizations (see Chapter 10), and so continue the debate on the sexuality of organization.

Bibliography

Abbey, A (1982) 'Sex Differences in Attribution for Friendly Behavior: Do Males Misperceive Females' Friendliness?', *Journal of Personality and Social Psychology*, 42(5):830–8.

Abbey, A. (1987) 'Misperceptions of Friendly Behavior as Sexual Interest: a Survey of Naturally Occurring Incidents', *Psychology of Women Quarterly*, 11(2):173–95.

Abbey, A., C. Cozzorelli, K. McLaughlin and R. Harnish (1987) 'The Effects of Clothing and Dyad Sex Composition on Perceptions of Sexual Intent: Do Women and Men Evaluate these Cues Differently?', *Journal of Applied Social Psychology*, 17:108–26.

Abbey, A. and C. Melby (1986) 'The Effects of Nonverbal Cues on Gender Differences in Perceptions of Sexual Intent', *Sex Roles*, 15(5/6):283–98.

Abella, R. S. (1984) *Equality in Employment*. A Royal Commission Report. Ottawa: Ministry of Supply and Services Canada.

Abernathy, W. J., K. B. Clark and A. M. Kantrow (1983) *Industrial Renaissance. Producing a Competitive Future for America*. New York: Basic Books.

Adams, M. L. (1989) 'There's No Place Like Home: On the Place of Identity in Feminist Politics', *Feminist Review*, 31:22–33.

Alliance Against Sexual Coercion (1980) *Sexual Harassment: an Annotated Bibliography*. Cambridge, MA.: Alliance Against Sexual Coercion.

Alliance Against Sexual Coercion (1981) 'Organizing against Sexual Harassment', *Radical America*, 15:17–36.

American Federation of State, County and Municipal Employees (n.d.) *On-the-Job Sexual Harassment: What the Union Can Do*. Washington, DC: AFSCME.

Ardener, S. (1978) *Defining Females: the Nature of Women in Society*. London: Croom Helm.

Ardill, S. and S. O'Sullivan (1986) 'Upsetting an Applecart: Difference, Desire and Lesbian Sadomasochism', *Feminist Review*, 23:31–57.

Armstrong, P. and H. Armstrong (1983) *A Working Majority*. Ottawa: Canadian Advisory Council on the Status of Women.

Bachrach, P. and M. S. Baratz (1962) 'Two Faces of Power', *American Political Science Review*, 56(4):947–52.

Bachrach, P. and M. S. Baratz (1963) 'Decisions and Nondecisions: an Analytical Framework', *American Political Science Review*, 57(3):632–42.

Balsamo, A. (1985) 'Beyond Female as Variable: Constructing a Feminist Perspective on Organizational Analysis', Paper prepared for the conference 'Critical Perspectives in Organizational Analysis', September.

Barker, J. and H. Downing (1980) 'Word Processing and the Transformation of Patriarchal Relations of Control in the Office', *Capital and Class*, Special issue 10 (Spring):64–99.

Bibliography 183

Barrett, M. (1988) *Women's Oppression Today*, 2nd edn. London: Verso.
Barrett, M. and M. McIntosh (1982) *The Anti-Social Family*. London: Verso.
Barron, R. and G. Norris (1976) 'Sexual Division and the Dual Labour Market', in D. Barker and S. Allen (eds) *Dependence and Exploitation in Work and Marriage*, pp. 47–69. London: Tavistock.
Bateson, G. (1972) *Steps to an Ecology of Mind*. New York: Ballantine.
Beard, K., H. Hawksworth, B. A. Heritage, M. Hopkin and S. Seal (n.d.) *Coping with Growing Up*. Produced by staff at Residential Unit for Mentally Handicapped Children and Young Adults, 18 Carlton Close, Hemsworth.
Beer, C., R. Jeffery and T. Munyard (1983) *Gay Workers: Trade Unions and the Law*. (1st published 1981). London: NCCL.
Bell, A. P. and M. S. Weinberg (1978) *Homosexualities: a Study of Diversity among Men and Women*. New York: Simon and Schuster.
Bem, S. L. (1974) 'The Measurement of Psychological Androgyny', *Journal of Consulting and Clincial Psychology*, 42:155–62.
Bem, S. L. (1981) 'Gender Schema Theory: a Cognitive Account of Sex-typing', *Psychological Review*, 88:354–64.
Benjamin, J. (1984) 'Master and Slave: the Fantasy of Erotic Domination', in A. Snitow, C. Stansell and S. Thompson (eds) *Desire: the Politics of Sexuality*, pp. 280–99. London: Virago. New York: Monthly Review Press.
Benson, J. K. (1977) 'Organizations: a Dialectical View', *Administrative Science Quarterly*, 22:1–22.
Benson, S. P. (1986) *Counter Cultures: Saleswomen, Managers, and Customers in American Department Stores, 1890–1940*. Urbana and Chicago: University of Illinois Press.
Bernardin, H. (ed.) (1982) *Women in the Work Force*. New York: Praeger.
Bilton, T., K. Bonnett, P. Jones, M. Stanworth, K. Sheard and A. Webster (1983) *Introductory Sociology*. London: Macmillan.
Bittner, E. (1965) 'The Concept of Organization', *Social Research*, 32(3):239–55.
Blau, P. M. and M M. Meyer (1971) *Bureaucracy in Modern Society*. New York: Random House.
Blau, P. and W. R. Scott (1963) *Formal Organizations*. Boston and London: Routledge & Kegan Paul.
Blauner, R. (1967) *Alienation and Freedom*. Chicago: University of Chicago Press.
Blumstein, P. and P. Schwartz (1983) *American Couples*. New York: William Morrow.
Bologh, R. W. (1987) 'Max Weber on Erotic Love: a Feminist Inquiry', in S. Whimster and S. Lash (eds) *Max Weber, Rationality and Modernity*, pp. 242–58. London: Allen & Unwin.
Borisoff, D. and L. Merrill (1985) *The Power to Communicate. Gender Differences as Barriers*. Illinois: Waveland Press.
Boseley, S. (1983) 'Disabled Sit in over Hostel Sacking', *The Guardian*, 29 Oct.:3.
Braverman, H. (1974) *Labor and Monopoly Capital*. New York: Monthly Review Press.
Brittan, A. B. (1989) *Masculinity and Power*. Oxford: Basil Blackwell.
Brooks, V. (1981) *Minority Stress and Lesbian Women*. Lexington, MA: Lexington.
Broverman, I. K., D. M. Broverman, F. E. Clarkson, P. S. Rosenkrantz and S. F. Vogel (1981) 'Sex-Role Stereotypes and Clinical Judgements', in E. Howell and M. Bayes (eds) *Women and Mental Health*, pp. 86–97. New York: Basic Books.

Bruegel, I. (1979) 'Women as a Reserve Army of Labour: a Note on Recent British Experience', *Feminist Review*, 3:12–23.
Burrell, G. (1984) 'Sex and Organizational Analysis', *Organization Studies*, 5(2):97–118.
Burrell, G. (1988) 'Modernism, Post-Modernism and Organizational Analysis 2: the Contribution of Michel Foucault', *Organization Studies*, 9(2):221–36.
Burrell, G. and G. Morgan (1979) *Sociological Paradigms and Organizational Analysis*. London: Heinemann.
Campaign for Homosexual Equality (1981) *What About the Gay Workers?*. London: CHE.
Carothers, S. C. and P. Crull (1984) 'Contrasting Sexual Harassment in Female and Male Dominated Occupations', in K. Brodkin-Sacha and D. Remy (eds) *My Troubles are Going to have Trouble with Me*, pp. 219–28. New Brunswick, NJ: Rutgers University Press.
Chafetz, J., P. Sampson, P. Beck and J. West (1974) 'A Study of Homosexual Women', *Social Work*, 19(6):714–23.
Chatov, R. (1981) 'Cooperation between Government and Business', in P. C. Nystrom and W. H. Starbuck (eds) *Handbook of Organizational Design, Vol. 2*, pp. 487–502. New York: Oxford University Press.
Cheek, D. (1976) *Assertive Black . . . Puzzled White*. San Luis Obispo, CA: Impact Publishers.
Chodorow, N. (1971) 'Being and Doing: a Cross-Cultural Examination of the Socialization of Males and Females', in V. Gornick and B. K. Moran (eds) *Women in Sexist Society*, pp. 259–91. New York: New American Library.
Chodorow, N. (1978) *The Reproduction of Mothering: Psychoanalysis and the Sociology of Gender*. Berkeley, CA: University of California Press.
Clark, L. M. G. and L. Lange (1979) *The Sexism of Social and Political Theory*. Toronto: University of Toronto Press.
Clegg, S. (1981) 'Organization and Control', *Administrative Science Quarterly*, 26:545–62.
Clegg, S. and D. Dunkerley (1980) *Organization, Class and Control*. London: Routledge & Kegan Paul.
Clegg, S. and W. Higgins (1987) 'Against the Current: Organizational Sociology and Socialism', *Organization Studies*, 8(3):201–21.
Cockburn, C. (1983) *Brothers. Male Dominance and Technological Change*. London: Pluto Press.
Cockburn, C. (1988) 'Masculinity, the Left and Feminism', in R. Chapman and J. Rutherford (eds) *Male Order: Unwrapping Masculinity*, pp. 303–29. London: Lawrence & Wishart.
Cockburn, C. (1989) 'Equal Opportunities: the Short and Long Agendas', *Industrial Relations Journal*, 20(3).
Cockburn, C. (1990) 'Men's Power in Organizations: "Equal Opportunities" Intervenes', in J. Hearn and D. H. J. Morgan (eds) *Men, Masculinity and Social Theories*. London/Winchester, MA.: Unwin Hyman.
Cohen, A. and B. A. Gutek (1985) 'Dimensions of Perceptions of Social–Sexual Behavior in a Work Setting', *Sex Roles*, 13:317–27.
Coles, F. S. (1985) 'Sexual Harassment: Complainant Definitions and Agency Responses', *Labor Law Journal*, 36(6):369–76.
Coley, L and R. Marler (1987) 'Responding to the Sexuality of People with a Mental Handicap', in G. Horobin (ed) *Sex, Gender and Care Work, Research Highlights*

Bibliography 185

in Social Work, No. 15, pp 66–81. New York: St Martin's. London: Jessica Kingsley.
Collins, E. G. C. (1983) 'Managers and Lovers', *Harvard Business Review*, 61(5):141–53.
Collinson, D. L. (1981) 'Managing the Shopfloor', unpublished Msc thesis, UMIST, Manchester, UK.
Collinson, D. L. (1988a) 'Engineering Humour: Masculinity, Joking and Conflict in Shopfloor Relations', *Organization Studies*, 9(2):181–99.
Collinson, D. L. (1988b) *Barriers to Fair Selection: a Multi-Sector Study of Recruitment Practices*. London: Equal Opportunities Commission/HMSO.
Collinson, D. L. (1988c) 'Managing to Discriminate: Power and Agency in the Recruitment Process', unpublished PhD dissertion, Manchester School of Management, UMIST, Manchester, UK.
Community Care (1988) 'Row Prompts Complaints Review' (8 Sept.):1.
Connell, R. W. (1983) *Which Way is Up?* London, Boston, Sydney: Allen & Unwin.
Connell, R. W. (1985) 'Theorising Gender', *Sociology* 19(2):260–72.
Connell, R. W. (1987) *Gender and Power*. Cambridge: Polity Press.
Constantinople, A. (1973) 'Maculinity–Feminity: an Exception to a Famous Dictum', *Psychological Bulletin*, 80:389–407.
Cooper, R. and G. Burrell (1988) 'Modernism, Postmodernism and Organizational Analysis: an Introduction', *Organization Studies*, 9(1):91–112.
Cooper, C. and M. Davidson (1982) *High Pressure. Working Lives of Women Managers*. Glasgow: Collins/Fontana.
Coward, R. (1982) 'Sexual Violence and Sexuality', *Feminist Review*, 11:9–22.
Coward, R. (1984) *Female Desire. Women's Sexuality Today*. London: Collins/Paladin.
Cox, A. (1982) *The Cox Report on the American Corporation*. Chicago: Delacorte.
Creed, B. (1984) 'The Women's Romance as Sexual Fantasy: "Mills & Boon"', in Women and Labour Publications Collective, *All Her Labours: Embroidering the Framework*, pp. 47–67. Sydney: Hale & Iremonger.
Crompton, R. and G. Jones (1984) *White-Collar Proletariat*. London: Macmillan.
Crozier, M. (1964) *The Bureaucratic Phenomenon*. London: Tavistock. Chicago: University of Chicago Press.
Crull, P. (1982) 'Stress Effects of Sexual Harassment on the Job: Implications for Counseling', *American Journal of Orthopsychiatry*, 52(3):539–94.
Daniels, K. (ed.) (1984) *So Much Hard Work. Women and Prostitution in Australian History*. Sydney: Collins/Fontana.
Davis, L. (1980) 'Sex and the Residential Setting', in R. G. Walton and D. Elliott (eds) *Residential Care: a Reader*, pp. 263–72. Oxford: Pergamon.
Davis, S. M. (1984) *Managing Corporate Culture*. Cambridge, MA: Ballinger.
Deal, T. E. and A. A. Kennedy (1982) *Corporate Cultures*. Reading, MA: Addison-Wesley.
Deaux, K. (1985) 'Sex and Gender', *Annual Review of Psychology*, 36:49–81.
Deaux, K. and L. L. Lewis (1984) 'The Structure of Gender Stereotypes: Interrelationships among Components and Gender Labels', *Journal of Personality and Social Psychology*, 46:991–1004.
De Beauvoir, S. (1972) *The Second Sex* (1st edn 1949). Harmondsworth, Middlesex: Penguin Books.
Delacoste, F. and P. Alexander (eds) (1988) *Sex Work: Writings by Women in the Sex Industry*. London: Virago.

D'Emilio, J. and E. Freedman (1988) *Intimate Matters: a History of Sexuality in America*. New York: Harper & Row.

Denhart, R. B. (1981) *In the Shadow of Organization*. Lawrence, KS: Regents Press.

Dennis, N., F. Henriques and C. Slaughter (1969) *Coal is our Life*. London: Eyre & Spottiswoode.

Diamond, I. and L. Quinby (1984) 'American Feminism in the Age of the Body', *Signs*, 10(1):119–25.

Dubeck, P. J. (1979) 'Sexism in Recruiting Management Personnel for a Manufacturing Firm', in R. Alverez and Associates, *Discrimination in Organizations*, pp. 88–99. London: Jossey-Bass.

Dunwoody-Miller, V. and B. A. Gutek (1985) *S.H.E. Project Report: Sexual Harassment in the State Workforce: Results of a Survey*. Sacramento, CA: Sexual Harassment in Employment Project of the California Commission on the Status of Women.

Dworkin, A. (1981) *Pornography: Men Possessing Women*. London: The Women's Press.

Edwards, R. (1979) *Contested Terrain*. New York: Basic Books.

Ehrenreich, B. and D. English (1979) *For Her Own Good. 150 Years of the Experts' Advice to Women*. London: Pluto Press.

Eichler, M. (1980) *The Double Standard*. New York: St Martin's.

Eldridge, J. E. T. and A. D. Crombie (1974) *A Sociology of Organizations*. London: Allen & Unwin.

Elshtain, J. B. (1981) *Public Man, Private Woman*. Oxford: Martin Robertson.

Engels, F. (1972) *The Origins of the Family, Private Property and the State* (1st published 1884). London: Lawrence & Wishart.

Engels, F. (1975) 'The Condition of the Working-Class in England' (1st published 1845), in K. Marx and F. Engels, *Collected Works*, Vol. 4, pp. 295–596. London: Lawrence & Wishart.

Equal Employment Opportunity Commission (1980) 'Guidelines on Discrimination on the Basis of Sex' (29 CFR Part 1604), *Federal Register*, 45 (219).

Farley, L. (1978) *Sexual Shakedown: the Sexual Harassment of Women on the Job*. London: Melbourne House. New York: McGraw Hill.

Featherstone, M. (1988) 'In Pursuit of the Postmodern: an Introduction', *Theory, Culture & Society*, 5(2/3):195–215.

Feminist Review Collective (1982) 'Editorial', *Feminist Review*, 11:1–4.

Ferguson, A. (1984) 'Sex War: the Debate between Radical and Libertarian Feminists', *Signs*, 10(1):106–12.

Ferguson, K. E. (1984) *The Feminist Case against Bureaucracy*. Philadelphia, PA: Temple University Press.

Ferguson, K. E. (1987) 'Work, Text, and Act in Discourses of Organization', *Women and Politics*, 7(2):1–21.

Ferguson, K. E. (1988) 'Subject-centredness in Feminist Discourse', in K. B. Jones and A. G. Jónasdóttir (eds) *The Political Interests of Gender, Developing Theory and Research with a Feminist Face*, pp. 66–78. London, Newbury Park: Sage.

Finch, J. and D. Groves (1982) 'By Women for Women: Caring for the Frail Elderly', *Women's Studies International Forum*, 5 (5):427–38.

Fine, G. A. (1987) 'One of the Boys: Women in Male Dominated Settings', in M. S. Kimmel (ed.) *Changing Men: New Directions in Research on Men and Masculinity*, pp. 131–47. London: Sage.

Bibliography 187

Foucault, M. (1976) *The Archaeology of Knowledge* (1st published 1969). London: Tavistock.

Foucault, M. (1977) *Discipline and Punish: the Birth of the Prison* (1st published 1975). Harmondsworth, Middlesex: Allen Lane, Penguin Books. New York: Vintage Books.

Foucault, M. (1979) *The History of Sexuality*, Vol. 1 (1st published 1976). New York: Vintage Books.

Foucault, M. (1988) 'Technologies of the Self', in L. H. Martin, H. Gutman and P. H. Hutton (eds) *Technologies of the Self, a Seminar with Michel Foucault*, pp. 16–49. Boston: University of Massachusetts Press. London: Tavistock.

Foushee, H. C., R. L. Helmreich and J. T. Spence (1979) 'Implicit Theories of Masculinity and Femininity: Dualistic or Bipolar?', *Psychology of Women Quarterly*, 3:259–69.

Franklin, U. M. (1985) *Will Women Change Technology or Will Technology Change Women?* Ottawa, Ont.: Canadian Research Institute for the Advancement of Women, Paper No. 9.

Gagnon, J. and W. Simon (1973) *Sexual Conduct, the Social Sources of Human Sexuality*. Chicago: Aldine.

Game, A. and R. Pringle (1983) *Gender at Work*. Sydney, London, Boston: Allen & Unwin.

Game, A. and R. Pringle (1986) 'Beyond *Gender at Work*: Secretaries', in N. Grieve and A. Burns (eds) *Australian Women: New Feminist Perspectives*, pp. 273–91. Melbourne: Oxford University Press.

Gerth, H. H. and C. W. Mills (eds) (1958) *From Max Weber: Essays in Sociology*. New York: Galaxy.

Gilligan, C. (1982) *In a Different Voice. Psychological Theory and Women's Development*. Cambridge, MA: Harvard University Press.

Giorgi, A. (1975) *Duquesne Studies in Phenomenological Psychology*, Vol. 2. Atlantic Highlands, NJ: Humanities Press.

Glass, S. P. and T. L. Wright (1985) 'Sex Differences in Type of Extramarital Involvement and Marital Dissatisfaction', *Sex Roles*, 12(9/10):1101–20.

GLC (Greater London Council) (1985) *Danger! . . . Heterosexism at Work*. London: GLC.

Glenn, Evelyn Nakano and Roslyn L. Feldberg (1979) 'Women as Mediators in the Labor Process', paper presented to the American Sociological Association Meeting, Boston, MA.

Glennon, L. M. (1983) 'Synthesism: a Case of Feminist Methodology', in G. Morgan (ed.) *Beyond Method*, pp. 260–71. London: Sage.

Goffman, E. (1961) *Asylums*. Harmondsworth, Middlesex: Penguin Books. New York: Doubleday.

Goffman, E. (1963) *Stigma*. Englewood Cliffs, NJ: Prentice-Hall.

Goodchilds, J. D. and G. L. Zellman (1984) 'Sexual Signaling and Adolescent Aggression in Adolescent Relationships', in N. M. Malamuth and E. Donnerstein (eds) *Pornography and Sexual Aggression*, pp. 233–43. Orlando, FL: Academic Press.

Gordon, L. (1981) 'The Politics of Sexual Harassment', *Radical America*, 15:7–16.

Gould, R. E. (1974) 'Measuring Masculinity by the Size of a Paycheck', in J. H. Pleck and J. Sawyer (eds) *Men and Masculinity*, pp. 96–100. Englewood Cliffs, NJ: Prentice-Hall.

Grady, K.E. (1977) 'Sex as a Social Label: the Illusion of Sex Differences', unpublished PhD dissertation, City University, New York.

Grauerholz, E. and R. T. Serpe (1985) 'Initiation and Response: the Dynamics of Sexual Interaction', *Sex Roles*, 12(9/10): 1041–59.

Gray, S. (1984) 'Romance in the Workplace: Corporate Rules for the Game of Love', *Business Week*, 2847:70–1.

Gray, S. (1987) 'Sharing the Shopfloor', in M. Kaufman (ed.) *Beyond Patriarchy. Essays by Men on Pleasure, Power and Change*, pp. 216–34. Toronto: Oxford University Press.

Greenglass, E. (1982) *A World of Difference: Gender Roles in Perspective*. Toronto: John Wiley.

Grosz, E. (1987) 'Feminist Theory and the Challenge to Knowledge', *Women's Studies International Forum*, 10:475–80.

The Guardian (1988) 'Children's Home Staff Harassed Over Sex Claim' (2 Sept.):20.

Gutek, B. A. (1985) *Sex and the Workplace: Impact of Sexual Behavior and Harassment on Women, Men and Organizations*. San Francisco, CA: Jossey-Bass.

Gutek, B. A. and A. Cohen (1987) 'Sex Ratios, Sex Role Spillover, and Sex at Work: a Comparison of Men's and Women's Experiences', *Human Relations*, 40(2):97–115.

Gutek, B. A., A. Cohen and A. Konrad (forthcoming) *Sex Composition and Sex: Predicting Social–Sexual Behavior in the Workplace*.

Gutek, B. A. and V. Dunwoody (1987) 'Understanding Sex in the Workplace', in A. Stromberg, L. Larwood and B. A. Gutek (eds) *Women and Work: an Annual Review*, Vol. 2, pp. 249–69. Newbury Park: Sage.

Gutek, B. A. and B. Morasch (1982) 'Sex Ratios, Sex-Role Spillover and Sexual Harassment of Women at Work', *Journal of Social Issues*, 38(4):55–74.

Gutek, B. A., B. Morasch and A. Cohen (1983) 'Interpreting Social Sexual Behavior in the Work Setting', *Journal of Vocational Behavior*, 22(1):30–48.

Gutek, B. A. and C. Nakamura (1982) 'Gender Roles and Sexuality in the World of Work', in El Allgeier and N. McCormick (eds) *Gender Roles and Sexual Behavior*, pp. 182–201. Palo Alto, CA: Mayfield.

Gutek, B. A., C. Y. Nakamura, M. Gahart, I. Handschumacher and D. Russell (1980) 'Sexuality and the Workplace', *Basic and Applied Social Psychology*, 1:255–65.

Hakim, C. (1979) *Occupational Segregation: A Comparative Study of the Degree and Pattern of the Differentiation between Men and Women's Work in Britain, the United States and Other Countries*, Department of Employment Research Paper, No. 9. London: Department of Employment.

Hall, M. (1981) 'Gays in Corporations: the Invisible Minority', unpublished PhD dissertation, Union Graduate School, San Francisco, CA.

Hall, M. (1986) 'The Lesbian Corporate Experience', *Journal of Homosexuality*, 12(3/4):59–75.

Harragan, B. L. (1977) *Games Mother Never Taught You: Corporate Gamesmanship for Women*. New York: Warner Books.

Harrison, R. and R. Lee (1986) 'Love at Work', *Personnel Management*, Jan.: 20–4.

Hasenfeld, Y. (1972) 'People Processing Organizations', *American Sociological Review*, 37(3):256–63.

Haug, F. et al. (1987) *Female Sexualization. A Collective Work of Memory*. London: Verso (1st published in German 1983).

Hearn, J. (1985) 'Men's Sexuality at Work', in A. Metcalf and M. Humphries (eds) *The Sexuality of Men*, pp. 110–28. London: Pluto Press.
Hearn, J. (1987) *The Gender of Oppression: Men, Masculinity and the Critique of Marxism*. Brighton: Wheatsheaf. New York: St Martin's.
Hearn, J. and P. W. Parkin (1983) 'Gender and Organizations: a Selective Review and a Critique of a Neglected Area', *Organization Studies*, 4(3):219–42.
Hearn, J. and P. W. Parkin (1987) *'Sex' at 'Work'. The Power and Paradox of Organisation Sexuality*. Brighton: Wheatsheaf. New York: St Martin's.
Hearn, J. and P. W. Parkin (1988) 'Women, Men and Leadership: a Critical Review of Assumptions, Practices, and Change in the Industrialized Nations', in N. J. Adler and D. Izraeli (eds) *Women in Management Worldwide*, pp. 17–40. New York: M. E. Sharpe.
Hegel, G. (1949) *Phenomenology of Mind* (1st published 1807). London: Allen & Unwin.
Henley, N. M. (1977) *Body Politics. Power, Sex and Nonverbal Communication*. Englewood Cliffs, NJ: Prentice-Hall.
Hennig, M. and A. Jardim (1977) *The Managerial Woman*. New York: Anchor Books.
Hess, B. H. and M. M. Ferree (1987) *Analyzing Gender. A Handbook of Social Science Research*. Newbury Park, CA: Sage.
Hochschild, A. R. (1983) *The Managed Heart*. Berkeley, CA: University of California Press.
Hofstede, G. (1984) *Culture's Consequences*. London: Sage.
Hogbacka, R., I. Kandolin, E. Haavio-Mannila and K. Kauppinen-Toropainen (1987) *Sexual Harassment*. Equality Publications. Series E. Abstracts 2/1987. Helsinki: Ministry of Social Affairs, Finland.
Hoiberg, A. (ed.) (1982) *Women and the World of Work*. New York: Plenum Press.
Hollway, W. (1983) 'Heterosexual Sex: Power and Desire for the Other', in S. Cartledge and J. Ryan (eds) *Sex and Love. New Thoughts on Old Contradictions*, pp. 124–40. London: The Women's Press.
Hollway, W. (1984) 'Gender Difference and the Production of Subjectivity', in J. Henriques, W. Hollway, C. Urwin, C. Venn and V. Walkerdine, *Changing the Subject*, pp. 227–63. London: Methuen.
Holter, H. (ed.) (1984) *Patriarchy in a Welfare Society*. Oslo: Universitetsforlaget.
Homans, H. (1987) 'Man-Made Myths: the Reality of Being a Woman Scientist in the NHS', in A. Spencer and D. Podmore (eds) *In a Man's World: Essays on Women in Male-Dominated Professions*, pp. 87–112. London: Tavistock.
Horn, P. D. and J. C. Horn (1982) *Sex in the Office . . . Power and Passion in the Workplace*. Reading, MA: Addison-Wesley.
Howe, D. (1986) 'The Segregation of Women and Their Work in the Personal Social Services', *Critical Social Policy*, 5(3):21–35.
Hughes Report (1986) *Report of the Committee of Enquiry into Children's Homes and Hostels*. Belfast: HMSO.
Jay, A (1972) *Corporation Man*. London: Cape.
Jay, K. and A. Young (1972) *Out of the Closets*. Reading, MA: Addison-Wesley.
Jensen, I. and B. A. Gutek (1982) 'Attributions and Assignment of Responsibility in Sexual Harassment', *Journal of Social Issues*, 38(4):121–36.
Jones, B. (1972) 'Sex in the Office', *National Times*, 12 June.
Kahn-Hut, R., A. Kaplan-Daniels and R. Colvard (eds) (1982) *Women and Work: Problems and Perspectives*. New York: Oxford University Press.

Kanter, R. M. (1975) 'Women in Organizations: Sex Roles, Group Dynamics, and Change Strategies', in A. Sargent (ed.) *Beyond Sex Roles*. St. Paul, MN: West.

Kanter, R. M. (1977) *Men and Women of the Corporation*. New York: Basic Books.

Kanter, R. M. (1983) *The Change Masters. Corporate Entrepreneurship at Work*. New York: Simon and Schuster. London: Allen & Unwin.

Karr, R. G. (1978) 'Homosexual Labeling and the Male Role', *Journal of Social Issues*, 34(3):73–83.

Katz, D. and R. L. Kahn (1978) *The Social Psychology of Organizations* (1st published 1966). New York: John Wiley.

Keller, E. F. (1987) 'The Gender/Science System: Or is Sex to Gender as Nature is to Science', *Hypatia*, 2(3):37–49.

Kelly, L. (1987) 'The Continuum of Sexual Violence', in J. Hanmer and M. Maynard (eds) *Women, Violence and Social Control*, pp. 46–60. London: Macmillan.

Kerr, C. and A. Siegel (1954) 'The Interindustry Propensity to Strike – an International Comparison', in A. Kornhauser (ed.) *Industrial Conflict*, pp. 189–212. New York: McGraw-Hill.

Kessler, S. J. and W. McKenna (1978) *Gender: an Ethnomethodological Approach*. New York: John Wiley.

Khan, A. and A. J. Mills (1988) 'Retirement and Sex Discrimination', *Solicitors Journal*, 132(22):805–8.

Kilroe, S. and R. Wiener (1988) *Sexual Encounters in Health Care. A Training Manual*. Leeds: Leeds Polytechnic.

Kinsey, A. C., W. B. Pomeroy and C. E. Martin (1948) *Sexual Behavior in the Human Male*. Philadelphia, PA: Saunders.

Kleinberg, S. (1987) 'The New Masculinity of Gay Men, and Beyond', in M. Kaufman (ed.) *Beyond Patriarchy. Essays by Men on Pleasure, Power, and Change*, pp. 120–38. Toronto: Oxford University Press.

Kohn, M. M. (1971) 'Bureaucratic Man: a Portrait and an Interpretation', *American Sociological Review*, 36(3):461–74.

Konrad, A. M. and B. A. Gutek (1986) 'Impact of Work Experiences on Attitudes towards Sexual Harassment', *Administrative Science Quarterly*, 31:422–38.

Korda, M. (1972) *Male Chauvinism! How it Works*. New York: Random House.

Kristeva, J. (1980) *Desire in Language. A Semiotic Approach to Literature and Art*. Oxford: Basil Blackwell.

Kroker, A. and D. Cook (1988) *The Post-Modern Scene. Excremental Culture and Hyper-Aesthetics*. London: Macmillan.

Laing, R. (1970) *The Divided Self*. New York: Pantheon.

Laws, J. L. (1979) *The Second X: Sex Role and Social Role*. New York: Elsevier.

Laws, J. L. and P. Schwartz (1977) *Sexual Scripts: the Social Construction of Female Sexuality*. Hinsdale, IL: Dryden.

Leeds TUCRIC (1983) *Sexual Harassment of Women at Work*. Leeds: TUCRIC.

Levine, M. P. (1979) 'Employment Discrimination against Gay Men', *International Review of Modern Sociology*, 9(5/7):151–63.

Levine, M. P. and R. Leonard (1984) 'Discrimination against Lesbians in the Work Force'. *Signs*, 9(4):700–9.

Lindsey, K. (1977) 'Sexual Harassment on the Job, and How to Stop it', *Ms. Magazine*, 6(5):47–51, 73–8.

Lipman-Blumen, J. (1984) *Gender Roles and Power*. Englewood Cliffs, NJ: Prentice-Hall.

Lippert, J. (1977) 'Sexuality and Consumption', in J. Snodgrass (ed.) *A Book of Readings for Men against Sexism*, pp. 207–13. Albion, CA: Times Change.
Lockwood, D. (1958) *The Blackcoated Worker*. London: Unwin University Books.
Lowe, G. S. (1987) *Women in the Administrative Revolution. The Feminization of Clerical Work*. Cambridge: Polity Press. Toronto: University of Toronto Press.
Lupton, T. (1963) *On the Shop Floor*. Oxford: Pergamon.
Lyotard, J.-F. (1982) *The Post Modern Condition*. Manchester: Manchester University Press.
Mackie, M. (1987) *Constructing Women and Men. Gender Socialization*. Toronto: Holt, Rinehart and Winston.
MacKinnon, C. A. (1979) *Sexual Harassment of Working Women*. New Haven, CT: Yale University Press.
MacKinnon, C. A. (1982) 'Feminism, Marxism, Method and the State: an Agenda for Theory', *Signs*, 7(3):515–44.
MacKinnon, C. A. (1983) 'Feminism, Marxism, Method and the State: Toward Feminist Jurisprudence', *Signs*, 8(4):635–58.
Major, B., P. J. Carnevale and K. Deaux (1981) 'A Different Perspective on Androgyny: Evaluations of Masculine and Feminine Personality Characteristics', *Journal of Personality and Social Psychology*, 41:988–1001.
Marcuse, H. (1968) *One Dimensional Man*. London: Sphere Books.
Mayo, E. (1960) *The Human Problems of an Industrial Civilisation* (1st published 1933). New York: Viking.
McConaghy, N. (1967) 'Penile Volume Change to Moving Pictures of Male and Female Nudes in Heterosexual and Homosexual Males', *Behavior, Research and Therapy*, 5:43–8.
McLane, H. (1980) *Selecting, Developing and Retaining Women Executives*. New York: Van Nostrand.
Meehan, E. M. (1985) *Women's Rights at Work*. London: Macmillan.
Merleau-Ponty, M. (1962) *Phenomenology of Perception*. Atlantic Highlands, NJ: Humanities Press.
Mieli, M. (1980) *Homosexuality and Liberation—Elements of a Gay Critique*, London: Gay Men's Press.
Miller, J. B. (1976) *Toward a New Psychology of Women*. Boston, MA: Beacon Press.
Mills, A. J. (1987) 'Interview: Gareth Morgan', *Aurora*, 11(2):42–6.
Mills, A. J. (1988a) 'Organizational Acculturation and Gender Discrimination', in P. K. Kresl (ed.) *Canadian Issues, X(1) — Women and the Workplace*, pp. 1–22. Montreal: Association of Canadian Studies/International Council for Canadian Studies.
Mills, A. J. (1988b) 'Organization, Gender and Culture', *Organization Studies*, 9(3):351–69.
Minson, J. (1981) 'The Assertion of Homosexuality', *m/f*, 5/6:19–39.
Mitchell, J. (1975) *Feminism and Psychoanalysis*. Harmondsworth, Middlesex: Penguin Books.
Molloy, J. T. (1977) *The Woman's Dress for Success Book*. New York: Warner Books.
Morgan, D. H. J. (1981) 'Men, Masculinity and the Process of Sociological Inquiry', in H. Roberts (ed.) *Doing Feminist Research*, pp. 83–113. London: Routledge & Kegan Paul.

Morgan, G. (1980) 'Paradigms, Metaphors and Puzzle Solving in Organization Theory', *Administrative Science Quarterly*, 25:605–22.
Morgan, G. (1986) *Images of Organization*. London: Sage.
Morin, S. (1975) 'Attitudes toward Homosexuality and Social Distance', paper presented at the meeting of the American Psychological Association (Sept.), Chicago.
Morris, M. (1988) *The Pirate's Fiancé—Feminism, Reading, Postmodernism*. London, New York: Verso.
Moss, P. and N. Fonda (eds) (1980) *Work and the Family*. London: Temple Smith.
Murphy, G. (1988) 'The Effect of Heterosexism on Social Services', unpublished MA thesis, University of Bradford, Bradford, UK.
Neugarten, D. A. and J. M. Shafritz (eds) (1980) *Sexuality in Organizations. Romantic and Coercive Behaviors at Work*. Oak Park, IL: Moore.
Nieva, V. F. and B. A. Gutek (1981) *Women and Work: a Psychological Perspective*. New York: Praeger.
Noe, R. A. (1988) 'Women and Mentoring: a Review and Research Agenda', *Academy of Management Journal*, 13(1):65–78.
Oakley, A. (1972) *Sex, Gender and Society*. London: Temple Smith.
Oakley, A. (1981) *Subject Women*. New York: Pantheon.
O'Brien, M. (1981) *The Politics of Reproduction*. London: Routledge & Kegan Paul.
O'Farrell, B. and S. L. Harlan (1982) 'Craftworkers and Clerks: the Effects of Male Co-worker Hostility on Women's Satisfaction with Non-Traditional Jobs', *Social Problems*, 29:252–64.
Ouchi, W. (1981) *Theory Z: How American Business can Meet the Japanese Challenge*. Reading, MA: Addison-Wesley.
Pateman, C. (1988) *The Sexual Contract*. London: Polity Press.
Pearson, J. C. (1985) *Gender and Communication*. Iowa: Wm. C. Brown.
Peters, T. J. and R. H. Waterman (1982) *In Search of Excellence*. New York: Harper & Row.
Plummer, K. (1975) *Sexual Stigma, an Interactionist Account*. London: Routledge & Kegan Paul.
Pollert, A. (1981) *Girls, Wives, Factory Lives*. London: Macmillan.
Pringle, R. (1989) *Secretaries Talk: Sexuality, Power and Work*. London: Verso.
Quinn, R. E. (1977) 'Coping with Cupid: the Formation, Impact and Management of Romantic Relationships in Organizations', *Administrative Science Quarterly*, 22:30–45.
Rakow, L. F. (1986) 'Rethinking Gender Research in Communication', *Journal of Communication*, 36(4):11–24.
Réage, P. (1965) *The Story of O* (trans. S. d'Estree). New York: Grove Press.
Reiter, Esther (1986) 'Life in a Fast-Food Factory', in Heron, C. and R. Storey (eds) *On the Job*, pp. 309–26. Kingston and Montreal: McGill/Queen's.
Rich, A. (1984) 'Compulsory Heterosexuality and Lesbian Existence' (1st published 1980), in A. Snitow, C. Stansell and S. Thompson (eds) *Desire: the Politics of Sexuality*, pp. 212–41. London: Virago. New York: Monthly Review Press.
Riley, P. (1983) 'A Structurationist Account of Political Culture', *Administrative Science Quarterly*, 28:414–37.
Rosaldo, M. Z. (1974) 'Women, Culture and Society: a Theoretical Overview', in M. Z. Rosaldo and L. Lamphere (eds) *Women, Culture and Society*, pp. 17–42. Stanford, CA: Stanford University Press.

Rose, M. (1975) *Industrial Behaviour: Theoretical Development since Taylor.* London: Allen Lane.

Rubin, G. (1984) 'Thinking Sex: Notes for a Radical Theory for the Politics of Sexuality', in C. S. Vance (ed.) *Pleasure and Danger: Exploring Female Sexuality,* pp. 267–319. Boston, MA: London: Routledge & Kegan Paul.

Rubin, G., D. English and A. Hollibaugh (1981) 'Talking Sex: a Conversation on Sexuality and Feminism', *Socialist Review,* 58(11/4):43–62.

Ruble, T. L. (1983) 'Sex Stereotypes: Issues of Change in the 1970s', *Sex Roles,* 9(3):397–402.

Ryan, M. P. (1979) *Womanhood in America.* New York: New Viewpoints.

Saal, F. E. (1986) 'Males' Misperceptions of Females' Friendliness: Replication and Extension', paper presesnted at the Midwestern Psychological Association (May), Chicago.

Safran, C. (1976) 'What Men do to Women on the Job: a Shocking Look at Sexual Harassment', *Redbook Magazine,* 149:217–23.

Saghir, M. T. and E. Robins (1973) *Male and Female Homosexualities: a Comprehensive Investigation.* Baltimore, MD: Williams & Wilkins.

Sargent, A. (1983) *The Androgynous Manager.* New York: AMACOM.

Schein, Edgar H. (1985) *Organizational Culture and Leadership.* London: Jossey-Bass.

Schneider, B. E. (1981) 'Coming Out at Work: Detriments and Consequences of Lesbians' Openness at their Workplaces', paper presented at the Annual Meeting of the Society for the Study of Social Problems, Toronto.

Schneider, B. E. (1982) 'Consciousness about Sexual Harassment among Heterosexual and Lesbian Women Workers', *Journal of Social Issues,* 38(4):75–98.

Schneider, B. E. (1984) 'The Office Affair: Myth and Reality for Heterosexual and Lesbian Women Workers', *Sociological Perspectives,* 27(4):443–64.

Schneider, B. E. and M. Gould (1987) 'Female Sexuality: Looking Back into the Future', in B. H. Hess and M. M. Ferree (eds) *Analyzing Gender. A Handbook of Social Science Research,* pp. 120–53. Newbury Park, CA: Sage.

Scollard, J. R. (1983) *No-Nonsense Management Tips for Women.* New York: Pocket Books.

Scott, J. W. (1986) 'Gender: a Useful Category of Historical Analysis', *American Historical Review,* 91(5):1053–75.

Segal, L. (1987) *Is the Future Female?* London: Virago.

Sennett, R. and J. Cobb (1977) *The Hidden Injuries of Class.* London: Cambridge University Press.

Sharron, H. (1983) 'Getting Personal', *Social Work Today,* 15(3) (20 Sept.):4.

Sheriff, P. and E. J. Campbell (1981) 'La place des femmes: un dossier sur la sociologie des organisations', *Sociologie et sociétés,* 13:113–30.

Silverman, D. (1970) *The Theory of Organizations.* London: Heinemann.

Silverman, K. (1984) 'Histoire d'O: the Construction of a Female Subject', in C. Vance (ed.) *Pleasure and Danger. Exploring Female Sexuality,* pp. 320–49. Boston, MA. London: Routledge & Kegan Paul.

Simpson, R. L. and I. H. Simpson (1969) 'Women and Bureaucracy in the Semi-Professions', in A. Etzioni (ed.) *The Semi-Professions and their Organization,* pp. 196–265. New York: The Free Press.

Simpson, S., M. McCarrey and H. P. Edwards (1987) 'Relationship of Supervisors' Sex-Role Stereotypes to Performance Evaluation of Male and Female Subordinates in Nontraditional Jobs', *Canadian Journal of Administrative Sciences*, 4(1):15–30.

Smircich, L. (1985) 'Is the Concept of Culture a Paradigm for Understanding Organizations and Ourselves?', in P. J. Frost, L. F. Moore, M. R. Louis, C. C. Lundberg and J. Martin (eds) *Organizational Culture*, pp. 55–72. London: Sage.

Smith, D. E. (1975) 'An Analysis of Ideological Structures and how Women are Excluded: Considerations for Academic Women', *Canadian Review of Sociology and Anthropology*, 12(4), part 1:353–69.

Social Work Today (1988) 'New Complaints Procedure for Children in Care' (22 Sept.) 20(4):3.

Spence, J. T. and R. L. Helmreich (1978) *Masculinity and Femininity*. Austin, TX: University of Texas Press.

Spender, D. (1981) 'The Gatekeepers: a Feminist Critique of Academic Publishing', in H. Roberts (ed.) *Doing Feminist Research*, pp. 186–202. London: Routledge & Kegan Paul.

Stacey, M. and C. Davies (1983) *Division of Labour in Child Health Care: Final Report to the SSRC 1983* (Dec.). Coventry: University of Warwick.

Stacey, M. and M. Price (1981) *Women, Power and Politics*. London: Tavistock.

Stanley, L. (1984) 'Whales and Minnows: Some Sexual Theorists and their Followers and how they Contribute to Making Feminism Invisible', *Women's Studies International Forum*, 7(1):53–62.

Struminger, L. S. (1979) *Women and the Making of the Working Class: Lyon 1830–1870*. Vermont: Eden Press.

Tancred-Sheriff, P. (1985) 'Women's Experience, Women's Knowledge and the Power of Knowledge' *Atlantis*, 10:106–17.

Taylor, N. (ed.) (1986) *All in a Day's Work. A Report on Anti-Lesbian Discrimination in Employment and Unemployment in London*. London: Lesbian Employment Rights.

Thompson, P. (1983) *The Nature of Work*. London and Basingstoke: Macmillan.

Tolman, R. M., D. D. Mowry, L. E. Jones and J. Brekke (1986) 'Developing a Profeminist Commitment among Men in Social Work', in N. Van Den Bergh and L. B. Cooper (eds) *Feminist Visions for Social Work*, pp. 61–79. Silver Springs, MD: NASW.

Tresemer, D. W. (1975) 'Assumptions Made about Gender Roles', in M. Millman and R. M. Kanter (eds) *Another Voice: Feminist Perspectives on Social Life and Social Science*, pp. 308–39. New York: Doubleday Anchor.

Vance, C. (ed.) (1984) *Pleasure and Danger. Exploring Female Sexuality*. Boston, MA. London: Routledge & Kegan Paul.

Voydanoff, P. (ed.) (1984) *Work and Family: Changing Roles of Men and Women*. Palo Alto, CA: Mayfield.

Walby, S. (1986) *Patriarchy at Work*. Cambridge: Polity Press.

Walby, S. (1988) 'Gender Politics and Social Theory', *Sociology*, 22(2):215–32.

Wallace, P. A. (ed.) (1982) *Women in the Workplace*. Boston, MA: Auburn House.

Warner, W., P. P. Van Riper, N. H. Martin and O. F. Collins (1982) 'Women Executives in the Federal Government', *Public Personnel Review*, October:227–34.

Weeks, J. (1986) *Sexuality*. London: Tavistock.

Wendell, J. (1988) 'Disclosing Lesbian Orientation', paper presented at the National Gay and Lesbian Health Conference, Boston, MA.

Wernick, A. (1987) 'From Voyeur to Narcissist: the Imagery of Men in Contemporary Advertising', in M. Kaufman (ed.) *Beyond Patriarchy. Essays by Men on Pleasure, Power and Change*, pp. 277-97. Toronto, New York: Oxford University Press.

Weston, K. M. and L. B. Rofel (1985) 'Sexuality, Class, and Conflict in a Lesbian Workplace', in E. B. Freedman, B. Gelpi et al. (eds) *The Lesbian Issue: Essays from Signs*, pp. 199-222. Chicago: University of Chicago Press.

White, K. (1987) 'Residential Care of Adolescents: Residents, Carers and Sexual Issues', in G. Horobin (ed.) *Sex, Gender and Care Work, Research Highlights in Social Work*, No. 15, pp. 52-65. New York: St Martin's. London: Jessica Kingsley.

Whyte, W. M. (1956) *The Organization Man*. New York: Simon and Schuster.

Wickham, G. (forthcoming) 'The Political Possibilities of Post-Modernism, *Economy and Society*, 19.

Williams, J. E. and D. L. Best (1982) *Measuring Sex Stereotypes: a Thirty-Nation Study*. Beverly Hills, CA: Sage.

Willis, P. E. (1977) *Learning to Labour*. Farnborough, Hampshire: Saxon House.

Wise, S. and L. Stanley (1984) 'Sexual Politics—an Editorial Introduction', *Women's Studies International Forum*, 7(1):1-6.

Wright, E. O., C. Costell, D. Hachen and J. Sprague (1982) 'The American Class Structure', *American Sociological Review*, 47(6):709-26.

Young, M. and P. Willmott (1962) *Family and Kinship in East London*. Harmondsworth, Middlesex: Penguin Books.

Zedeck, S. and S. Cascio (1984) 'Psychological Issues in Personnel Decisions', *Annual Review of Psychology*, 35:461-518.

Zilbergeld, B. (1978) *Male Sexuality*. Boston, MA: Little Brown.

Zita, J. N. (1982) 'Historical Amnesia and the Lesbian Continuum', in N. O. Keohane, M. Z. Rosaldo and B. C. Gelpi (eds) *Feminist Theory. A Critique of Ideology*, pp. 161-76. Brighton, Sussex: Harvester. Chicago: University of Chicago Press.

Index

Abbey, A. 60–2
Abella, R. S. 38, 40
Abernathy, W. J. 11
absenteeism 86
Adams, M. L. 28
AIDS 19, 56, 57
Alexander, P. 18
alienation 156
Alliance Against Sexual Coercion 20
androgyny 141
Ardener, S. 118
Ardill, S. 7, 27, 28
Armstrong, P. 55
authority 159, 161, 162

Bachrach, P. 117
Bales, R. F. 9
Balsamo, A. 54
Baratz, M. S. 117
Barker, J. 49, 54
Barrett, M. 38, 161
Barron, R. 118
Bateson, G. 136
Beard, K. 113, 117
Beer, C. 23
Bell, A. P. 24
Bem, S. L. 60
Benjamin, J. 174–6
Benson, J. K. 29, 36
Benson, S. P. 43, 48, 50, 52, 53
Bentham, J. 121
Bernadin, H. 141
Best, D. L. 59, 60
Bilton, T. 35
bisexuality 13
Bittner, E. 14
Blau, P. 18, 162
Blauner, R. 41
Blumstein, P. 128

Bologh, R. W. 177
Borisoff, D. 35
Boseley, S. 115
bosses 25, 54, 127, 142, 146, 149, 154, 158, 159, 161, 162, 165, 169, 170, 172, 175
  female 171, 173, 177
  male 169, 171, 173
Braverman, H. 38, 42, 45
Brittan, A. B. 93, 94
Brooks, V. 24
Broverman, I. K. 120
Bruegel, I. 118
bureaucracy 15, 159–62, 177
  control 47, 168
  discourse 39
  organization 92
  structure 159
  Weber's theory of 9
  welfare 110, 119, 120
Burrell, G. 12, 27, 29, 35, 43, 52, 57, 92, 141

Campaign for Homosexual Equality 23
Campbell, E. J. 9
capitalism 47, 48, 108, 161
  economy 50
  enterprise 53, 54
  industrial 37
  knowledge 49
  organizations 92
Carothers, S. C. 61, 88, 89
Cascio, S. 57
Chafetz, J. 24
Chatov, R. 57
Cheek, D. 135
Chodorow, N. 34, 126, 142, 174
Clark, L. M. G. 11, 118, 119
class 7, 8, 24, 30, 33, 88, 161, 168

Clegg, S. 29, 33, 38, 43
Cobb, J. 97
Cockburn, C. 15, 21, 23, 25, 88, 98
Cohen, A. 56, 58, 66
Coley, L. 113
Collins, E. C. G. 21
Collinson, D. L. 21, 91, 92, 95, 98, 108
community care 114
Connell, R. W. 27, 28, 108
Constantinople, A. 60
control 47, 53, 107
  activities 51
  adjunct 47–51, 55
  and gender characteristics 53
  and women 45
  and women's sexuality 52, 54
  and proportion of women, 51
  extra-organizational rules, 33, 36, 41
  managerial 49, 51, 98
  reproductive rules 33, 42
  rules of 45
  sexuality and women 46
  social-regulative rules 33, 38
  state rules 33, 39
  strategic rules 33, 41
  system 46, 47, 52, 55
  technical rules 33, 36
  types of organizational 49
  use of female sexuality 54
Cook, D. 181
Cooper, C. 34
Cooper, R. 11
Coward, R. 8, 27, 28, 35
Cox, A. 128
Creed, B. 167
Crombie, A. D. 34
Crompton, R. 29, 39, 49
Crozier, M. 10
Crull, P. 59, 61, 88, 89
culture 29, 30, 33, 34, 38, 39, 68, 97, 101, 103, 127, 137, 144, 148, 150, 153, 156, 161, 166
  analysis 166
  attributions 127
  barriers 39
  corporate 38
  male 153, 156
  male-dominated 101, 103, 144
  manual labour 97
  meanings 33
  norms 68
  of corporate women 148
  organizational 29, 30, 34, 36, 39, 40, 42, 43, 45, 58, 126, 140–2, 144, 146, 147, 150, 153, 156
  paradigm 30
  popular 150, 161
  significance 34
  values 34

Daniels, K. 163
Davidson, M. 34
Davies, C. 120
Davis, S. M. 40
Davis, L. 113
Deal, T. E. 42
Deaux, K. 60, 61
Delacoste, F. 18
De Beauvoir, S. 8
D'Emilio, J. 126
Dennis, N. 42
desexualization 12, 16, 27, 92, 149–51, 169, 176, 181
desire 2, 8, 27, 31, 94, 159, 166, 168, 176
Diamond, I. 7, 24
DiTomaso, N. 21, 52, 103
domination 140, 142, 159, 160, 166, 168
  erotic 175, 176
  male 35, 39, 93, 98, 107, 108, 118, 141, 142, 144–6, 166, 168, 174, 178
  of male sexuality 21
  organizational 178
  sexual 55, 178
Downing, H. 49, 54
Dubeck, P. J. 35
Dunkerley, D. 29
Dunwoody, V. 21, 56, 164
Dunwoody-Miller, V. 58, 59
Durkheim, E. 9
Dworkin, A. 6

Edwards, R. 46
Ehrenreich, B. 119
Eichler, M. 28, 142
Eldridge, J. E. T. 34
Elshtain, J. B. 118
Engels, F. 37
English, D. 119
epistemology 139
equality 141, 156
eroticism 125–7, 140, 143, 149, 175, 179

false consciousness 156
family 54, 94, 96, 117–19, 121, 123, 126, 142, 143, 158, 161, 168–70
 ideology 161
 metaphors 161
 products and services 47
 relations 173
 responsibilities 152
Farley, L. 20
Fayol, H. 9
Featherstone, M. 28
Feldberg, E. N. 47
female
 identity 174
 marital status differences 74, 76, 78
 subordinate occupational roles 72
Feminist Review Collective 27
feminism 3, 5–8, 19, 21, 26–30, 33, 43–5, 129, 137, 139, 142, 158, 160, 164–6, 168, 174, 176, 180
 materialist 6, 30, 33
 radical 168
 strategy 43
 studies 21, 28, 33, 45, 139, 141, 142
 writers 27
Ferguson, A. 6
Ferguson, K. E. 29, 35, 39, 180
Ferree, M. M. 28
Finch, J. 119
Fine, G. A. 98
Follett, M. P. 9
Fonda, N. 141
Foucault, M. 7, 8, 12, 13, 15, 32, 121, 158, 166–8, 174
Foushee, H. C. 60
Franklin, U, M. 144
Freedman, E. 126
Freud, S. 4

Gagnon, J. 4
Game, A. 15, 25, 92, 159, 177
gay
 liberation 5, 128, 133
 lifestyle 126
 men 6, 7, 18, 19, 22, 23, 119
gays 130–2, 134–7, 154
 see also homosexuality; lesbianism
gender 1–10, 13, 14, 16, 19, 21, 25, 26, 29–34, 36, 39, 42, 44, 45, 46, 51, 52, 56, 58, 68, 71–3, 77, 78, 108, 119, 120, 126, 130, 131, 135, 138, 140–2, 143–7, 149–51, 154–6, 158–61, 163, 164, 168, 174, 175, 179, 180
 asymmetry 34
 behaviour 146
 blindness 163, 180
 construction 30, 32, 44
 difference 126, 142, 143, 174
 differences in the workplace 72
 distortion in organizations 46, 52
 division of labour 33, 34, 119, 120
 expectations 138
 identity 8, 108, 140, 154, 156
 inequality 164
 management of 140
 norm 154
 power imbalance 14
 relations 1, 9, 10, 14, 21, 31, 73, 168, 180
 role expectations 58
 roles 68
 rules 30
 segregation at work 77, 78
 similarities 142
 socialization 34
 structure 140
Gerth, H. H. 159
Gilligan, C. 7, 140, 142
Giorgi, A. 129
Glass, S. P. 60
Greater London Council 23
Glenn, E. N. 47
Glennon, L. M. 30
Goffman, E. 121, 138
Goodchilds, J. D. 61
Gould, R. E. 27, 151
Grauerholz, E. 60
Gray, S. 21, 98
Greenglass, E. 141
Grosz, E. 179, 180
Groves, D. 119
Guardian, The 114, 116
Gutek, B. A. 20, 21, 46, 52, 56–9, 61, 62, 66, 80, 81, 88, 89, 91, 107, 143, 144, 164

Hakim, C. 93, 94
Hall, M. 24, 127, 147
Harlan, S. L. 68
Harragan, B. L. 148, 155
Harrison, R. 21

Hasenfeld, Y. 121
Haug, F. 181
Hearn, J. 5, 10, 19, 21, 25, 27, 29–31, 42, 52–4, 57, 62, 70, 91, 93, 98, 108, 110, 117, 118, 125, 141, 164
Hegel, G. 126
Helmreich, R. L. 60
Henley, N. M. 25, 32
Hennig, M. 142
Hess, B. H. 28
heterosexuality 4, 6, 13, 18, 20–3, 31, 56, 66, 91, 93, 112, 119, 125, 126, 129, 131, 133, 136, 138, 147, 155, 165, 174, 176, 179
  compulsory 158, 164–6
hierarchy 58, 59, 67, 108, 140, 142, 145, 159, 166, 179
  and sexual relationships 103, 107
Higgins, W. 43
history
  of sexuality and gender 5
Hobbes, T. 9
Hochschild, A. R. 35, 48, 52
Hofstede, G. 42
Hogbacka, R. 20
Hoiberg, A. 141
Hollway, W. 6, 93, 94, 170, 174
Holter, H. 28
Homans, H. 152
homophobia 116, 130, 135–7, 147, 148, 154
homosexuality 5, 6, 7, 13, 18, 19, 22, 23, 28, 32, 116, 119, 122, 125, 126, 131, 133–5, 137, 164–6
  and executives' attitudes 128
  perceptions of 135
  see also gays; lesbianism
Horn, J. C. 21
Horn, P. D.
Howe, D. 119
Hughes Report 113

ideology 142

Jardim, A. 142
Jay, A. 9
Jay, K. 136
Jensen, I. 56
job seniority 74, 75, 87
Jones, B. 158
Jones, G. 29, 39, 49

Kahn, D. 59
Kahn-Hut, R. 141
Kanter, R. M. 11, 65, 88, 142, 147, 152, 160, 177
Kantrow, A. M. 11
Karr, R. G. 135
Katz, D. 59
Keller, E. F. 8
Kelly, L. 6
Kennedy, A. A. 42
Kerr, C. 87
Khan, A. J. 41
Kilroe, S. 124
Kinsey, A. C. 60
Kleinberg, S. 7
Kohn, M. M. 9
Konrad, A. M. 56, 66, 80, 81, 88, 89
Korda, M. 163
Kramarae, C. 32
Kristeva, J. 8
Kroker, A. 181

labour 92
  domestic 46
  resistance 93, 94, 98
  women's wage 46
labour force 35, 36
  women's distribution 46, 48
  women's position 45
labour market 33, 118
  effects on women, minorities and men 73
labour process 19, 38, 45, 46, 51, 52, 92
Lacan, J. 8, 174
Laing, R. 138
Lange, L. 118, 119
Laws, J. L. 4
Lee, R. 21
Leeds TUCRIC 20, 21, 80
Leonard, R. 23, 24
lesbianism 5, 6, 7, 18, 19, 22–4, 61', 65, 119, 125, 126, 127–39, 147, 148, 154, 155, 165, 173, 174, 178
  and career limitations 134
  and consequences of disclosure 133
  and disclosure 132, 137
  and discrimination 24, 128, 130, 131, 135
  and non-disclosure 130, 131, 136
  see also homosexuality; gays
Levine, M. P. 23, 24

Index 201

Lewis, L. L. 60
Lipman-Blumen, J. 60, 64
Lippert, J. 24
Lockwood, D. 48
Lowe, G. S. 49
Lupton, T. 118
Lyotard, J.-F. 11, 15

McConaghy, N. 135
Machiavelli, N. 9
McIntosh, M. 161
Mackie, M. 34
MacKinnon, C. A. 3, 7, 8, 27, 35, 71, 163, 165, 179, 180
Mclane, H. 135
macromanipulation 64, 65
Major, B. 60
male
  communication style 39
  identity 97, 174
  individuation 126
  lack of trust of women workers 88
  marital status differences 75
  organizational analysis 26, 43
  organizational power 34
  sexual violence 6
  theories and theorists 1, 8
  values 34
management 1, 48–51, 53, 69, 74, 75, 77, 86, 92, 93, 97, 98, 107, 108, 115, 116, 123, 131, 140, 144, 146, 147, 152, 164, 169, 177
  attitude re harassment 86
  authority 48
  control 93, 107
  gender composition 75, 77
  identification with 48
  opposition to 48
  policies 164
managers 57, 59, 109, 110, 115, 139, 142–4, 148, 149, 152, 154, 155, 173, 178
  female 173, 178
  male 173
Marcuse, H. 163, 167
Marler, R. 113
Marx, K. 9
marxism 6
Mayo, E. 10
Meehan, E. M. 40, 41
Melby, C. 61

menstruation 150
Merleau-Ponty, M. 129
Merrill, L. 35
methodology 16, 17, 139, 142, 180
  and interdisciplinarity 179
  case studies 91
  empiricism 91
  experimental research 56
  naturalistic 129
  pluralism 16
  qualitative studies 91
  quantitative studies 56
Meyer, M. M. 162
micromanipulation 64, 65
Miller, J. B. 142
Mills, A. J. 29, 30, 35, 38, 41, 43, 52, 108
Mills, C. W. 159
Minson, J. 28
Mitchell, J. 4
modernism 12, 17, 19, 28, 180
Molloy, J. T. 150
morality 142
Morasch, B. 21, 56, 58
Morgan, D. 140
Morgan, G. 27, 29, 30, 34–6, 39, 43
Morin, S. 135
Morris, H. 180
Moss, P. 141
Murphy, G. 115

Nakamura, C. 56
Neugarten, D. A. 20
Nieva, V. F. 59
Noe, R. A. 39
Norris, G. 118

Oakley, A. 32
O'Brien, M. 118
O'Farrell, B. 68
organization 1, 10–20, 25, 26, 49, 50, 58, 62, 69, 70, 110, 126, 127, 138, 143–6, 150, 152, 153, 162
  ideal type 162
  of production 10–14, 16, 19, 20
  of sexuality 17, 18, 53, 55, 125
  sexuality 25, 110
organizational
  acculturation 42, 43
  activity 1

analysis 1, 10, 12, 13, 16, 17, 29, 30, 43
approach re women's inequality 45
behaviour 57, 65, 68
change 68
characteristics 141
environment 58, 68
experience 42, 140, 142
goals 18, 19, 63, 146
inclusion of women 39
life 9, 15, 22, 26, 35, 39, 122, 141–3, 151
literature 19
location of women 46, 51, 55
membership 140
mobility 148
networks 39
norms 59, 144, 154
participation 141
performance 141
policies 19, 113, 152, 181
politics 142
position 58, 143
power 35, 98, 107, 140–3, 152, 156, 159
practices 39, 41, 56, 91, 107, 108
processes 38
purposes 38
reality 43, 46, 140, 141
researchers 57, 67
responsibilities 152
rewards 63
roles 140
status 140, 145, 149, 156
structure 51, 59, 65, 68, 139, 141, 142, 144, 179
studies, 11, 14, 46, 142, 160
success 145, 151
system 145
organizations 1, 9, 14–16, 18–20, 22, 25, 27, 29–31, 34, 36, 37, 39, 43, 45, 51, 56, 58, 69, 91, 93, 108, 109, 115, 118, 124, 126, 129, 142, 143, 148, 158, 160, 178, 180
custodial 23
heterosexual 24
military 23
of production 47
religious 23
O'Sullivan, S. 7, 27, 28
Ouchi 11, 39, 42

Parkin, P. W. 5, 10, 19, 21, 23, 25, 27, 29–31, 42, 53, 54, 57, 70, 91, 108, 110, 111, 117, 125, 141, 164
Parsons, T. 9
Pateman, C. 161
patriarchy 9, 21, 108, 140, 142, 180
assumptions 109
ideology 174
structure 160, 161
Pearson, J. C. 39
Peters, T. J. 11
pleasure 8, 162, 163, 165–7, 172, 173, 175–7
Plummer, K. 31
politics
of sexuality and gender 5
Pollert, A. 21, 36, 43
pornography 166, 175
positivism 142
dominance of 142
postmodernism 16, 17, 19, 28, 158, 180
post-structuralism 5
power 3–6, 8, 14, 21, 25–7, 31, 32, 70–3, 84, 85, 88, 91, 93, 98, 99, 103, 107–10, 114, 118, 120–4, 140, 143, 144, 145, 148, 150–2, 158, 160–2, 164, 165, 166–8, 171, 173, 174, 176, 177, 181
abuse of 114
analysis 6
differences in organizations 73
economic 166
games 85
generic 110, 123
ideological 160
male 21, 72, 108, 122, 164, 165, 168
managerial 108
relations 4, 5, 31, 32, 162, 168
sexual 165, 166
social 166
structure 84
techniques 167
pregnancy 87, 113, 151, 152
Price, M. 118
Pringle, R. 15, 25, 54, 92, 159, 177
production 2, 98, 118
material means of 34
means of symbolic 34
of organization 2, 18, 26
of organizations 2, 26
social arrangements of 38

techniques 36
productivity 2, 11, 12
profeminist 1, 3, 26, 44, 180
professionals 143, 144
psychoanalysis 4, 5, 28, 158
 and feminist theory 174
public/private 13, 15, 22–4, 26, 27, 30, 33, 34, 52, 56, 57, 89, 110, 117–24, 159, 161, 162, 167, 169

Quinby, L. 7, 24
Quinn, R. E. 21, 93, 106

race/ethnicity 71, 73, 83, 84, 88
 differences in the workplace 78
 discrimination 82
Rakow, L. F. 32, 33, 36, 39
rationality 159, 161, 163, 167, 175, 177
 male 166
Réage, P. 166
Reiter, E. 48
reproduction 2, 11, 12, 118
 of organization 2, 9, 14–20, 26
 of organizations 2, 26
Rich, A. 6, 164, 165
Riley, P. 39, 142
Robins, E. 24
Rofel, L. B. 24
role
 analysis 59, 67
 sex vs work 61
Rosaldo, M. Z. 33, 34
Rose, M. 162
Rubin, G. 5, 18, 28, 166
Ruble, T. L. 60
Ryan, M. P. 37, 40, 41, 43

Saal, F. E. 61
sadomasochism 158, 173, 175, 176
 lesbian 176
Saghir, M. T. 24
Sargent, A. 141
Schneider, B. E. 24, 27, 59, 61, 65
Schwartz, P. 4, 128
science 11, 12, 15–17, 27, 140
Scollard, J. R. 150–2, 154
Scott, J. W. 18
secretaries 25, 54, 59, 93, 127, 142, 149, 158–62, 164, 165, 167–73, 175–8
Segal, L. 166
segregation

 sexual 52, 53
 women, in occupations and organizations 45
Sennett, R. 97
Serpe, R. T. 60
sex 31, 32
 biological 3
 differences 32
 male 4
sex discrimination 21, 26, 30, 42, 57, 71–3, 78, 81, 88, 146, 154, 156
 and age of women 82
 and homosexuals 23
 gender differences 78
 gender segregation and salary differences 80
 perceptions of 79
sex role
 spillover 52, 59, 68, 69, 125, 143
sexism 10, 42, 43, 99, 142, 156
 comments 99
 in research 142
 organizational practices 42
sexual
 abuse 113, 114, 121
 activities 92, 166
 assault 113
 attraction 170
 attractiveness 53, 65, 163
 body 22
 characteristics 154
 desirability 58
 discourses 91, 93–8, 103, 107, 109, 167, 168, 170, 171, 173
 division of labour 30, 37, 41, 164
 encounters 58
 ethics 166
 exploitation 115, 121, 122
 fantasies 162, 163
 games 176
 identity 7, 154, 156
 ideology 8
 interactions 158, 162
 metaphor 169
 minorities 166
 negotiations in the workplace 85, 86
 neutrality 155
 normalcy 126
 objects 167
 orientation 128, 135, 147, 154
 politics 7, 24, 123, 166, 176

power structure 163
practices 18
relations 12, 22, 113, 114, 122, 175
rumour 22
segregation 94
subjects 167
testing by supervisors and workers 84
time 22
values 166
violence 13, 20
sexual behaviour 8, 22, 56–9, 65–7, 70, 111, 113, 164
  at work, perceptions of 58
  definitions of women's 61
  guidelines 70
  male 93
  of men at work 62, 63
  pervasiveness of 66
  visibility of 67
sexual harassment 13, 14, 20–2, 26, 35, 56–8, 62, 66, 67, 69, 70, 71, 73, 78, 80, 81, 86, 88, 89, 93, 111, 115, 116, 121, 127, 141, 146, 154, 155, 162, 164, 165, 166, 167, 170, 177, 178
  avoidance 164
  control of women 54
  financial dependence of women 72, 86
  gender differences in perception 88
  organizational policies 68, 69
  perceptions of 80
  physical segregation at work 80
  working-class women 72
sexuality 1–20, 22, 25–7, 29–32, 35, 45, 46, 52–8, 61–3, 64–7, 71, 72, 81, 84, 89, 91–6, 98, 99, 103, 107, 108–15, 117, 119–24, 135, 139–44, 146–8, 149–51, 153–6, 158, 159, 161–9, 173–5, 176–81
  academic hostility towards 10
  and gender control 54
  and trivialization 65–7
  construction of 19
  control of 141
  dominance of male 94
  fear of 5
  female 55, 119, 167
  implicit organizational rules 112
  in organizations 178
  in residential organizations 110–14, 123, 124
  in the workplace 20, 93, 110, 163, 167, 177
  lack of organizational rules 112, 113, 115, 117, 122, 123
  male 94–6, 98, 99, 107, 108, 117, 122
  management of 140
  of organization 1, 2, 9, 10, 15–18, 20, 46
  of organizations 22, 55, 180, 181
  politicization of 117
  punitive 154–6
  suppression of 92
  sexualization 25, 26, 64, 69, 73, 74, 81, 88, 115, 150, 151, 153, 155, 158, 162, 178, 180, 181
  of authority 88
  of discourse 180
  of the workplace 73, 88
Shafritz, J. M. 20
Sharron, H. 115
Sheppard, D. 25, 65
Sheriff, P. 9
Siegel, A. 87
Silverman, D. 162
Silverman, K. 166, 175
Simmel, G. 9
Simon, W. 4
Simpson, I. H. 118
Simpson, R. L. 118
Simpson, S. 39
Smircich, L. 29, 30, 43
Smith, D. E. 10
Social Work Today 114
socialization 34
  and control 49
sociology
  occupational 45
Spence, J. T. 60
Spencer, H. 9
Spender, D. 10
Stacey, M. 118, 120
Stanley, L. 8
stereotypes 61–3, 146, 150, 156, 177
  female 35
  male 35
  sex 59, 60
  sexist 167
strategies 145, 148, 150, 151, 154, 168, 172–4, 177

blending in 146, 153
gender management 65, 144, 146, 147, 154, 156
managerial 92
managing pregnancy 152
precariousness of 147
rightful place 146, 155
used by lesbians 128, 131, 132, 135–8, 147, 154, 155
Strumingher, L. S. 36, 38, 43
subordination 35, 98, 107, 139, 140, 142

Tancred-Sheriff, P. 29, 30, 38
Taylor, N. 24, 116, 128
Taylor, F. W. 9
theory 10, 17, 180
  contract 161
  discourse 180
  feminist 1, 25, 180
  functionalism 9
  labour process 46, 51
  organization 1, 2, 9, 10, 13, 14, 16, 19, 20, 29, 42, 91, 180
  organizational 45, 179
  political 161
  postmodernist 25
  social 16
  systems 9
Thompson, P. 54
Thorne, B. 32
Tonnies, F. 9
Tresemer, D. W. 32

unions 20, 48, 74, 76–8, 87, 94, 98–101, 103, 107, 108
Urwick, L. F. 9

Vance, C. S. 166
violence 175

Voydanoff, P. 141

Walby, S. 28, 108
Wallace, P. A. 141
Warner, W. P. P. 135
Waterman, R. H. 11
Weber, M. 9, 21, 159–62, 167, 177
Weeks, J. 30–2
Weinberg, M. S. 24
Wendell, J. 128
Wernick A. 181
Weston, K. M. 24
White, K. 111, 112, 114, 121
Whyte, W. M. 9
Wickham, G. 28
Wiener, R. 124
Williams, J. E. 59, 60
Willis, P. E. 98, 118
Willmott, P. 42
Woodward, J. 9
workers 58, 110, 118
  adjunct control 50, 53
  clerical 47–9, 55
  sales and services 48, 49, 55
workplace 45, 71, 91, 98, 162, 164–6
  options for working-class women 74
  relations 161
  sexually heterogeneous 54
Wright, E. O. 35
Wright, T. L. 60

Young, A. 136
Young, M. 42

Zedeck, S. 57
Zellman, G. L. 61
Zilbergeld, B. 60
Zita, J. N. 179